D0557806

Basic Documents of American
Public Administration
1776-1950

Basic Documents of American
Public Administration
1776-1950

Selected and edited by
Frederick C. Mosher

HOLMES & MEIER PUBLISHERS, Inc.
New York · London

First published in the United States of America 1976 by
Holmes & Meier Publishers, Inc.
30 Irving Place
New York, N.Y. 10003

Great Britain:
Holmes & Meier Publishers, Ltd.
131 Trafalgar Road
Greenwich, London SE10 9TX

Copyright © Holmes & Meier Publishers, Inc. 1976
Second printing 1983
All rights reserved

LIBRARY OF CONGRESS CATALOGING IN PUBLICATION DATA

Main entry under title:

Basic documents of American public administration, 1776-1950.

    1. United States — Politics and government — Sources. 2. United
States — Executive departments — Management — History — Sources.
3. Civil service — United States — History — Sources.
I. Mosher, Frederick C.
JK411.B3   353   76-13866
ISBN 0-8419-0275-5
ISBN 0-8419-0276-3 pbk.

Printed in the United States of America

Contents

Preface

With the recent proliferation of texts and edited collections of readings in or related to public affairs and administration, one may reasonably question: why now this one? The rationale is that there is a serious lacuna in the spate of recent literature in its failure to treat seriously and systematically the *older* documents, official and unofficial, which have proven to have lasting impact upon knowledge and understanding in this field. Most of the current publications rely solely or primarily upon current problems, perspectives, and interests, sometimes supported by references to earlier precedents. These are valuable and indeed essential in the study of the field, but, unless they are frequently revised, they suffer early mortality. As situations change and as slogans and catchwords fade into obscurity, current works rapidly lose their currency. Even the most astute and perceptive scholars find it difficult to identify the concepts and the writings of recent months and years which will prove to have enduring impact. The best index of the continuing significance of any document is surely its demonstrated survival over time.

In my own study and teaching over many years, I have found it inconvenient, difficult, and sometimes impossible to find, study, and present the materials from the past which are truly essential to the learning of public administration. For the inquiring person in this field, whether student or practitioner, the bulk of these older materials are hard to find or obtain; in those places which lack adequate library facilities, they are not there to be found, even after the most painstaking search. This literature falls into two general classes: (1) official documents—constitutions, statutes, executive orders, official reports, court decisions, etc.; and (2) unofficial works—books, articles, monographs, etc.

This volume undertakes to present, in chronological order, the major official documents most relevant to the development of American public administration. (Court decisions are not included.) There will be a later volume on unofficial but significant publications. The material reproduced herein consists of documents which, with one slight exception (explained below), were adopted or issued by an official governmental agency in the United States and which have proven to have had enduring importance. All are still significant at the time of this writing, and most undoubtedly will continue to be so for some time in the future, even though some, such as the Northwest Ordinance and the Classification Act of 1923, have been rescinded or superseded.

This collection begins with the Declaration which proclaimed the independence of the United States of America in 1776 and closes with the concluding report of the First Hoover Commission, published in 1949. In other words, it is drawn from documents issued during the first century and three-quarters of the nation's history. The coverage is admittedly uneven because the development of public administration was uneven. Part I contains some of the basic documents of the pre-Constitutional and the organizing periods of the new Republic. There is then a skip of nearly a century to the beginnings around 1880 of what I have called the "Management Movement," the subject of Part II. There were obviously a great many events and documents in the intervening period, ranging through the establishment of judicial review, the formation of political parties, the revision of the Presidential election system, the maturing of the bureaucracy under President Jackson, the spoils system, the growing dominance of legislatures, the Civil War, the Emancipation Proclamation, the Morrill Act with its enormous impact on higher education, the opening up of the West and the considerable role of government in the process, and many others. Yet it was not in a positive sense a period which enveloped any consistent theme, philosophy, or even consciousness of public administration as discipline or profession. Rather, it set the stage and posed many of the problems for the public administration which was to emerge in subsequent years.

The period of the management movement, herein artificially defined as the half-century between about 1880 and 1930, encompassed the development, growth, and widening acceptance of patterns of values, doctrines, and techniques to guide the administrative side of government. It was a genuine social movement, grounded in reform, idealism, and yet pragmatism. For purposes of convenience in this volume, I have closed Part II with the beginning of the Great Depression and the dawn of the New Deal, which greatly changed the context within which the movement's elements would be applied in the future. Yet, its most mature expressions came later—in the late thirties and again, after World War II, in the late forties. By that time, it had grown from a "movement" to an accepted body of philosophy and doctrine, and, at this writing, it still is. After World War II, it was questioned, challenged, and even attacked from a number of directions: informal organization; human relations and later organizational development; economic analysis and Planning-Programming-Budgeting Systems (PPBS); participative management; administrative ecology; and perhaps most seriously, policy and politics in administration. In the Bicentennial era, a substitutive ethos may emerge. But the orthodox or "classical" theory—the product of the management movement—remains a powerful force in the interpretation and practice of public administration. In the words of Dwight Waldo,*

> not only is the classical theory still today the formal working theory of large numbers of persons technically concerned with administrative-organizational matters, both in the public and private spheres, but I expect it will be around a long, long time. This is not necessarily because it is "true," though I should say it has much truth in it, both descriptively and prescriptively; that is to say, both as a description of organizations as we find them in our society and as a prescription for achieving the goals of these organizations "efficiently." But in any event, a social theory widely held by the actors has a self-confirming tendency and the classical theory is now deeply ingrained in our culture.

Part III of this volume consists of documents issued or adopted during the second term of President Franklin D. Roosevelt, which expressed in official form the underlying tenets of the manage-

* "Organization Theory: An Elephantine Problem," *Public Administration Review*, XXI, no. 4 (1961), p. 220.

ment movement as applied to the national government. Part IV consists of selected documents between World War II and 1949. Most of them were consistent with the management movement and were formulations of proposals developed before or during the war.

The documents significant for public administration that might be included in a volume such as this would surely encompass several hundred thousands of pages, clearly impracticable for current publication. And it is doubtful that any two persons editing such a volume would agree on every entry or, more painfully, every exclusion. The dominating consideration of choice was that the volume, while within reasonable length, be useful to persons interested in, or teaching, or studying public administration by providing them basic documentary material and references, especially those that are not elsewhere readily available; that in doing so it suggest the documents of greatest significance; and that it put the various documents in appropriate relationship to each other, to the times which produced them, and to the consequences in subsequent years. The collection is not intended to provide a flowing and coherent history of public administration in the United States. It is rather perceived as a reference work of original documents which provide basic clauses and punctuation marks of that history with which students in the field should be acquainted.

In keeping with this general purpose, I have been guided by three more specific criteria—that the volume include:

> underlying statements of, and constraints upon, governmental purposes which are relevant to public administration; (e.g., the Declaration of Independence; the Constitution; the Report of the Brownlow Committee);

> enactments with enduring impact upon the organization and procedures of government in this country; (e.g., the acts establishing the original federal departments in 1789; the Civil Service Act of 1883; the Budget and Accounting Act of 1921; the Classification Act of 1923; the Employment Act of 1946; the Administrative Procedure Act of 1946);

> enactments which were "firsts" and precedents in their fields; (e.g., the acts establishing the original depart-

ments in 1789; the Civil Service Act of 1883; the Act to Regulate Commerce of 1887; the acts of 1947 and 1949 creating the Department of Defense).

Almost all of the documents reproduced in this volume pertain to and were issued by the federal government. This is despite the fact, discussed in the introduction to Part II, that the management movement, with the exception of civil service reform, really jumped off from the cities where, until the New Deal, most government and most misgovernment were. For purposes of this collection, it appeared that the more generally applicable federal documents would have greater value and greater interest than, for example, the first city manager ordinance of Staunton, Virginia, or the first classification ordinance in Chicago or the first budget of the Health Department of New York City. In lieu of such particularized local precedents, I have included, in Part II, major administrative sections of the Model City Charter, prepared and issued by the National Municipal League in 1916. It was not an official document, but it influenced an unmeasured number of official documents at all levels of government. More important for our purposes, it very nearly epitomized the orthodox doctrine of what was then perceived as good and right for governmental organization and administration.

Each of the four parts of this volume is introduced by an editorial statement consisting of two sections. First is a brief discussion of the period under consideration, its temporal boundaries and its social and political context. Second are a few sentences pertaining to each of the documents that follow, their origins, precedents, rationale, and impact. Few of the documents are quoted in full. They have been edited with some care in the interests of brevity, convenience, and relevance. I have tried to eliminate materials that are: not directly concerned with public administration; of only temporary or transitory significance; technical and legalistic. The deletions are noted in footnotes at the beginning of each document. Virtually all the documents are verbatim copies from the originals as they first appeared. They therefore reflect the practices in grammar, spelling, punctuation, capitalization, and style of their authors and of the time period in which they were written.

This collection would hardly have been possible without the

collaboration, conscious or unconscious, of quite a number of people. First are those many graduate students at the University of Virginia who were asked to labor through much of it as part of their course work and who offered comments and criticisms, sometimes caustic, of various inclusions and exclusions in earlier drafts. Second are a series of research assistants, likewise graduate students, who not only dug out and reproduced copies of all that follows, as well as a great many other documents that were deleted, but also offered suggestions, advice and editorial assistance. Among these was John M. Holmes, who made the original search and brought together the first draft. A number of others succeeded him and were of great assistance: Rita Epperson, George Gregory Raab, Laura Hudson Stevens, and Mary Stevens. I can hardly name all those who have contributed to the clerical and typing tasks, but would make particular acknowledgment to the one who put together the final draft, Susan Marks. Finally, I am most grateful to Professor Edith K. Mosher, to whom I am married, who helped, as she long has, with her advice, criticism, and suggestions.

But, try as I might, I cannot escape responsibility.

Basic Documents of American
Public Administration
1776-1950

PART I

The Foundations

The Foundations

The beginnings of American public administration stretch far back before the American Revolution, into English and, later, colonial experience and thought. The documents included in this section were a culmination of some centuries of philosophy, argument, compromise, confrontation, and war in or between Britain and America. The American colonies in the eighteenth century provided a hospitable climate for the cultivation of the developing philosophy of man and government. In the words of John Adams:*

> But what do we mean by the American Revolution? Do we mean the American war? The Revolution was effected before the war commenced. The Revolution was in the minds and hearts of the people; a change in their religious sentiments, of their duties and obligations. . . . This radical change in the principles, opinions, sentiments, and affections of the people was the real American Revolution.

The changing principles and opinions to which Adams alluded obviously included resistance and antagonism to an administration which was felt to be distant, oppressive, and beyond popular control or participation. Actually, there was very little affirmative guidance in the early American documents, either official or unofficial, on public administration. The word administration does not appear in any of them. Article II of the Constitution opens with the sentence: "The executive Power shall be vested in a President of the United States of America." But the meaning of the words "executive Power" is only partially explicated in subsequent sentences.

Article I of the Constitution enumerates in greater detail the powers of Congress. But nowhere in the Constitution or other of

* Letter from John Adams to Hezekia Niles, 1818.

the early documents does one find more than the most rudimentary elements of public administration as the subject is currently construed: organization and procedures; direction and control; planning; budgeting; the public service; etc. The omission did not occur because the founders were unaware of administration or its importance. For the closing day of the Constitutional Convention, Benjamin Franklin wrote an eloquent speech (delivered by another because of his illness), urging unanimity in agreement on the Constitution. His central argument was an apparent allusion to the famous couplet about forms of government and the dominance of good administration by Alexander Pope, published a half-century earlier. Franklin wrote:

> In these sentiments, Sir, I agree to this Constitution, with all its faults—if they are such; because I think a general government necessary for us, and there is no *form* of government but what may be a blessing to the people, if well administered; and I believe, farther, that this is likely to be well administered for a course of years. . . . I hope, therefore, for our own sakes, as a part of the people, and for the sake of our posterity, that we shall act heartily and unanimously in recommending this Constitution, wherever our influence may extend, and turn our future thoughts and endeavours to the means of having it *well administered.**

A few months later, Alexander Hamilton, in the *Federalist* No. 68, specifically disavowed the "political heresy" of Alexander Pope, but proceeded to assert that ". . . we may safely pronounce that the true test of a good government is its aptitude and tendency to produce a good administration."†

It is doubtful that a majority of Hamilton's contemporaries would have endorsed this statement; Franklin's was probably more acceptable since his use of "administered" apparently applied to the conduct of the government as a whole, not just the executive branch.

---

* As quoted in Thomas Fleming, ed., *Benjamin Franklin: A Biography in His Own Words,* vol. 2 (Newsweek Inc.), pp. 396-97.

† Clinton Rossiter, ed., *The Federalist Papers* (The New American Library, 1961), p. 414.

Current students of public administration may find solace and support in the statements of Hamilton and Franklin and in some lines from the Constitution. But the real legacies from our beginning period were quite different. In general terms, they were in two categories: first, a genuine and deserved *fear* of public administration, its potential infringements on liberty and threat of oppression; second, in the face of conflicting opinions at the time, an unwillingness or inability to settle matters "once and for all," a series of compromises in generalized language which left many matters open for future resolution.

The product of the first of these legacies was a whole series of limitations, procedural safeguards, and checks—checks on governments in general in their relations with the people, checks on one level of government against others, checks on one branch—perhaps particularly the executive (or administrative) branch—by the others. These ring through most of the pre-Constitutional documents and a good part of the Constitution itself, particularly its Bill of Rights. From the standpoint of activist public administrators, the guidance of the documents was more negative than positive: they stipulated more of what could not be done and more constraints on methods than they provided on what could be done and how to do it. This restraining thrust probably made the development of a positivist and unified public administration directed to achievement of purposes more difficult and later in coming. But many Americans would agree that it was and to a considerable degree remains essential to a free society.

The second legacy cited above, the omissions and ambiguities of some of the basic documents, was very likely one of the main reasons why the Constitution and the system of government which it established have been so flexible and so enduring. They left open for future invention and experimentation an almost limitless variety of opportunities and challenges which either could not be settled or could not be anticipated at the time. It is needless here to attempt an enumeration of the issues not resolved in the Constitution and the early laws. But it is true that they included almost all of the subjects and issues now enveloped in the field of public administration. The specific guidance was slight, but the general philosophy was clear. It was what we have more recently described as pragmatism.

1. DECLARATION OF INDEPENDENCE (1776)

It is appropriate to start this collection with the document that in fact proclaimed the United States of America as an independent governmental entity, but full acknowledgment should be made that the Declaration had many precedents extending over centuries. Its most immediate ancestor, the Virginia Declaration of Rights, drafted by George Mason, had been adopted less than a month earlier by the Virginia Convention, and it served as a model for guarantees of rights in other state constitutions and later for the first ten amendments of the federal Constitution. The bold and incisive eloquence of the Declaration of Independence in behalf of liberty and self-government and against tyranny has earned it inspirational immortality not only in the United States but around the world. Of its four parts—a brief preamble, a statement of philosophical principles, a listing of "injuries and usurpations" by the King of Great Britain, and a resounding declaration of independence*—the charges against the King are here omitted. Though of dominant concern in 1776, the alleged offenses (most of which were measures that had actually been enacted by the British Parliament) are now of mainly historical interest. The most enduring parts are the first and second.

2. NORTHWEST ORDINANCE OF 1787

Eight days after its adoption of the Declaration of Independence, an ad hoc committee presented to the Continental Congress a draft of Articles of Confederation for the new states. Adoption of the Articles was delayed almost to the effective end of the Revolution (March 1781, six months before Yorktown), partly if not principally because of disputes over the claims of some of the new states to the lands in the west. Among the deficiencies of the Articles as a viable framework for a central government was their vesting of all powers in a single body, the Congress, with no provisions for administration of the limited powers granted the Confederation. But during the eight years of its existence, the Congress of the

*Although, as historians have noted, the Congress had declared independence two days earlier, on July 2, 1776; the Declaration of July 4 was actually a document to set forth the reasons for declaring independence.

Confederation adopted some acts of far-reaching significance, and prominent among these were the ordinances of 1784, 1785, and 1787 dealing with territories ceded by individual states to the United States in the region north and west of the Ohio River. These ordinances established principles, techniques, and methods for the growth of the nation, not only in the Northwest Territory. The Ordinance of 1784 provided for the geographical division of the west into districts and for temporary districts ultimately eligible for statehood. The Ordinance of 1785 provided a uniform method for the subdividing and surveying of the uncharted territories. It also, for the first time, made grants of land by the federal government for the development of schools. The Ordinance of 1787, now generally known as the Northwest Ordinance, provided a temporary system of government for the territory consisting of a governor and three judges appointed by the Congress, and an elected house of representatives after the population reached a specified minimum. Of more enduring importance (and the only parts of the Ordinance included herein) were the provisions whereby the territories could later become not less than three nor more than five states on an equal footing with the original states; and the articles, which should "forever remain unalterable," guaranteeing basic liberties, education, "good faith" towards the Indians, and freedom from slavery. The Northwest Ordinance was reenacted with slight change by the first Congress after adoption of the Constitution.

3. Constitution of the United States (1789)

The most fundamental of all public documents in the United States, the Constitution, is here presented in full. Because of the pertinence of some recent amendments, all amendments approved to the date of this publication are included.

4. Acts Establishing Original Federal Administrative Agencies (1789)

Among the first orders of business of the first Congress under the Constitution was the setting up of the main departments of government, none of which had been specified in the Constitution.

The first two of these, the Department of Foreign Affairs *(4a)*—
which later the same year was renamed Department of State *(4b)* so
that it could accommodate domestic as well as foreign
responsibilities—and the Department of War *(4c)*, were granted
extraordinarily broad and general powers in their respective
realms. Both, however, were enjoined to conduct their business "in
such manner as the President of the United States shall from time
to time order or instruct." In other words, the first Congress
acknowledged the special powers and prerogatives of the President
in the fields of defense and foreign affairs.

The Act establishing the Treasury Department *(4d)* was far
different. It provided in some detail for subordinate officers and
their powers within the Department and established the basic elements of the federal financial system. Thus did the Congress
express its immediate concern and powers over the public finances
and also its greater prerogatives in domestic than in foreign policy.
It is interesting that this Act provided an early, if not the first,
prohibition against conflicts of interest of public officials.

The office of Attorney General *(4e)* seems to have been created
almost as an afterthought to the establishment of the federal
judiciary. The Attorney General was perceived as a part-time ad-
viser to the government and occasional advocate before the Supreme Court on a retainer, expected to make a large part of his
livelihood in private practice. He was provided virtually no staff
and had no powers with regard to the U.S. attorneys in the field. It
was not until 1870 that the Department of Justice was established,
with the Attorney General serving as its head.

Shortly after the first Congress was organized, it became em-
broiled in a vigorous debate over the President's power to remove
heads of departments who had been appointed by him with
Senatorial consent. This issue, which had been left unsettled in the
Constitution and went to the heart of the President's control over
administration, was resolved in favor of the administrative authority of the President. All of the acts establishing the first three
departments specifically acknowledged the President's power to
remove their heads without consent of the Senate.

1. Declaration of Independence*
In Congress, July 4, 1776

When in the Course of human events, it becomes necessary for one people to dissolve the political bands which have connected them with another, and to assume among the powers of the earth, the separate and equal station to which the Laws of Nature and of Nature's God entitle them, a decent respect to the opinions of mankind requires that they should declare the causes which impel them to the separation.—We hold these truths to be self-evident, that all men are created equal, that they are endowed by their Creator with certain unalienable Rights, that among these are Life, Liberty and the pursuit of Happiness.—That to secure these rights, Governments are instituted among Men, deriving their just powers from the consent of the governed,—That whenever any Form of Government becomes destructive of these ends, it is the Right of the People to alter or to abolish it, and to institute new Government, laying its foundation on such principles and organizing its powers in such form, as to them shall seem most likely to effect their Safety and Happiness. Prudence, indeed, will dictate that Governments long established should not be changed for light and transient causes; and accordingly all experience hath shown, that mankind are more disposed to suffer, while evils are sufferable, than to right themselves by abolishing the forms to which they are accustomed. But when a long train of abuses and usurpations, pursuing invariably the same Object evinces a design to reduce them under absolute Despotism, it is their right, it is their duty, to throw off such Government, and to provide new Guards for their future

---

* Not including the lengthy bill of particulars against the King of Great Britain.

security.—Such has been the patient sufferance of these Colonies; and such is now the necessity which constrains them to alter their former Systems of Government. . . .

WE, THEREFORE, the REPRESENTATIVES of the UNITED STATES OF AMERICA, in General Congress, Assembled, appealing to the Supreme Judge of the world for the rectitude of our intentions, do, in the Name, and by Authority of the good People of these Colonies, solemnly publish and declare, That these United Colonies are, and of Right ought to be FREE AND INDEPENDENT STATES; that they are Absolved from all Allegiance to the British Crown, and that all political connection between them and the State of Great Britain, is and ought to be totally dissolved; and that as Free and Independent States, they have full Power to levy War, conclude Peace, contract Alliances, establish Commerce, and to do all other Acts and Things which Independent States may of right do.—And for the support of this Declaration, with a firm reliance on the protection of Divine Providence, we mutually pledge to each other our Lives, our Fortunes and our sacred Honor.

---

2. Northwest Ordinance of 1787*
Officially entitled: Ordinance of 1787, July 13, 1787

AN ORDINANCE FOR THE GOVERNMENT OF THE TERRITORY OF THE
UNITED STATES NORTHWEST OF THE RIVER OHIO

Section 1. *Be it ordained by the United States in Congress assembled,* That the said Territory, for the purpose of temporary government, be one district, subject, however, to be divided into two districts, as future circumstances may, in the opinion of Congress, make it expedient.

Sec. 13. And for extending the fundamental principles of civil and religious liberty, which form the basis whereon these republics, their laws and constitutions, are erected; to fix and establish those principles as the basis of all laws, constitutions, and governments, which forever hereafter

* Excluded are sections 2 through 12, which provided in some detail for the government of the territory in the interim period before states were created, and those sentences of Article V which set forth tentative boundaries of the projected new states.

shall be formed in the said territories; to provide, also, for the establishment of States, and permanent government therein, and for their admission to a share in the Federal councils on an equal footing with the original States, at as early periods as may be consistent with the general interest:

Sec. 14. It is hereby ordained and declared, by the authority aforesaid, that the following articles shall be considered as articles of compact, between the original States and the people and States in the said territory, and forever remain unalterable, unless by common consent, to wit:

Article I

No person, demeaning himself in a peaceable and orderly manner, shall ever be molested on account of his mode of worship, or religious sentiments, in the said territory.

Article II

The inhabitants of the said territory shall always be entitled to the benefits of the writs of *habeas corpus,* and of the trial by jury; of a proportionate representation of the people in the legislature, and of judicial proceedings according to the course of the common law. All persons shall be bailable, unless for capital offences, where the proof shall be evident, or the presumption great. All fines shall be moderate; and no cruel or unusual punishment shall be inflicted. No man shall be deprived of his liberty or property, but by the judgment of his peers, or the law of the land, and should the public exigencies make it necessary, for the common preservation, to take any person's property, or to demand his particular services, full compensation shall be made for the same. And, in the just preservation of rights and property, it is understood and declared, that no law ought ever to be made or have force in the said territory, that shall, in any manner whatever, interfere with or affect private contracts, or engagements, *bona fide,* and without fraud previously formed.

Article III

Religion, morality, and knowledge being necessary to good government and the happiness of mankind, schools and the means of education shall forever be encouraged. The utmost good faith shall always be observed towards the Indians; their lands and property shall never be taken from them without their consent; and in their property, rights, and liberty they never shall be invaded or disturbed unless in just and lawful wars authorized by Congress; but laws founded in justice and humanity shall, from time to time, be made, for preventing wrongs being done to them, and for preserving peace and friendship with them.

Article IV

The said territory, and the States which may be formed therein shall forever remain a part of this confederacy of the United States of America, subject to the articles of Confederation, and to such alterations therein as shall be constitutionally made; and to all the acts and ordinances of the United States in Congress assembled, conformable thereto. The inhabitants and settlers in the said territory shall be subject to pay a part of the Federal debts, contracted, or to be contracted, and a proportional part of the expenses of government to be apportioned on them by Congress, according to the same common rule and measure by which apportionments thereof shall be made on the other States; and the taxes for paying their proportion shall be laid and levied by the authority and direction of the legislatures of the district, or districts, or new States, as in the original States, within the time agreed upon by the United States in Congress assembled. The legislatures of those districts, or new States, shall never interfere with the primary disposal of the soil by the United States in Congress assembled, nor with any regulations Congress may find necessary for securing the title in such soil to the *bona-fide* purchasers. No tax shall be imposed on lands the property of the United States; and in no case shall non-resident proprietors be taxed higher than residents. The navigable waters leading into the Mississippi and Saint Lawrence, and the carrying places between the same, shall be common highways, and forever free, as well to the inhabitants of the said territory as to the citizens of the United States, and those of any other States that may be admitted into the confederacy, without any tax, impost, or duty therefor.

Article V

. . . And whenever any of the said States shall have sixty thousand free inhabitants therein, such State shall be admitted by its delegates, into the Congress of the United States, on an equal footing with the original States, in all respects whatever; and shall be at liberty to form a permanent constitution and State government: *Provided,* The constitution and government, so to be formed, shall be republican, and in conformity to the principles contained in these articles, and, so far as it can be consistent with the general interest of the confederacy, such admission shall be allowed at an earlier period, and when there may be a less number of free inhabitants in the State than sixty thousand.

Article VI

There shall be neither slavery nor involuntary servitude in the said territory, otherwise than in the punishment of crimes, whereof the party shall have been duly convicted: *Provided always,* That any person escaping into the same, from whom labor or service is lawfully claimed in any one of the original States, such fugitive may be lawfully reclaimed, and conveyed to the person claiming his or her labor or service as aforesaid.

Be it ordained by the authority aforesaid, That the resolutions of the 23rd of April, 1784, relative to the subject of this ordinance, be, and the same are hereby, repealed, and declared null and void.

Done by the United States, in Congress assembled, the 13th day of July, in the year of our Lord 1787, and of their sovereignty and independence the twelfth.

---

3. Constitution of the United States (1789)

WE THE PEOPLE of the United States, in Order to form a more perfect Union, establish Justice, insure domestic Tranquility, provide for the common defence, promote the general Welfare, and secure the Blessings of Liberty to ourselves and our Posterity, do ordain and establish this Constitution for the United States of America.

Article I

Section 1. All legislative Powers herein granted shall be vested in a Congress of the United States, which shall consist of a Senate and House of Representatives.

Section 2. The House of Representatives shall be composed of Members chosen every second Year by the People of the several States, and the Electors in each State shall have the Qualifications requisite for Electors of the most numerous Branch of the State Legislature.

No person shall be a Representative who shall not have attained to the Age of twenty five Years, and been seven Years a Citizen of the United States, and who shall not, when elected, be an Inhabitant of that State in which he shall be chosen.

[Representatives and direct Taxes shall be apportioned among the several States which may be included within this Union, according to their respective Numbers, which shall be determined by adding to the whole Number of free Persons, including those bound to Service for a Term of

Years, and excluding Indians not taxed, three fifths of all other Persons.]*
The actual Enumeration shall be made within three Years after the first
Meeting of the Congress of the United States, and within every sub-
sequent Term of ten Years, in such Manner as they shall by Law direct.
The Number of Representatives shall not exceed one for every thirty
Thousand, but each State shall have at Least one Representative; and
until such enumeration shall be made, the State of New Hampshire shall
be entitled to chuse three, Massachusetts eight, Rhode-Island and Provi-
dence Plantations one, Connecticut five, New-York six, New Jersey four,
Pennsylvania eight, Delaware one, Maryland six, Virginia ten, North
Carolina five, South Carolina five, and Georgia three.

When vacancies happen in the Representation from any State, the
Executive Authority thereof shall issue Writs of Election to fill such
Vacancies.

The House of Representatives shall chuse their Speaker and other
Officers; and shall have the sole Power of Impeachment.

Section 3. The Senate of the United States shall be composed of two
Senators from each State, [chosen by the Legislature thereof,]† for six
Years; and each Senator shall have one Vote.

Immediately after they shall be assembled in Consequence of the first
Election, they shall be divided as equally as may be into three Classes. The
Seats of the Senators of the first Class shall be vacated at the Expiration of
the second Year, of the second Class at the Expiration of the fourth Year,
and of the third Class at the Expiration of the sixth Year, so that one third
may be chosen every second Year; [and if Vacancies happen by Resignation, or otherwise, during the Recess of the Legislature of any State, the
Executive thereof may make temporary Appointments until the next
Meeting of the Legislature, which shall then fill such Vacancies].§

No Person shall be a Senator who shall not have attained to the Age of
thirty Years, and been nine Years a Citizen of the United States, and who
shall not, when elected, be an Inhabitant of that State for which he shall be
chosen.

The Vice President of the United States shall be President of the Senate,
but shall have no Vote, unless they be equally divided.

The Senate shall chuse their other Officers, and also a President pro
tempore, in the Absence of the Vice President, or when he shall exercise
the Office of President of the United States.

* Changed by section 2 of the fourteenth amendment. (Brackets are used herein to
indicate passages in the Constitution and Amendments that have been changed, superseded, or repealed.)

† Changed by section 1 of the seventeenth amendment.

§ Changed by clause 2 of the seventeenth amendment.

The Senate shall have the sole Power to try all Impeachments. When sitting for that Purpose, they shall be on Oath or Affirmation. When the President of the United States is tried, the Chief Justice shall preside: And no Person shall be convicted without the Concurrence of two thirds of the Members present.

Judgment in Cases of Impeachment shall not extend further than to removal from Office, and disqualification to hold and enjoy any Office of honor, Trust or Profit under the United States: but the Party convicted shall nevertheless be liable and subject to Indictment, Trial, Judgment and Punishment, according to Law.

Section 4. The Times, Places and Manner of holding Elections for Senators and Representatives, shall be prescribed in each State by the Legislature thereof; but the Congress may at any time by Law make or alter such Regulations, except as to the Places of chusing Senators.

The Congress shall assemble at least once in every Year, and such Meeting shall [be on the first Monday in December,]* unless they shall by Law appoint a different Day.

Section 5. Each House shall be the Judge of the Elections, Returns and Qualifications of its own Members, and a Majority of each shall constitute a Quorum to do Business; but a smaller Number may adjourn from day to day, and may be authorized to compel the Attendance of absent Members, in such Manner, and under such Penalties as each House may provide.

Each House may determine the Rules of its Proceedings, punish its Members for disorderly Behaviour, and, with the Concurrence of two thirds, expel a Member.

Each House shall keep a Journal of its Proceedings, and from time to time publish the same, excepting such Parts as may in their Judgment require Secrecy; and the Yeas and Nays of the Members of either House on any question shall, at the Desire of one fifth of those Present, be entered on the Journal.

Neither House, during the Session of Congress, shall, without the Consent of the other, adjourn for more than three days, nor to any other Place than that in which the two Houses shall be sitting.

Section 6. The Senators and Representatives shall receive a Compensation for their Services, to be ascertained by Law, and paid out of the Treasury of the United States. They shall in all Cases, except Treason, Felony and Breach of the Peace, be privileged from Arrest during their Attendance at the Session of their respective Houses, and in going to and

* Changed by section 2 of the twentieth amendment.

returning from the same; and for any Speech or Debate in either House, they shall not be questioned in any other Place.

No Senator or Representative shall, during the Time for which he was elected, be appointed to any civil Office under the Authority of the United States, which shall have been created, or the Emoluments whereof shall have been encreased during such time; and no Person holding any Office under the United States, shall be a Member of either House during his Continuance in Office.

Section 7. All Bills for raising Revenue shall originate in the House of Representatives; but the Senate may propose or concur with Amendments as on other Bills.

Every Bill which shall have passed the House of Representatives and the Senate, shall, before it become a Law, be presented to the President of the United States; If he approve he shall sign it, but if not he shall return it, with his Objections to that House in which it shall have originated, who shall enter the Objections at large on their Journal, and proceed to reconsider it. If after such Reconsideration two thirds of that House shall agree to pass the Bill, it shall be sent, together with the Objections, to the other House, by which it shall likewise be reconsidered, and if approved by two thirds of that House, it shall become a Law. But in all such Cases the Votes of both Houses shall be determined by yeas and Nays, and the Names of the Persons voting for and against the Bill shall be entered on the Journal of each House respectively. If any Bill shall not be returned by the President within ten Days (Sundays excepted) after it shall have been presented to him, the Same shall be a Law, in like Manner as if he had signed it, unless the Congress by their Adjournment prevent its Return, in which Case it shall not be a Law.

Every Order, Resolution, or Vote to which the Concurrence of the Senate and House of Representatives may be necessary (except on a question of Adjournment) shall be presented to the President of the United States; and before the Same shall take Effect, shall be approved by him, or being disapproved by him, shall be repassed by two thirds of the Senate and House of Representatives, according to the Rules and Limitations prescribed in the Case of a Bill.

Section 8. The Congress shall have Power To lay and collect Taxes, Duties, Imposts and Excises, to pay the Debts and provide for the common Defence and general Welfare of the United States; but all Duties, Imposts and Excises shall be uniform throughout the United States;

To borrow Money on the credit of the United States;

To regulate Commerce with foreign Nations, and among the several States, and with the Indian Tribes;

To establish an uniform Rule of Naturalization, and uniform Laws on the subject of Bankruptcies throughout the United States;

To coin Money, regulate the Value thereof, and of foreign Coin, and fix the Standard of Weights and Measures;

To provide for the Punishment of counterfeiting the Securities and current Coin of the United States;

To establish Post Offices and post Roads;

To promote the Progress of Science and useful Arts, by securing for limited Times to Authors and Inventors the exclusive Right to their respective Writings and Discoveries;

To constitute Tribunals inferior to the supreme Court;

To define and punish Piracies and Felonies committed on the high Seas, and Offences against the Law of Nations;

To declare War, grant Letters of Marque and Reprisal, and make Rules concerning Captures on Land and Water;

To raise and support Armies, but no Appropriation of Money to that Use shall be for a longer Term than two Years;

To provide and maintain a Navy;

To make Rules for the Government and Regulation of the land and naval Forces;

To provide for calling forth the Militia to execute the Laws of the Union, suppress Insurrections and repel Invasions;

To provide for organizing, arming, and disciplining, the Militia, and for governing such Part of them as may be employed in the Service of the United States, reserving to the States respectively, the Appointment of the Officers, and the Authority of training the Militia according to the discipline prescribed by Congress;

To exercise exclusive Legislation in all Cases whatsoever, over such District (not exceeding ten Miles square) as may, by Cession of particular States, and the Acceptance of Congress, become the Seat of the Government of the United States, and to exercise like Authority over all Places purchased by the Consent of the Legislature of the State in which the Same shall be, for the Erection of Forts, Magazines, Arsenals, dock-Yards, and other needful Buildings;—And

To make all Laws which shall be necessary and proper for carrying into Execution the foregoing Powers, and all other Powers vested by this Constitution in the Government of the United States, or in any Department or Officer thereof.

Section 9. The Migration or Importation of such Persons as any of the States now existing shall think proper to admit, shall not be prohibited by the Congress prior to the Year one thousand eight hundred and eight, but a Tax or duty may be imposed on such Importation, not exceeding ten dollars for each Person.

The Privilege of the Writ of Habeas Corpus shall not be suspended, unless when in Cases of Rebellion or Invasion the public Safety may require it.

No Bill of Attainder or ex post facto Law shall be passed.

* No Capitation, or other direct, Tax shall be laid, unless in Proportion to the Census or Enumeration herein before directed to be taken.

No Tax or Duty shall be laid on Articles exported from any State.

No Preference shall be given by any Regulation of Commerce or Revenue to the Ports of one State over those of another: nor shall Vessels bound to, or from, one State, be obliged to enter, clear, or pay Duties in another.

No Money shall be drawn from the Treasury, but in Consequence of Appropriations made by Law; and a regular Statement and Account of the Receipts and Expenditures of all public Money shall be published from time to time.

No Title of Nobility shall be granted by the United States: And no Person holding any Office of Profit or Trust under them, shall, without the Consent of the Congress, accept of any present, Emolument, Office, or Title, of any kind whatever, from any King, Prince, or foreign State.

Section 10. No State shall enter into any Treaty, Alliance, or Confederation; grant Letters of Marque and Reprisal; coin Money; emit Bills of Credit; make any Thing but gold and silver Coin a Tender in Payment of Debts; pass any Bill of Attainder, ex post facto Law, or Law impairing the Obligation of Contracts, or grant any Title of Nobility.

No State shall, without the Consent of the Congress, lay any Imposts or Duties on Imports or Exports, except what may be absolutely necessary for executing it's inspection Laws: and the net Produce of all Duties and Imposts, laid by any State on Imports or Exports, shall be for the Use of the Treasury of the United States; and all such Laws shall be subject to the Revision and Controul of the Congress.

No State shall, without the Consent of Congress, lay any Duty of Tonnage, keep Troops, or Ships of War in time of Peace, enter into any Agreement or Compact with another State, or with a foreign Power, or engage in War, unless actually invaded, or in such imminent Danger as will not admit of delay.

Article II

Section 1. The executive Power shall be vested in a President of the United States of America. He shall hold his Office during the Term of

* See the sixteenth amendment.

four Years, and, together with the Vice President, chosen for the same Term, be elected, as follows

Each State shall appoint, in such Manner as the Legislature thereof may direct, a Number of Electors, equal to the whole Number of Senators and Representatives to which the State may be entitled in the Congress: but no Senator or Representative, or Person holding an Office of Trust or Profit under the United States, shall be appointed an Elector.

[The Electors shall meet in their respective States, and vote by Ballot for two Persons, of whom one at least shall not be an Inhabitant of the same State with themselves. And they shall make a List of all the Persons voted for, and of the Number of Votes for each; which List they shall sign and certify, and transmit sealed to the Seat of the Government of the United States, directed to the President of the Senate. The President of the Senate shall, in the Presence of the Senate and House of Representatives, open all the Certificates, and the Votes shall then be counted. The Person having the greatest Number of Votes shall be the President, if such Number be a Majority of the whole Number of Electors appointed; and if there be more than one who have such Majority, and have an equal Number of Votes, then the House of Representatives shall immediately chuse by Ballot one of them for President; and if no Person have a Majority, then from the five highest on the List the said House shall in like Manner chuse the President. But in chusing the President, the Votes shall be taken by States, the Representation from each State having one Vote; A quorum for this Purpose shall consist of a Member or Members from two thirds of the States, and a Majority of all the States shall be necessary to a Choice. In every Case, after the Choice of the President, the Person having the greatest Number of Votes of the Electors shall be the Vice President. But if there should remain two or more who have equal Votes, the Senate shall chuse from them by Ballot the Vice President.]*

The Congress may determine the Time of chusing the Electors, and the Day on which they shall give their Votes; which Day shall be the same throughout the United States.

No Person except a natural born Citizen, or a Citizen of the United States, at the time of the Adoption of this Constitution, shall be eligible to the Office of President; neither shall any Person be eligible to that Office who shall not have attained to the Age of thirty five Years, and been fourteen Years a Resident within the United States.

In Case of the Removal of the President from Office, or of his Death, Resignation, or Inability to discharge the Powers and Duties of the said Office,† the Same shall devolve on the Vice President, and the Congress

* Superseded by the twelfth amendment.

† This provision has been affected by the twenty-fifth amendment.

may by Law provide for the Case of Removal, Death, Resignation or Inability, both of the President and Vice President, declaring what Officer shall then act as President, and such Officer shall act accordingly, until the Disability be removed, or a President shall be elected.

The President shall, at stated Times, receive for his Services, a Compensation, which shall neither be encreased nor diminished during the Period for which he shall have been elected, and he shall not receive within that Period any other Emolument from the United States, or any of them.

Before he enter on the Execution of his Office, he shall take the following Oath or Affirmation:—"I do solemnly swear (or affirm) that I will faithfully execute the Office of President of the United States, and will to the best of my Ability, preserve, protect and defend the Constitution of the United States."

Section 2. The President shall be Commander in Chief of the Army and Navy of the United States, and of the Militia of the several States, when called into the actual Service of the United States; he may require the Opinion, in writing, of the principal Officer in each of the executive Departments, upon any Subject relating to the Duties of their respective Offices, and he shall have Power to grant Reprieves and Pardons for Offences against the United States, except in Cases of Impeachment.

He shall have Power, by and with the Advice and Consent of the Senate, to make Treaties, provided two thirds of the Senators present concur; and he shall nominate, and by and with the Advice and Consent of the Senate, shall appoint Ambassadors, other public Ministers and Consuls, Judges of the supreme Court, and all other Officers of the United States, whose Appointments are not herein otherwise provided for, and which shall be established by Law: but the Congress may by Law vest the Appointment of such inferior Officers, as they think proper, in the President alone, in the Courts of Law, or in the Heads of Departments.

The President shall have Power to fill up all Vacancies that may happen during the Recess of the Senate, by granting Commissions which shall expire at the End of their next Session.

Section 3. He shall from time to time give to the Congress Information of the State of the Union, and recommend to their Consideration such Measures as he shall judge necessary and expedient; he may, on extraordinary Occasions, convene both Houses, or either of them, and in Case of Disagreement between them, with Respect to the Time of Adjournment, he may adjourn them to such Time as he shall think proper; he shall receive Ambassadors and other public Ministers; he shall take Care that the Laws be faithfully executed, and shall Commission all the Officers of the United States.

Section 4. The President, Vice President and all civil Officers of the United States, shall be removed from Office on Impeachment for, and Conviction of, Treason, Bribery, or other high Crimes and Misdemeanors.

Article III

Section 1. The judicial Power of the United States, shall be vested in one supreme Court, and in such inferior Courts as the Congress may from time to time ordain and establish. The Judges, both of the supreme and inferior Courts, shall hold their Offices during good Behaviour, and shall, at stated Times, receive for their Services, a Compensation, which shall not be diminished during their Continuance in Office.

Section 2. The judicial Power shall extend to all Cases, in Law and Equity, arising under this Constitution, the Laws of the United States, and Treaties made, or which shall be made, under their Authority;—to all Cases affecting Ambassadors, other public Ministers and Consuls;—to all Cases of admiralty and maritime Jurisdiction;—to Controversies to which the United States shall be a Party;—to Controversies between two or more States;—between a State and Citizens of another State;*—between Citizens of different States,—between Citizens of the same State claiming Lands under Grants of different States, and between a State, or the Citizens thereof, and foreign States, Citizens or Subjects.

In all Cases affecting Ambassadors, other public Ministers and Consuls, and those in which a State shall be Party, the supreme Court shall have original Jurisdiction. In all the other Cases before mentioned, the supreme Court shall have appellate Jurisdiction, both as to Law and Fact, with such Exceptions, and under such Regulations as the Congress shall make.

The Trial of all Crimes, except in Cases of Impeachment, shall be by Jury; and such Trial shall be held in the State where the said Crimes shall have been committed; but when not committed within any State, the Trial shall be at such Place or Places as the Congress may by Law have directed.

Section 3. Treason against the United States, shall consist only in levying War against them, or in adhering to their Enemies, giving them Aid and Comfort. No Person shall be convicted of Treason unless on the Testimony of two Witnesses to the same overt Act, or on Confession in open Court.

The Congress shall have Power to declare the Punishment of Treason, but no Attainder of Treason shall work Corruption of Blood, or Forfeiture except during the Life of the Person attainted.

* This clause has been affected by the eleventh amendment.

Article IV

Section 1. Full Faith and Credit shall be given in each State to the public Acts, Records, and judicial Proceedings of every other State. And the Congress may by general Laws prescribe the Manner in which such Acts, Records and Proceedings shall be proved, and the Effect thereof.

Section 2. The Citizens of each State shall be entitled to all Privileges and Immunities of Citizens in the several States.

A Person charged in any State with Treason, Felony, or other Crime, who shall flee from Justice, and be found in another State, shall on Demand of the executive Authority of the State from which he fled, be delivered up, to be removed to the State having Jurisdiction of the Crime.

[No Person held to Service or Labour in one State, under the Laws thereof, escaping into another, shall, in Consequence of any Law or Regulation therein, be discharged from such Service or Labour, but shall be delivered up on Claim of the Party to whom such Service or Labour may be due.]*

Section 3. New States may be admitted by the Congress into this Union; but no new State shall be formed or erected within the Jurisdiction of any other State; nor any State be formed by the Junction of two or more States, or Parts of States, without the Consent of the Legislatures of the States concerned as well as of the Congress.

The Congress shall have Power to dispose of and make all needful Rules and Regulations respecting the Territory or other Property belonging to the United States; and nothing in this Constitution shall be so construed as to Prejudice any Claims of the United States, or of any particular State.

Section 4. The United States shall guarantee to every State in this Union a Republican Form of Government, and shall protect each of them against Invasion; and on Application of the Legislature, or of the Executive (when the Legislature cannot be convened) against domestic Violence.

Article V

The Congress, whenever two thirds of both Houses shall deem it necessary, shall propose Amendments to this Constitution, or, on the Application of the Legislatures of two thirds of the several States, shall call a Convention for proposing Amendments, which, in either Case, shall be valid to all Intents and Purposes, as Part of this Constitution, when ratified by the Legislatures of three fourths of the several States, or by

* Superseded by the thirteenth amendment.

Conventions in three fourths thereof, as the one or the other Mode of Ratification may be proposed by the Congress; Provided [that no Amendment which may be made prior to the Year One thousand eight hundred and eight shall in any Manner affect the first and fourth Clauses in the Ninth Section of the first Article; and]* that no State, without its Consent, shall be deprived of its equal Suffrage in the Senate.

Article VI

All Debts contracted and Engagements entered into, before the Adoption of this Constitution, shall be as valid against the United States under this Constitution, as under the Confederation.

This Constitution, and the Laws of the United States which shall be made in Pursuance thereof; and all Treaties made, or which shall be made, under the Authority of the United States, shall be the supreme Law of the Land; and the Judges in every State shall be bound thereby, any Thing in the Constitution or Laws of any State to the Contrary notwithstanding.

The Senators and Representatives before mentioned, and the Members of the several State Legislatures, and all executive and judicial Officers, both of the United States and of the several States, shall be bound by Oath or Affirmation, to support this Constitution; but no religious Test shall ever be required as a Qualification to any Office or public Trust under the United States.

Article VII

The Ratification of the Conventions of nine States, shall be sufficient for the Establishment of this Constitution between the States so ratifying the Same.

Done in Convention by the Unanimous Consent of the States present the Seventeenth Day of September in the Year of our Lord one thousand seven hundred and Eighty seven and of the Independence of the United States of America the Twelfth in witness whereof We have hereunto subscribed our Names.

* Obsolete.

Amendments

Article I*

Congress shall make no law respecting an establishment of religion, or prohibiting the free exercise thereof; or abridging the freedom of speech, or of the press; or the right of the people peaceably to assemble, and to petition the Government for a redress of grievances.

Article II

A well regulated Militia, being necessary to the security of a free State, the right of the people to keep and bear Arms, shall not be infringed.

Article III

No Soldier shall, in time of peace be quartered in any house, without the consent of the Owner, nor in time of war, but in a manner to be prescribed by law.

Article IV

The right of the people to be secure in their persons, houses, papers, and effects, against unreasonable searches and seizures, shall not be violated, and no Warrants shall issue, but upon probable cause, supported by Oath or affirmation, and particularly describing the place to be searched, and the persons or things to be seized.

Article V

No person shall be held to answer for a capital, or otherwise infamous crime, unless on a presentment or indictment of a Grand Jury, except in cases arising in the land or naval forces, or in the Militia, when in actual service in time of War or public danger; nor shall any person be subject for the same offence to be twice put in jeopardy of life or limb; nor shall be compelled in any criminal case to be a witness against himself, nor be deprived of life, liberty, or property, without due process of law; nor shall private property be taken for public use without just compensation.

* Ratification of the first ten amendments was completed on December 15, 1791. Dates given in parentheses for subsequent amendments are those on which the amendments were declared effective.

Article VI

In all criminal prosecutions, the accused shall enjoy the right to a speedy and public trial, by an impartial jury of the State and district wherein the crime shall have been committed, which district shall have been previously ascertained by law, and to be informed of the nature and cause of the accusation; to be confronted with the witnesses against him; to have compulsory process for obtaining Witnesses in his favor, and to have the assistance of counsel for his defence.

Article VII

In Suits at common law, where the value in controversy shall exceed twenty dollars, the right of trial by jury shall be preserved, and no fact tried by a jury, shall be otherwise reexamined in any Court of the United States, than according to the rules of the common law.

Article VIII

Excessive bail shall not be required, nor excessive fines imposed, nor cruel and unusual punishments inflicted.

Article IX

The enumeration in the Constitution, of certain rights, shall not be construed to deny or disparage others retained by the people.

Article X

The powers not delegated to the United States by the Constitution, nor prohibited by it to the States, are reserved to the States respectively, or to the people.

Article XI (January 8, 1798)

The Judicial power of the United States shall not be construed to extend to any suit in law or equity, commenced or prosecuted against one of the United States by Citizens of another State, or by Citizens or Subjects of any Foreign State.

Article XII (September 25, 1804)

The electors shall meet in their respective states and vote by ballot for President and Vice-President, one of whom, at least, shall not be an inhabitant of the same state with themselves; they shall name in their ballots the person voted for as President, and in distinct ballots the person voted for as Vice-President, and they shall make distinct lists of all persons voted for as President, and of all persons voted for as Vice-President, and of the number of votes for each, which lists they shall sign and certify, and transmit sealed to the seat of the government of the United States, directed to the President of the Senate;—The President of the Senate shall, in the presence of the Senate and House of Representatives, open all the certificates and the votes shall then be counted;—The person having the greatest number of votes for President, shall be the President, if such number be a majority of the whole number of Electors appointed; and if no person have such majority, then from the persons having the highest numbers not exceeding three on the list of those voted for as President, the House of Representatives shall choose immediately, by ballot, the President. But in choosing the President, the votes shall be taken by states, the representation from each state having one vote; a quorum for this purpose shall consist of a member or members from two-thirds of the states, and a majority of all the states shall be necessary to a choice. [And if the House of Representatives shall not choose a President whenever the right of choice shall devolve upon them, before the fourth day of March next following, then the Vice-President shall act as President, as in the case of the death or other constitutional disability of the President.]* The person having the greatest number of votes as Vice-President, shall be the Vice-President, if such number be a majority of the whole number of Electors appointed, and if no person have a majority, then from the two highest numbers on the list, the Senate shall choose the Vice-President; a quorum for the purpose shall consist of two-thirds of the whole number of Senators, and a majority of the whole number shall be necessary to a choice. But no person constitutionally ineligible to the office of President shall be eligible to that of Vice-President of the United States.

Article XIII (December 18, 1865)

Section 1. Neither slavery nor involuntary servitude, except as a punishment for crime whereof the party shall have been duly convicted, shall exist within the United States, or any place subject to their jurisdiction.

Section 2. Congress shall have power to enforce this article by appropriate legislation.

Article XIV (July 28, 1868)

Section 1. All persons born or naturalized in the United States, and subject to the jurisdiction thereof, are citizens of the United States and of

---

* Superseded by section 3 of the twentieth amendment.

the State wherein they reside. No State shall make or enforce any law which shall abridge the privileges or immunities of citizens of the United States; nor shall any State deprive any person of life, liberty, or property, without due process of law; nor deny to any person within its jurisdiction the equal protection of the laws.

Section 2. Representatives shall be apportioned among the several States according to their respective numbers, counting the whole number of persons in each State, excluding Indians not taxed. But when the right to vote at any election for the choice of electors for President and Vice President of the United States, Representatives in Congress, the Executive and Judicial officers of a State, or the members of the Legislature thereof, is denied to any of the male inhabitants of such State, being twenty-one years of age,* and citizens of the United States, or in any way abridged, except for participation in rebellion, or other crime, the basis of representation therein shall be reduced in the proportion which the number of such male citizens shall bear to the whole number of male citizens twenty-one years of age in such State.

Section 3. No person shall be a Senator or Representative in Congress, or elector of President and Vice President, or hold any office, civil or military, under the United States, or under any State, who, having previously taken an oath, as a member of Congress, or as an officer of the United States, or as a member of any State legislature, or as an executive or judicial officer of any State, to support the Constitution of the United States, shall have engaged in insurrection or rebellion against the same, or given aid or comfort to the enemies thereof. But Congress may by a vote of two-thirds of each House, remove such disability.

Section 4. The validity of the public debt of the United States, authorized by law, including debts incurred for payment of pensions and bounties for services in suppressing insurrection or rebellion, shall not be questioned. But neither the United States nor any State shall assume or pay any debt or obligation incurred in aid of insurrection or rebellion against the United States, or any claim for the loss or emancipation of any slave; but all such debts, obligations and claims shall be held illegal and void.

Section 5. The Congress shall have power to enforce, by appropriate legislation, the provisions of this article.

---

* See the twenty-sixth amendment.

Article XV (March 30, 1870)

Section 1. The right of citizens of the United States to vote shall not be denied or abridged by the United States or by any State on account of race, color, or previous condition of servitude.

Section 2. The Congress shall have power to enforce this article by appropriate legislation.

Article XVI (February 25, 1913)

The Congress shall have power to lay and collect taxes on incomes, from whatever source derived, without apportionment among the several States, and without regard to any census or enumeration.

Article XVII (May 31, 1913)

The Senate of the United States shall be composed of two Senators from each State, elected by the people thereof, for six years; and each Senator shall have one vote. The electors in each State shall have the qualifications requisite for electors of the most numerous branch of the State legislatures.

When vacancies happen in the representation of any State in the Senate, the executive authority of such State shall issue writs of election to fill such vacancies: *Provided,* That the legislature of any State may empower the executive thereof to make temporary appointments until the people fill the vacancies by election as the legislature may direct.

This amendment shall not be so construed as to affect the election or term of any Senator chosen before it becomes valid as part of the Constitution.

[Article XVIII (January 29, 1919)

[Section 1. After one year from the ratification of this article the manufacture, sale, or transportation of intoxicating liquors within, the importation thereof into, or the exportation thereof from the United States and all territory subject to the jurisdiction thereof for beverage purposes is hereby prohibited.

[Section 2. The Congress and the several States shall have concurrent power to enforce this article by appropriate legislation.

[Section 3. This article shall be inoperative unless it shall have been ratified as an amendment to the Constitution by the legislatures of the several States, as provided in the Constitution, within seven years from the date of the submission hereof to the States by the Congress.]*

* Repealed by section 1 of the twenty-first amendment.

Article XIX (August 18, 1920)

The right of citizens of the United States to vote shall not be denied or abridged by the United States or by any State on account of sex.

Congress shall have power to enforce this article by appropriate legislation.

Article XX (February 6, 1933)

Section 1. The terms of the President and Vice President shall end at noon on the 20th day of January, and the terms of Senators and Representatives at noon on the 3d day of January, of the years in which such terms would have ended if this article had not been ratified; and the terms of their successors shall then begin.

Section 2. The Congress shall assemble at least once in every year, and such meeting shall begin at noon on the 3d day of January, unless they shall by law appoint a different day.

Section 3. If, at the time fixed for the beginning of the term of the President, the President elect shall have died, the Vice President elect shall become President. If a President shall not have been chosen before the time fixed for the beginning of his term, or if the President elect shall have failed to qualify, then the Vice President elect shall act as President until a President shall have qualified; and the Congress may by law provide for the case wherein neither a President elect nor a Vice President elect shall have qualified, declaring who shall then act as President, or the manner in which one who is to act shall be selected, and such person shall act accordingly until a President or Vice President shall have qualified.

Section 4. The Congress may by law provide for the case of the death of any of the persons from whom the House of Representatives may choose a President whenever the right of choice shall have devolved upon them, and for the case of the death of any of the persons from whom the Senate may choose a Vice President whenever the right of choice shall have devolved upon them.

Section 5. Sections 1 and 2 shall take effect on the 15th day of October following the ratification of this article.

Section 6. This article shall be inoperative unless it shall have been ratified as an amendment to the Constitution by the legislatures of three-fourths of the several States within seven years from the date of its submission.

Article XXI (December 5, 1933)

Section 1. The eighteenth article of amendment to the Constitution of the United States is hereby repealed.

Section 2. The transportation or importation into any State, Territory, or possession of the United States for delivery or use therein of intoxicating liquors, in violation of the laws thereof, is hereby prohibited.

Section 3. This article shall be inoperative unless it shall have been ratified as an amendment to the Constitution by conventions in the several States, as provided in the Constitution, within seven years from the date of the submission hereof to the States by the Congress.

Article XXII (February 26, 1951)

Section 1. No person shall be elected to the office of the President more than twice, and no person who has held the office of President, or acted as President, for more than two years of a term to which some other person was elected President shall be elected to the office of the President more than once. But this Article shall not apply to any person holding the office of President when this Article was proposed by the Congress, and shall not prevent any person who may be holding the office of President, or acting as President, during the term within which this Article becomes operative from holding the office of President or acting as President during the remainder of such term.

Section 2. This article shall be inoperative unless it shall have been ratified as an amendment to the Constitution by the legislatures of three-fourths of the several States within seven years from the date of its submission to the States by the Congress.

Article XXIII (March 29, 1961)

Section 1. The District constituting the seat of Government of the United States shall appoint in such manner as the Congress may direct:
A number of electors of President and Vice President equal to the whole number of Senators and Representatives in Congress to which the District would be entitled if it were a State, but in no event more than the least populous State; they shall be in addition to those appointed by the States, but they shall be considered, for the purposes of the election of President and Vice President, to be electors appointed by a State; and they shall meet in the District and perform such duties as provided by the twelfth article of amendment.

Section 2. The Congress shall have power to enforce this article by appropriate legislation.

Article XXIV (February 4, 1964)

Section 1. The right of citizens of the United States to vote in any primary or other election for President or Vice President, for electors for President or Vice President, or for Senator or Representative in Congress, shall not be denied or abridged by the United States or any State by reason of failure to pay any poll tax or other tax.

Sec. 2. The Congress shall have power to enforce this article by appropriate legislation.

Article XXV (February 23, 1967)

Section 1. In case of removal of the President from office or of his death or resignation, the Vice President shall become President.

Sec. 2. Whenever there is a vacancy in the office of the Vice President, the President shall nominate a Vice President who shall take office upon confirmation by a majority vote of both Houses of Congress.

Sec. 3. Whenever the President transmits to the President pro tempore of the Senate and the Speaker of the House of Representatives his written declaration that he is unable to discharge the powers and duties of his office, and until he transmits to them a written declaration to the contrary, such powers and duties shall be discharged by the Vice President as Acting President.

Sec. 4. Whenever the Vice President and a majority of either the principal officers of the executive departments or of such other body as Congress may by law provide, transmit to the President pro tempore of the Senate and the Speaker of the House of Representatives their written declaration that the President is unable to discharge the powers and duties of his office, the Vice President shall immediately assume the powers and duties of the office as Acting President.

Thereafter, when the President transmits to the President pro tempore of the Senate and the Speaker of the House of Representatives his written declaration that no inability exists, he shall resume the powers and duties of his office unless the Vice President and a majority of either the principal officers of the executive departments or of such other body as Congress may by law provide, transmit within four days to the President pro tempore of the Senate and the Speaker of the House of Representatives their written declaration that the President is unable to discharge the powers and duties of his office. Thereupon Congress shall decide the issue, assembling within forty-eight hours for that purpose if not in session. If the Congress, within twenty-one days after receipt of the latter written declaration, or, if Congress is not in session, within twenty-one days after Congress is required to assemble, determines by two-thirds vote of both Houses that the President is unable to discharge the powers and duties of his office, the Vice President shall continue to discharge the same as Acting President; otherwise, the President shall resume the powers and duties of his office.

Article XXVI (July 5, 1971)

Section 1. The right of citizens of the United States, who are eighteen years of age or older, to vote shall not be denied or abridged by the United States or by any State on account of age.

Sec. 2. The Congress shall have power to enforce this article by appropriate legislation.

---

4. Acts Establishing Original Federal Administrative Agencies (1789)

a. Department of Foreign Affairs

AN ACT FOR ESTABLISHING AN EXECUTIVE DEPARTMENT,
TO BE DENOMINATED THE DEPARTMENT OF
FOREIGN AFFAIRS, JULY 27, 1789*

Section 1. *Be it enacted by the Senate and House of Representatives of the United States of America in Congress assembled,* That there shall be an Executive department, to be denominated the Department of Foreign Affairs, and that there shall be a principal officer therein, to be called the Secretary for the Department of Foreign Affairs, who shall perform and execute such duties as shall from time to time be enjoined on or intrusted to him by the President of the United States, agreeable to the Constitution, relative to correspondences, commissions or instructions to or with public ministers or consuls, from the United States, or to negotiations with public ministers

---

* 1 Stat. 4 (1789).

from foreign states or princes, or to memorials or other applications from foreign public ministers or other foreigners, or to such other matters respecting foreign affairs, as the President of the United States shall assign to the said department; and furthermore, that the said principal officer shall conduct the business of the said department in such manner as the President of the United States shall from time to time order or instruct.

Sec. 2. *And be it further enacted,* That there shall be in the said department, an inferior officer, to be appointed by the said principal officer, and to be employed therein as he shall deem proper, and to be called the chief Clerk in the Department of Foreign Affairs, and who, whenever the said principal officer shall be removed from office by the President of the United States, or in any other case of vacancy, shall during such vacancy have the charge and custody of all records, books, and papers appertaining to the said department.

Sec. 3. *And be it further enacted,* That the said principal officer, and every other person to be appointed or employed in the said department, shall, before he enters on the execution of his office or employment, take an oath or affirmation, well and faithfully to execute the trust committed to him.

Sec. 4. *And be it further enacted,* That the Secretary for the Department of Foreign Affairs, to be appointed in consequence of this act, shall forthwith after his appointment, be entitled to have the custody and charge of all records, books and papers in the office of Secretary for the Department of Foreign Affairs, heretofore established by the United States in Congress assembled.

b. Department of State

AN ACT TO PROVIDE FOR THE SAFE-KEEPING OF THE ACTS,
RECORDS AND SEAL OF THE UNITED STATES,
AND FOR OTHER PURPOSES, SEPTEMBER 15, 1789*

Section 1. *Be it enacted by the Senate and House of Representatives of the United States of America in Congress assembled,* That the Executive department, denominated the Department of Foreign Affairs, shall hereafter be denominated the Department of State, and the principal officer therein shall hereafter be called the Secretary of State.

Sec. 2. *And be it further enacted,* That whenever a bill, order, resolution, or vote of the Senate and House of Representatives, having been approved and signed by the President of the United States, or not having been returned by him with his objections, shall become a law, or take effect, it shall forthwith thereafter be received by the said Secretary from the President; and whenever a bill, order, resolution, or vote, shall be returned by the President with his objections, and shall, on being reconsidered be agreed to be passed, and be approved by two-thirds of both Houses of Congress, and thereby become a law or take effect, it shall, in such case, be received by the said Secretary from the President of the Senate, or the speaker of the House of Representatives, in whichsoever House it shall last have been so approved; and the said Secretary shall, as soon as conveniently may be, after he shall receive the same, cause every such law, order, resolution, and vote, to be published in at least three of the public newspapers printed within the United States, and shall also cause one printed copy to be delivered to each Senator and Representative of the United States, and two printed copies duly authenticated to be sent to the Executive authority of each State; and he shall carefully preserve the originals, and shall cause the same to be recorded in books to be provided for the purpose.

Sec. 3. *And be it further enacted,* That the seal heretofore used by the United States in Congress assembled, shall be, and hereby is declared to be, the seal of the United States.

Sec. 4. *And be it further enacted,* That the said Secretary shall keep the said seal, and shall make out and record, and shall affix the said seal to all civil commissions, to officers of the United States, to be appointed by the

---

* 1 Stat. 14 (1789). Sections 5, 6, and 7, providing procedural details, are here omitted.

President by and with the advice and consent of the Senate, or by the President alone. *Provided,* That the said seal shall not be affixed to any commission, before the same shall have been signed by the President of the United States, nor to any other instrument or act, without the special warrant of the President therefor.

---

c. Department of War

AN ACT TO ESTABLISH AN EXECUTIVE DEPARTMENT, TO BE
DENOMINATED THE DEPARTMENT OF WAR, AUGUST 7, 1789*

Section 1. *Be it enacted by the Senate and House of Representatives of the United States of America in Congress assembled,* That there shall be an executive department to be denominated the Department of War, and that there shall be a principal officer therein, to be called the Secretary for the Department of War, who shall perform and execute such duties as shall from time to time be enjoined on, or entrusted to him by the President of the United States, agreeably to the Constitution, relative to military commissions, or to the land or naval forces, ships, or warlike stores of the United States, or to such other matters respecting military or naval affairs, as the President of the United States shall assign to the said department, or relative to the granting of lands to persons entitled thereto, for military services rendered to the United States, or relative to Indian affairs; and furthermore, that the said principal officer shall conduct the business of the said department in such manner, as the President of the United States shall from time to time order or instruct.

Sec. 2. *And be it further enacted,* That there shall be in the said department an inferior officer, to be appointed by the said principal officer, to be employed therein as he shall deem proper, and to be called the chief clerk in the department of war, and who, whenever the said principal officer shall be removed from office by the President of the United States, or in any other case of vacancy, shall, during such vacancy, have the charge and custody of all records, books and papers, appertaining to the said department.

* 1 Stat. 7 (1789).

Sec. 3. *And be it further enacted,* That the said principal officer, and every other person to be appointed or employed in the said department, shall, before he enters on the execution of his office or employment, take an oath or affirmation well and faithfully to execute the trust committed to him.

Sec. 4. *And be it further enacted,* That the Secretary for the department of war, to be appointed in consequence of this act, shall forthwith after his appointment, be entitled to have the custody and charge of all records, books and papers in the office of Secretary for the department of war, heretofore established by the United States in Congress assembled.

---

d. Treasury Department

AN ACT TO ESTABLISH THE TREASURY DEPARTMENT,
SEPTEMBER 2, 1789*

Section 1. *Be it enacted by the Senate and House of Representatives of the United States of America in Congress assembled,* That there shall be a Department of Treasury, in which shall be the following officers, namely: A Secretary of the Treasury, to be deemed head of the department; a Comptroller, an Auditor, a Treasurer, a Register, and an Assistant to the Secretary of the Treasury, which assistant shall be appointed by the said Secretary.

Sec. 2. *And be it further enacted,* That it shall be the duty of the Secretary of the Treasury to digest and prepare plans for the improvement and management of the revenue, and for the support of public credit; to prepare and report estimates of the public revenue, and the public expenditures; to superintend the collection of the revenue; to decide on the forms of keeping and stating accounts and making returns, and to grant under the limitations herein established, or to be hereafter provided, all warrants for monies to be issued from the Treasury, in pursuance of appropriations by law; to execute such services relative to the sale of the lands belonging to the United States, as may be by law required of him; to

* 1 Stat. 12 (1789).

make report, and give information to either branch of the legislature, in person or in writing (as he may be required), respecting all matters referred to him by the Senate or House of Representatives, or which shall appertain to his office; and generally to perform all such services relative to the finances, as he shall be directed to perform.

Sec. 3. *And be it further enacted,* That it shall be the duty of the Comptroller to superintend the adjustment and preservation of the public accounts; to examine all accounts settled by the Auditor, and certify the balances arising thereon to the Register; to countersign all warrants drawn by the Secretary of the Treasury, which shall be warranted by law; to report to the Secretary the official forms of all papers to be issued in the different offices for collecting the public revenue, and the manner and form of keeping and stating the accounts of the several persons employed therein. He shall moreover provide for the regular and punctual payment of all monies which may be collected, and shall direct prosecutions for all delinquencies of officers of the revenue, and for debts that are, or shall be due to the United States.

Sec. 4. *And be it further enacted,* That it shall be the duty of the Treasurer to receive and keep the monies of the United States, and to disburse the same upon warrants drawn by the Secretary of the Treasury, countersigned by the Comptroller, recorded by the Register, and not otherwise; he shall take receipts for all monies paid by him, and all receipts for monies received by him shall be endorsed upon warrants signed by the Secretary of the Treasury, without which warrant, so signed, no acknowledgment for money received into the public Treasury shall be valid. And the said Treasurer shall render his accounts to the Comptroller quarterly, (or oftener if required), and shall transmit a copy thereof, when settled, to the Secretary of the Treasury. He shall moreover, on the third day of every session of Congress, lay before the Senate and House of Representatives, fair and accurate copies of all accounts by him from time (to time) rendered to, and settled with the Comptroller as aforesaid, as also, a true and perfect account of the state of the Treasury. He shall, at all times, submit to the Secretary of the Treasury, and the Comptroller, or either of them, the inspections of the monies in his hands; and shall, prior to the entering upon the duties of his office, give bond, with sufficient sureties, to be approved by the Secretary of the Treasury and Comptroller, in the sum of one hundred and fifty thousand dollars, payable to the United States, with condition for the faithful performance of the duties of his office, and for the fidelity of the persons to be by him employed, which bond shall be lodged in the office of the Comptroller of the Treasury of the United States.

Sec. 5. *And be it further enacted,* That it shall be the duty of the Auditor to receive all public accounts, and after examination to certify the balance, and transmit the accounts with the vouchers and certificates to the Comptroller for his decision thereon: *Provided,* That if any person whose account shall be so audited, be dissatisfied therewith, he may within six months appeal to the Comptroller against such settlement.

Sec. 6. *And be it further enacted,* That it shall be the duty of the Register to keep all accounts of the receipts and expenditures of the public money, and of all debts due to or from the United States; to receive from the Comptroller the accounts which shall have been finally adjusted, and to preserve such accounts with their vouchers and certificates; to record all warrants for the receipt or payment of monies at the Treasury, certify the same thereon, and to transmit to the Secretary of the Treasury, copies of the certificates of balances of accounts adjusted as is herein directed.

Sec. 7. *And be it further enacted,* That whenever the Secretary shall be removed from office by the President of the United States, or in any other case of vacancy in the office of Secretary, the Assistant shall, during the vacancy, have the charge and custody of the records, books, and papers appertaining to the said office.

Sec. 8. *And be it further enacted,* That no person appointed to any office instituted by this act, shall directly or indirectly be concerned or interested in carrying on the business of trade or commerce, or be owner in whole or in part of any sea-vessel, or purchase by himself, or another in trust for him, any public lands or other public property, or be concerned in the purchase or disposal of any public securities of any state or of the United States, or take or apply to his own use, any emolument or gain for negotiating or transacting any business in the said department, other than what shall be allowed by law; and if any person shall offend against any of the prohibitions of this act, he shall be deemed guilty of a high misdemeanor, and forfeit to the United States the penalty of three thousand dollars, and shall upon conviction be removed from office, and forever thereafter incapable of holding any office under the United States: *Provided,* That if any other person than a public prosecutor shall give information of any such offence, upon which a prosecution and conviction shall be had, one half the aforesaid penalty of three thousand dollars, when recovered, shall be for the use of the person giving such information.

e. Office of Attorney General

AN ACT TO ESTABLISH THE JUDICIAL COURTS
OF THE UNITED STATES, SEPTEMBER 24, 1789*

Sec. 35. *And be it further enacted,* That in all courts of the United States, the parties may plead and manage their own causes personally or by the assistance of such counsel or attorneys at law as by the rules of the said courts respectively shall be permitted to manage and conduct causes therein. And there shall be appointed in each district a meet person learned in the law to act as attorney for the United States in such district, who shall be sworn or affirmed to the faithful executions of his office, whose duty it shall be to prosecute in such district all delinquents for crimes and offences, cognizable under the authority of the United States, and all civil actions in which the United States shall be concerned, except before the supreme court in the district in which that court shall be holden. And he shall receive as a compensation for his services such fees as shall be taxed therefor in the respective courts before which the suits or prosecutions shall be. And there shall also be appointed a meet person, learned in the law, to act as attorney-general for the United States, who shall be sworn or affirmed to a faithful execution of his office; whose duty it shall be to prosecute and conduct all suits in the Supreme Court in which the United States shall be concerned, and to give his advice and opinion upon questions of law when required by the President of the United States, or when requested by the heads of any of the departments, touching any matters that may concern their departments, and shall receive such compensation for his services as shall by law be provided.

---

* 1 Stat. 20, sec. 35 (1789). The excluded sections, 1 through 34, established the Federal Court System.

PART II

The Management Movement

The Management Movement

American governmental experience during the nation's first century offers rather little guidance or precedent for modern public administration, either as a field of study or as a professional activity. True, many of the leaders in Washington, in the states, and in the cities, proved to be effective administrators, and some of them spent the larger part of their working lives in administrative work. In the first several decades, a good many could regard their public service as a duty, as a "calling," and a few passed along some useful insights in their memoirs and other writings. But on the whole, we gained rather little in the way of a core of knowledge and understanding about the administrative side of government. In fact, the meaning of "administration" itself was ambiguous. In this neglect, we fell behind most of the countries in the industrializing West: the Germans and Austrians had their cameralism; most of the European continent had undergone the Napoleonic era of rationalizing and legalizing administrative structures and processes; even Britain had experienced its great reforms in budgeting and personnel.

The relative slowness of the development in this country of a true field of public administration may be—and has been—attributed to many factors. Among them were: the open frontier; the reliance upon private enterprise in the development and exploitation of the nation; the fear, inherited from colonial experience, of executive (or administrative) oppression, and the derivative negative stance toward administrative growth and power; the fact that rather few public organizations were of sufficient size to make their administration a matter of serious concern.

Other more strictly governmental factors contributed. One was of course the federal system, then construed as what we now call dual federalism, whereby the national and the state governments had relatively (but never totally) restricted and exclusive areas of operation, and wherein the great bulk of common services were

43

provided by hundreds and later thousands of local units. A second was the doctrine of separation of powers, particularly between the executives (the President, the state governors, the city mayors) and the legislatures (the Congress, the state legislatures, the city councils). The doctrine was not clear—and is still not clear—as to the powers and responsibilities of the executive and the legislative branches with respect to the administration of public programs. During much of the nineteenth century, and with the exceptions of the Jackson administration and in wartime, the balance tended in the direction of the legislative and away from the executive in both the nation and the states, thus inhibiting the development of integrated, coordinated, and unified administrations.

Another factor was the development of political parties and of their interest and involvement in day-to-day administrative matters. This tendency was accentuated by the doctrine of simplicity of government work, itself a rationale for frequent rotation in office and tenure limited to periods of sympathetic political affiliation. The doctrine was most plainly stated by President Andrew Jackson in his first annual message to Congress in 1829: "The duties of all public offices are, or at least admit of being made, so plain and simple that men of intelligence may readily qualify themselves for their performance; and I cannot but believe that more is lost by the long continuance of men in office than is generally to be gained by their experience."*

Administrative systems characterized by fragmentation of activities among thousands of more or less autonomous governmental units, most of them small, by fragmented leadership between executive and legislative and within the legislatures, by political infiltration in operations, and by the spoils system are not fertile ground for the cultivation of a sound public administration.

The developments here summarized as the "management movement" were, in considerable degree, a *response* to the conditions described above: fragmentation of responsibilities; lack of unified leadership; political corruption; and spoils. They were spawned in an era of reform, of progressivism, of growing professionalism and occupational specialism, and of faith in rationality

---

* James D. Richardson, *Messages and Papers of the Presidents*, vol. 2 (Bureau of National Literature and Art, 1903), p. 449.

and applied science. They were paralleled, to some extent anticipated, in the private sector by business reform and scientific management.

Despite the fact that the bulk of the documents reproduced in
this section were produced by the national government, most of the
doctrines which they reflect were in fact developed and first
applied in local and, to a lesser extent, state governments. The bulk
of governmental activity was local, as was the bulk of corruption
and maladministration. A number of private organizations at city,
state, and nation-wide levels directed their efforts to one or several
facets of governmental reform. Perhaps most noteworthy among
these were those indigenous American institutions known as
bureaus of municipal research, the first and most noteworthy of
which was that of New York City, founded in 1906 as the Bureau of
City Betterment, incorporated a year later as the Bureau of Municipal Research, and a few years later associated with the Training
School for Public Service. The purposes of the New York Bureau,
as stated in its Articles of Incorporation, are quite a good summa-
tion of the nature of the management movement as a whole:*

> To promote efficient and economical municipal gov-
> ernment; to promote adoption of scientific methods of
> accounting and of reporting the details of municipal
> business, with a view to facilitating the work of public
> officials; to secure constructive publicity in matters per-
> taining to municipal problems; to collect, to classify, to
> analyze, to correlate, to interpret and to publish facts as
> to the administration of municipal government.

The New York Bureau, like a few other seed-planting organizations of its kind, did not confine its attention to its city nor to cities in
general. It made studies in cities across the country, in states, and in
the national government, and it spawned sister bureaus in many
other places. For example, its second director had chaired President Taft's Commission on Economy and Efficiency, and a later
director served as a member of President F. D. Roosevelt's three-
man Committee on Administrative Management (reports of both

---

* Bureau of Municipal Research, New York, *Municipal Research*, no. 61, May 1915.

groups quoted below); it did the staff work for the New York State Constitutional Convention in 1915 and for a number of other states as well; and it conducted the basic investigations which led to the Classification Act of 1923.

Although the seeds of what came to be known as public administration were planted before the Civil War, the management movement itself may for convenience be considered to have started during the last two decades of the nineteenth century. It matured during the first third of the twentieth century. Although some of its culminating acts and expressions were produced during the New Deal period (see Part III), the movement itself had then become engulfed by the overwhelming concerns of the Great Depression and the redirection of the whole governmental system which resulted from that cataclysm.

The movement had three principal elements. First was *personnel reform,* the development of stable civil services premised on merit. Second was organizational and procedural reform, the main feature of which was *recognition of chief executives as the heads of administration,* to be made effective through integration of related activities in departments and other units, hierarchical structures of authority and responsibility, the concept of staff, and modernization and rationalization of procedures and methods. Third was the planning and control of public finances, more specifically, *the budget.*

1. THE CIVIL SERVICE SYSTEM

Although agitation against the spoils system had been building for more than a generation and, during that period, a few positive, usually temporary, actions had been taken to purge it, the first general and official step in this country was the passage during the Grant administration of a civil service reform bill. Enacted in 1871 as a rider to an appropriation bill, it consisted of one very long sentence:*

> That the President of the United States be, and he is hereby, authorized to prescribe such rules and regula-

---

* 16 Stat. 514 (1871).

tions for the admission of persons into the civil service of the United States as will best promote the efficiency thereof, and ascertain the fitness of each candidate in respect to age, health, character, knowledge, and ability for the branch of service into which he seeks to enter; and for this purpose the President is authorized to employ suitable persons to conduct said inquiries, to prescribe their duties, and to establish regulations for the conduct of persons who may receive appointments in the civil service.

Pursuant to this Act, the President set up the first Civil Service Commission, which embarked on a program considerably broader and more ambitious than that contemplated by the Pendleton Act a dozen years later, but its effectiveness was virtually nullified by the twice repeated failure of Congress to appropriate any funds for it. It went out of existence in 1875.

But the momentum for civil service reform increased during the years that followed. President Rutherford B. Hayes requested that Dorman B. Eaton, a New York lawyer and reformer, make a study and report on British experience with civil service reform. Eaton, who had been second chairman of Grant's Civil Service Commission and who was later to recommend the language of what came to be known as the Pendleton Act and to become first chairman of the permanent Civil Service Commission, submitted his report in 1879. The lengthy report, later published commercially and widely disseminated, set forth its conclusions and recommendations for an American merit system in several paragraphs, which are reproduced below *(1a)*.

The Civil Service (Pendleton) Act *(1b)* of 1883, though initially imitative of the British system, departed from it in many important respects. It addressed itself to only a few elements of public personnel administration as we now understand it, and applied to only a small minority of American public servants. Yet it formed the precedent and the basis for American personnel administration—and still does. Further, over the years, its influence has been widely diffused among the majority of American states and many of their local jurisdictions. It remains unquestionably one of the most important administrative statutes in American history.

2. Act to Regulate Commerce (1887)

In 1887, the Congress created the Interstate Commerce Commission in pursuance of its Constitutional power to regulate commerce. The Commission's principal initial concern was with railroad rates, but a variety of legislation in succeeding decades extended it to other modes and practices in interstate transportation. Modeled to some extent on a great number of regulatory commissions in the states and perhaps to a limited extent on the U.S. Civil Service Commission, which had been created four years earlier, it was the first of the federal regulatory commissions operating today and set the pattern of those semi-autonomous agencies which have sometimes been labeled the fourth branch of government.

3. Establishment of the General Staff of the Army

An organizational change of a different kind occurred a few years later. Thanks to the total ineptness of the Spanish forces, the United States emerged victorious in the short and one-sided Spanish-American War of 1898. But one feature of that war which became painfully evident and was widely publicized was the ineffectiveness and lack of coordination in the administration of the U.S. Army. Shortly thereafter, President McKinley appointed as Secretary of War, Elihu Root, a prominent New York attorney with no prior knowledge or experience in military affairs. Root undertook to educate himself about not only the deficiencies of the Army but also the organizational practices of major military forces in other nations, notably Germany, France, and Britain. His studies led him to the conviction that what was needed was a central agency for planning strategy, for programming, and for coordinating execution (a general staff), and a central officer with power over not only the armies in the field but also the various bureaus and services which provided their support (a chief of staff). By 1902, he was prepared to recommend such to the President and the Congress *(3a);* and the following year, the Congress acted affirmatively on his recommendations by passing the Act Creating the General Staff *(3b).*

The establishment of the General Staff had a significance which went well beyond the administration of the Army. The staff idea unquestionably carried over to civilian government at all levels, partly indeed through the person of Elihu Root himself. It was repeatedly referred to as a model in subsequent reforms of civil agencies—the Bureau of the Budget; budget, finance, and administrative offices in state and local governments; and offices of the heads of large departments.

4. REPORT OF THE (TAFT) COMMISSION ON ECONOMY AND EFFICIENCY: THE NEED FOR A NATIONAL BUDGET (1912)

The Army's General Staff may or may not have *directly* influenced the Commission on Economy and Efficiency set up by President Taft in 1910, but the central philosophy of the two with regard to the authority and responsibility of the President for national public administration was consistent. Between the Civil War and the opening of the twentieth century, there had been no fewer than four different Congressional committees to examine and make recommendations with regard to the efficiency of the administration. Best known of these were the Cockrell Committee (of senators, 1887-89) and the Dockery-Cockrell Joint Commission (of senators and representatives, 1893-95), which concentrated on rather detailed matters of internal departmental administration and accounting. All of these implicitly or explicitly affirmed the responsibility of the Congress with regard to national administration and virtually ignored any role in these matters on the part of the President.

President Theodore Roosevelt took an opposite view, more nearly in keeping with Alexander Hamilton's emphasis on "energy in the Executive." He urged that the President be granted and exert authority for reorganization and management of the administrative agencies. Early in his first elected term he established, without Congressional sanction, a Commission on Department Methods (1905-1909), better known as the Keep Commission for its chairman, Charles H. Keep, then Assistant Secretary of the Treasury. It was composed of high but sub-cabinet officials in the administration, and its work was entirely "in-house." It produced an impressive number of reports and recommendations, some of which—like personnel classification and the Federal Register— were implemented in later decades. But Congress, jealous of such Executive intrusion, acted on none of its legislative recommendations.

President Taft, more judicious than Roosevelt, requested that Congress establish and fund a Commission on Economy and Efficiency, to be appointed by the President. Unlike any of its predecessors, this group included outstanding reformers and scholars in political science. It endorsed the concept of Presidential responsibility for administration. It recommended Presidential initiative in regard to reorganization, a Bureau of the Budget reporting to the President, and a managerial staff under the Bureau for continuing studies of efficiency. Most of all, it urged what later came to be known as the executive budget, to be employed not only as a financial tool but as an instrument for recommending policies and programs. An independent Bureau of Efficiency was established in 1916—and abolished in 1933. But the central idea of an executive budget was not authorized until 1921, almost a decade after the Taft Commission's report. Meanwhile, however, the concept spread far and wide among state and local governments.

5. MODEL CITY CHARTER OF THE NATIONAL MUNICIPAL LEAGUE (1916)

The National Municipal League was, and remains at this writing, an outstanding citizens' voluntary organization dedicated to the reform and improvement of government at local and state levels. Organized in 1894 primarily to counter municipal corruption, it periodically developed, disseminated, and promoted model state constitutions, model legislation in various fields, and model city charters. Though not in any usual sense "official," these had great influence on the reform of cities and states, some of which adopted significant parts of them virtually without change. In 1916, the National Municipal League issued its second Model City Charter along with a Model Home Rule Amendment for state constitutions. The documents had been prepared during the previous three years by a committee of twelve prominent citizens, of whom five were or had been professors of political science. The Model City Charter is a good representation of the acme of the management movement in the cities and of governmental reform generally. Among its features were provisions for: initiative, referendum, and recall; a relatively small city council, elected at large or, in large cities, in relatively large districts; proportional representation (optional); all powers vested in the council, except where otherwise provided in the charter itself; a mayor, chosen from its own membership by the council; a strict separation of policy (the council's province) and administration (the city manager's province); a civil service system, governed by a virtually autonomous civil service board; a city planning board, likewise virtually autonomous, but with powers limited to advising and making recommendations to the council.

It is interesting that the 1916 Model City Charter, only a fraction of which is reproduced here, was about three times the length of the original Constitution of the United States.

6. BUDGET AND ACCOUNTING ACT (1921)

A direct though belated product of the Taft Commission on Economy and Efficiency was this monumental Act of 1921, signed by President Harding. It established the Bureau of the Budget and placed it in the Treasury Department; it was later transferred, in 1939, to the Executive Office of the President. Still later, in 1970, it became the Office of Management and Budget. The Act also created the office of Comptroller General in charge of a newly established General Accounting Office, both considered as agents of Congress rather than the President. President Wilson had vetoed an almost identical bill on the grounds that deprivation of Presidential power to remove the Comptroller General (who was given a fixed term of fifteen years) was a violation of the Constitution. One of the most perceptive of observers and students of American government has described the Budget and Accounting Act of 1921 as "probably the greatest landmark of our administrative history except for the Constitution itself."*

7. CLASSIFICATION ACT (1923)

Although there had been complaints since the eighteenth century about inadequacy and inequities in compensation of employees at all levels of government, and despite a number of recommenda-

---

* Herbert Emmerich, *Federal Organization and Administrative Management* (University of Alabama Press, 1971), pp. 40-41.

tions and a few tentative steps to ameliorate them, it was not until the second decade of the twentieth century that the concepts of position classification and "equal pay for equal work" were given general application. As was true of other elements of managerial reform, position classification was first adopted at the municipal level—in this instance, the City of Chicago in 1912. Classification spread rapidly in the periods before and after World War I among cities and states. It was not until the close of that war that the Congress set up a Joint Commission on Reclassification whose report in 1920 set forth a plan for a classification system for the national government. Its proposals provided the basis for the Classification Act of 1923. The Act provided for administration by an *ex officio* Personnel Classification Board, but its powers and responsibilities were later (in 1932) transferred to the Civil Service Commission.* Initially applicable only to employees in Washington, the Congress in 1940 authorized the President to extend it to the field service so that it was made applicable to the great bulk of the Federal civil service.† Position classification became a focal tool of management, not only in the various facets of personnel administration but also in relation to organization planning and control, budgeting, and work measurement and evaluation.

* 47 Stat. 416, Title V, secs. 505-509 (1932).
† The Ramspeck Act, 54 Stat. 1211 (1940).

1. The Civil Service System

a. Report Concerning Civil Service in Great Britain

Excerpt of Report by Dorman Eaton (1879)*

Chapter XXXIII

THE BEARING OF BRITISH EXPERIENCE
UPON CIVIL SERVICE REFORM IN THE UNITED STATES

... Still ... there remain the direct questions: Has the new system been adequately tested? Is it adapted to our constitutions and social life? Is it republican in spirit and consistent with the practical administration of government under our institutions? Have we the public intelligence and virtue which warrant the attempt to carry forward such a reform?

Some of these questions, I must think, have been sufficiently answered, if indeed it were possible to hesitate as to the answer to be given; and the others can be more intelligently considered if we have distinctly before our minds the principles and conclusions which have become accepted in the later experience of Great Britain. They may be briefly stated as follows:

1. Public office creates a relation of trust and duty of a kind which requires all authority and influence pertaining to it to be exercised with the same absolute conformity to moral standards, to the spirit of the constitution and the laws, and to the common interests of the people, which may be insisted upon in the use of public money or any other common property of the people; and, therefore, whatever difficulty may attend the practical application of the rule of duty, it is identically the

---

* U.S., Congress, House, H.R. Ex. Doc. 1, part 7, 46th Cong., 2d sess., 1879, pp. 215-17.

same whether it be applied to property or to official discretion. There can in principle be no official discretion to disregard common interests or to grant official favors to persons or to parties.

2. So far as any right is involved, in filling offices, it is the right of the people to have the worthiest citizens in the public service for the general welfare; and the privilege of sharing the honors and profits of holding office appertains equally to every citizen, in proportion to his measure of character and capacity which qualify him for such service.

4. [sic] The ability, attainments, and character requisite for the fit discharge of official duties of any kind,—in other words, the personal merits of the candidate—are *in themselves the highest claim* upon an office.

5. Party government and the salutary activity of parties are not super-seded, but they are made purer and more efficient, by the *merit system* of office, which brings larger capacity and higher character to their support.

6. Government by parties is enfeebled and debased by reliance upon a partisan system of appointments and removals; and, for its most vigorous life and salutary influence, it is only needful for the party majority to select, as the representatives of its views and the executors of its policy, the few high officers with whom rests the power to direct the national affairs, and to instruct and keep in the line of their duty the whole body of their subordinates through whose administrative work that policy is to be carried into effect.

7. Patronage in the hands of members of the legislature, which origi-nated in a usurpation of executive functions, increases the expenses of administration, is degrading and demoralizing to those who possess it, is disastrous to legislation, tends to impair the counterpoise and stability of the government; and it cannot withstand the criticism of an intelligent people when they fairly comprehend its character and consequences.

8. Examinations (in connection with investigations of character) may be so conducted as to ascertain, with far greater certainty than by any other means, the persons who are the most fit for the public service; and the worthiest thus disclosed may be selected for the public service by a just and non-partisan method, which the most enlightened public opinion will heartily approve.

9. Open competition presents at once the most just and practicable means of supplying fit persons for appointment. It is proved to have given the best public servants; it makes an end of patronage; and, besides being based on equal rights and common justice, it has been found to be the surest safeguard against both partisan coercion and official favoritism.

10. Such methods, which leave to parties and party government their true functions in unimpaired vigor, tend to reduce manipulation, in-trigue, and every form of corruption in politics to their smallest propor-

tions. They also reward learning, give more importance to character and principles, and make political life more attractive to all worthy citizens.

11. Regarded as a whole, the new system has raised the ambition and advanced both the self-respect and the popular estimation of those in the public service, while it has encouraged general education, arrested demoralizing solicitation for office, and promoted economy, efficiency, and fidelity in public affairs.

12. A system is entirely practicable under which official salaries shall increase during the more active years of life, and through which a retiring allowance is retained to be paid upon the officer leaving the public service; and such a system appears to contribute to economy and fidelity in administration.

13. Open competition is as fatal to all the conditions of a bureaucracy, as it is to patronage, nepotism and every form of favoritism, in the public service.

14. The merit system, by raising the character and capacity of the subordinate service, and by accustoming the people to consider personal worth and sound principles, rather than selfish interest and adroit management, as the controlling elements of success in politics, has also invigorated national patriotism, raised the standard of statesmanship, and caused political leaders to look more to the better sentiments and the higher intelligence for support.

---

b. Civil Service (Pendleton) Act (1883)

An Act to Regulate and Improve the Civil Service of the United States*

Be it enacted by the Senate and House of Representatives of the United States of America in Congress assembled, That the President is authorized to appoint, by and with the advice and consent of the Senate, three persons, not more than two of whom shall be adherents of the same party, as Civil Service Commissioners, and said three commissioners shall constitute the United States Civil Service Commission. Said commissioners shall hold no other official place under the United States.

---

* 22 Stat. 27 (1883). Section 4, which covers office space, is omitted.

The President may remove any commissioner; and any vacancy in the position of commissioner shall be so filled by the President, by and with the advice and consent of the Senate, as to conform to said conditions for the first selection of commissioners.

The commissioners shall each receive a salary of three thousand five hundred dollars a year. And each of said commissioners shall be paid his necessary traveling expenses incurred in the discharge of his duty as a commissioner.

Sec. 2. That it shall be the duty of said commissioners:

First. To aid the President, as he may request, in preparing suitable rules for carrying this act into effect, and when said rules shall have been promulgated it shall be the duty of all officers of the United States in the departments and offices to which any such rules may relate to aid, in all proper ways, in carrying said rules, and any modifications thereof, into effect.

Second. And, among other things, said rules shall provide and declare, as nearly as the conditions of good administration will warrant, as follows:

First, for open, competitive examinations for testing the fitness of applicants for the public service now classified or to be classified hereunder. Such examinations shall be practical in their character, and so far as may be shall relate to those matters which will fairly test the relative capacity and fitness of the persons examined to discharge the duties of the service into which they seek to be appointed.

Second, that all the offices, places, and employments so arranged or to be arranged in classes shall be filled by selections according to grade from among those graded highest as the results of such competitive examinations.

Third, appointments to the public service aforesaid in the departments at Washington shall be apportioned among the several States and Territories and the District of Columbia upon the basis of population as ascertained at the last preceding census. Every application for an examination shall contain, among other things, a statement, under oath, setting forth his or her actual bona fide residence at the time of making the application, as well as how long he or she has been a resident of such place.

Fourth, that there shall be a period of probation before any absolute appointment or employment aforesaid.

Fifth, that no person in the public service is for that reason under any obligations to contribute to any political fund, or to render any political service, and that he will not be removed or otherwise prejudiced for refusing to do so.

Sixth, that no person in said service has any right to use his official authority or influence to coerce the political action of any person or body.

Seventh, there shall be non-competitive examinations in all proper cases before the commission, when competent persons do not compete, after notice has been given of the existence of the vacancy, under such rules as may be prescribed by the commissioners as to the manner of giving notice.

Eighth, that notice shall be given in writing by the appointing power to said commission of the persons selected for appointment or employment from among those who have been examined, of the place of residence of such persons, of the rejection of any such persons after probation, of transfers, resignations, and removals, and of the date thereof, and a record of the same shall be kept by said commission. And any necessary exceptions from said eight fundamental provisions of the rules shall be set forth in connection with such rules, and the reasons therefor shall be stated in the annual reports of the commission.

Third. Said commission shall, subject to the rules that may be made by the President, make regulations for, and have control of, such examinations, and, through its members or the examiners, it shall supervise and preserve the records of the same; and said commission shall keep minutes of its own proceedings.

Fourth. Said commission may make investigations concerning the facts, and may report upon all matters touching the enforcement and effects of said rules and regulations, and concerning the action of any examiner or board of examiners hereinafter provided for, and its own subordinates, and those in the public service, in respect to the execution of this act.

Fifth. Said commission shall make an annual report to the President for transmission to Congress, showing its own action, the rules and regulations and the exceptions thereto in force, the practical effects thereof, and any suggestions it may approve for the more effectual accomplishment of the purposes of this act.

Sec. 3. That said commission is authorized to employ a chief examiner, a part of whose duty it shall be, under its direction, to act with the examining boards, so far as practicable, whether at Washington or elsewhere, and to secure accuracy, uniformity, and justice in all their proceedings, which shall be at all times open to him. The chief examiner shall be entitled to receive a salary at the rate of three thousand dollars a year, and he shall be paid his necessary traveling expenses incurred in the discharge of his duty. The commission shall have a secretary, to be appointed by the President, who shall receive a salary of one thousand six hundred dollars per annum. It may, when necessary, employ a stenographer, and a messenger, who shall be paid, when employed, the former at the rate of one thousand six hundred dollars a year, and the latter at the rate of six hundred dollars a year. The commission shall, at Washington, and in one or more places in each State and Territory where examinations are to take place, designate and select a suitable number of persons, not less than three, in the official service of the United States, residing in said State or Territory, after consulting the head of the department or office in which such persons serve, to be members of boards of examiners, and may at any time substitute any other person in said service living in such State or Territory in the place of any one so selected. Such boards of examiners shall be so located as to make it reasonably convenient and inexpensive for applicants to attend before them; and where there are persons to be examined in any State or Territory, examinations shall be held therein at least twice in each year. It shall be the duty of the collector, postmaster, and other officers of the United States, at any place outside of the District of Columbia where examinations are directed by the President or by said board to be held, to allow the reasonable use of the public buildings for holding such examinations, and in all proper ways to facilitate the same.

Sec. 5. That any said commissioner, examiner, copyist, or messenger, or any person in the public service who shall willfully and corruptly, by himself or in co-operation with one or more other persons, defeat, deceive, or obstruct any person in respect of his or her right of examination according to any such rules or regulations, or who shall willfully, corruptly, and falsely mark, grade, estimate, or report upon the examination or proper standing of any person examined hereunder, or aid in so doing, or who shall willfully and corruptly make any false representations concerning the same or concerning the person examined, or who shall willfully and corruptly furnish to any person any special or secret information for the purpose of either improving or injuring the prospects or chances of any person so examined, or to be examined, being appointed, employed, or promoted, shall for each such offense be deemed guilty of a misdemeanor, and upon conviction thereof, shall be punished by a fine of not less than one hundred dollars, nor more than one thousand dollars, or by imprisonment not less than ten days, nor more than one year, or by both such fine and imprisonment.

Sec. 6. That within sixty days after the passage of this act it shall be the duty of the Secretary of the Treasury, in as near conformity as may be to the classification of certain clerks now existing under the one hundred and sixty-third section of the Revised Statutes, to arrange in classes the several clerks and persons employed by the collector, naval officer, surveyor, and appraisers, or either of them, or being in the public service, at their respective offices in each customs district where the whole number of said clerks and persons shall be all together as many as fifty. And thereafter, from time to time, on the direction of the President, said Secretary shall make the like classification or arrangement of clerks and persons so employed, in connection with any said office or offices, in any other customs district. And, upon like request, and for the purposes of this act, said Secretary shall arrange in one or more of said classes, or of existing classes, any other clerks, agents, or persons employed under his department in any said district not now classified; and every such arrangement and classification upon being made shall be reported to the President.

Second. Within said sixty days it shall be the duty of the Postmaster-General, in general conformity to said one hundred and sixty-third section, to separately arrange in classes the several clerks and persons employed, or in the public service, at each post-office, or under any postmaster of the United States, where the whole number of said clerks and persons shall together amount to as many as fifty. And thereafter, from time to time, on the direction of the President, it shall be the duty of the Postmaster-General to arrange in like classes the clerks and persons so employed in the postal service in connection with any other post-office; and every such arrangement and classification upon being made shall be reported to the President.

Third. That from time to time said Secretary, the Postmaster-General, and each of the heads of departments mentioned in the one hundred and fifty-eighth section of the Revised Statutes, and each head of an office, shall, on the direction of the President, and for facilitating the execution of this act, respectively revise any then existing classification or arrangement of those in their respective departments and offices, and shall, for the purposes of the examination herein provided for, include in one or more of such classes, so far as practicable, subordinate places, clerks, and officers in the public service pertaining to their respective departments not before classified for examination.

Sec. 7. That after the expiration of six months from the passage of this act no officer or clerk shall be appointed, and no person shall be employed to enter or be promoted in either of the said classes now existing, or that may be arranged hereunder pursuant to said rules, until he has passed an examination, or is shown to be specially exempted from such examination in conformity herewith. But nothing herein contained shall be construed to take from those honorably discharged from the military or naval service any preference conferred by the seventeen hundred and fifty-fourth section of the Revised Statutes, nor to take from the President any authority not inconsistent with this act conferred by the seventeen hundred and fifty-third section of said statutes; nor shall any officer not in the executive branch of the government, or any person merely employed as a laborer or workman, be required to be classified hereunder; nor, unless by direction of the Senate, shall any person who has been nominated for confirmation by the Senate be required to be classified or to pass an examination.

Sec. 8. That no person habitually using intoxicating beverages to excess shall be appointed to, or retained in, any office, appointment, or employment to which the provisions of this act are applicable.

Sec. 9. That whenever there are already two or more members of a family in the public service in the grades covered by this act, no other member of such family shall be eligible to appointment to any of said grades.

Sec. 10. That no recommendation of any person who shall apply for office or place under the provisions of this act which may be given by any Senator or member of the House of Representatives, except as to the character or residence of the applicant, shall be received or considered by any person concerned in making any examination or appointment under this act.

Sec. 11. That no Senator, or Representative, or Territorial Delegate of the Congress, or Senator, Representative, or Delegate elect, or any officer or employee of either of said houses, and no executive, judicial, military, or naval officer of the United States, and no clerk or employee of any department, branch or bureau of the executive, judicial, or military or naval service of the United States, shall, directly or indirectly, solicit or receive, or be in any manner concerned in soliciting or receiving, any assessment, subscription, or contribution for any political purpose whatever, from any officer, clerk, or employee of the United States, or any department, branch, or bureau thereof, or from any person receiving any salary or compensation from moneys derived from the Treasury of the United States.

Sec. 12. That no person shall, in any room or building occupied in the discharge of official duties by any officer or employee of the United States mentioned in this act, or in any navy-yard, fort, or arsenal, solicit in any manner whatever, or receive any contribution of money or any other thing of value for any political purpose whatever.

Sec. 13. No officer or employee of the United States mentioned in this act shall discharge, or promote, or degrade, or in manner change the official rank or compensation of any other officer or employee, or promise or threaten so to do, for giving or withholding or neglecting to make any contribution of money or other valuable thing for any political purpose.

Sec. 14. That no officer, clerk, or other person in the service of the United States shall, directly or indirectly, give or hand over to any other officer, clerk, or person in the service of the United States, or to any Senator or Member of the House of Representatives, or Territorial Delegate, any money or other valuable thing on account of or to be applied to the promotion of any political object whatever.

Sec. 15. That any person who shall be guilty of violating any provision of the four foregoing sections shall be deemed guilty of a misdemeanor, and shall, on conviction thereof, be punished by a fine not exceeding five thousand dollars, or by imprisonment for a term not exceeding three years, or by such fine and imprisonment both, in the discretion of the court.

2. Act to Regulate Commerce (1887)*

Sec. 11. That a Commission is hereby created and established to be known as the Inter-State Commerce Commission, which shall be composed of five Commissioners, who shall be appointed by the President, by and with the advice and consent of the Senate. The Commissioners first appointed under this act shall continue in office for the term of two, three, four, five, and six years, respectively, from the first day of January, anno Domini

* 24 Stat. 104 (1887). Excluded are sections 1 through 10, which do not pertain to the establishment of the Interstate Commerce Commission, and sections 18, 19, 23 and 24, which contain details on internal administration, funding, and implementation.

eighteen hundred and eighty-seven, the term of each to be designated by the President; but their successors shall be appointed for terms of six years, except that any person chosen to fill a vacancy shall be appointed only for the unexpired term of the Commissioner whom he shall succeed. Any Commissioner may be removed by the President for inefficiency, neglect of duty, or malfeasance in office. Not more than three of the Commissioners shall be appointed from the same political party. No person in the employ of or holding any official relation to any common carrier subject to the provisions of this act, or owning stock or bonds thereof, or who is in any manner pecuniarily interested therein, shall enter upon the duties of or hold such office. Said Commissioners shall not engage in any other business, vocation, or employment. No vacancy in the commission shall impair the right of the remaining Commissioners to exercise all the powers of the Commission.

Sec. 12. That the Commission hereby created shall have authority to inquire into the management of the business of all common carriers subject to the provisions of this act, and shall keep itself informed as to the manner and method in which the same is conducted, and shall have the right to obtain from such common carriers full and complete information necessary to enable the Commission to perform the duties and carry out the objects for which it was created; and for the purposes of this act the Commission shall have power to require the attendance and testimony of witnesses and the production of all books, papers, tariffs, contracts, agreements, and documents relating to any matter under investigation, and to that end may invoke the aid of any court of the United States in requiring the attendance and testimony of witnesses and the production of books, papers, and documents under the provisions of this section.

And any of the circuit courts of the United States within the jurisdiction of which such inquiry is carried on may, in case of contumacy or refusal to obey a subpoena issued to any common carrier subject to the provisions of this act, or other person, issue an order requiring such common carrier or other person to appear before said Commission (and produce books and papers if so ordered) and give evidence touching the matter in question; and any failure to obey such order of the court may be punished by such court as a contempt thereof. The claim that any such testimony or evidence may tend to criminate the person giving such evidence shall not excuse such witness from testifying; but such evidence or testimony shall not be used against such person on the trial of any criminal proceeding.

Sec. 13. That any person, firm, corporation, or association, or any mercantile, agricultural, or manufacturing society, or any body politic or municipal organization complaining of anything done or omitted to be done by any common carrier subject to the provisions of this act in contravention of the provisions thereof, may apply to said Commission by petition, which shall briefly state the facts; whereupon a statement of the charges thus made shall be forwarded by the Commission to such common carrier, who shall be called upon to satisfy the complaint or to answer the same in writing within a reasonable time, to be specified by the Commission. If such common carrier, within the time specified, shall make reparation for the injury alleged to have been done, said carrier shall be relieved of liability to the complainant only for the particular violation of law thus complained of. If such carrier shall not satisfy the complaint within the time specified, or there shall appear to be any reasonable ground for investigating said complaint, it shall be the duty of the Commission to investigate the matters complained of in such manner and by such means as it shall deem proper.

Said Commission shall in like manner investigate any complaint forwarded by the railroad commissioner or railroad commission of any State or Territory, at the request of such commissioner or commission, and may institute any inquiry on its own motion in the same manner and to the same effect as though complaint had been made.

No complaint shall at any time be dismissed because of the absence of direct damage to the complainant.

Sec. 14. That whenever an investigation shall be made by said Commission, it shall be its duty to make a report in writing in respect thereto, which shall include the findings of fact upon which the conclusions of the Commission are based, together with its recommendation as to what reparation, if any, should be made by the common carrier to any party or parties who may be found to have been injured; and such findings so made shall thereafter, in all judicial proceedings, be deemed prima facie evidence as to each and every fact found.

All reports of investigations made by the Commission shall be entered of record, and a copy thereof shall be furnished to the party who may have complained, and to any common carrier that may have been complained of.

Sec. 15. That if in any case in which an investigation shall be made by said Commission it shall be made to appear to the satisfaction of the Commission, either by the testimony of witnesses or other evidence, that anything has been done or omitted to be done in violation of the provisions of this act, or of any law cognizable by said Commission, by any common carrier, or that any injury or damage has been sustained by the party or parties complaining, or by other parties aggrieved in consequence of any such violation, it shall be the duty of the Commission to forthwith cause a copy of its report in respect thereto to be delivered to such common carrier, together with a notice to said common carrier to cease and desist from such violation, or to make reparation for the injury so found to have been done, or both, within a reasonable time, to be specified by the Commission; and if, within the time specified, it shall be made to appear to the Commission that such common carrier has ceased from such violation of law, and has made reparation for the injury found to have been done, in compliance with the report and notice of the Commission, or to the satisfaction of the party complaining, a statement to that effect shall be entered of record by the Commission, and the said common carrier shall thereupon be relieved from further liability or penalty for such particular violation of law.

Sec. 16. That whenever any common carrier, as defined in and subject to the provisions of this act, shall violate or refuse or neglect to obey any lawful order or requirement of the Commission in this act named, it shall be the duty of the Commission, and lawful for any company or person interested in such order or requirement, to apply, in a summary way, by petition, to the circuit court of the United States sitting in equity in the judicial district in which the common carrier complained of has its principal office, or in which the violation or disobedience of such order or requirement shall happen, alleging such violation or disobedience, as the case may be; and the said court shall have power to hear and determine the matter, on such short notice to the common carrier complained of as the court shall deem reasonable; and such notice may be served on such common carrier, his or its officers, agents, or servants, in such manner as the court shall direct; and said court shall proceed to hear and determine the matter speedily as a court of equity, and without the formal pleadings and proceedings applicable to ordinary suits in equity, but in such manner as to do justice in the premises; and to this end such court shall have power, if it think fit, to direct and prosecute, in such mode and by such persons as it may appoint, all such inquiries as the court may think needful to enable it to form a just judgment in the matter of such petition; and on such hearings the report of said Commission shall be prima facie evidence of the matters therein stated; and if it be made to appear to such court, on such hearing or on report of any such person or persons, that the lawful order or requirement of said Commission drawn in question has been violated or disobeyed, it shall be lawful for such court to issue a writ of injunction or other proper process, mandatory or otherwise, to restrain such common carrier from further continuing such violation or disobedience of such order or requirement of said Commission, and enjoining obedience to the same; and in case of any disobedience of any such writ of injunction or other proper process, mandatory or otherwise, it shall be lawful for such court to issue writs of attachment, or any other process of said court incident or applicable to writs of injunction or other proper process, mandatory or otherwise, against such common carrier, and if a corporation, against one or more of the directors, officers, or agents of the same, or against any owner, lessee, trustee, receiver, or other person failing to obey such writ of injunction or other proper process, mandatory or otherwise; and said court may, if it shall think fit, make an order directing such common carrier or other person so disobeying such writ of injunction or other proper process, mandatory or otherwise, to pay such sum of money not exceeding for each carrier or person in default the sum of five hundred dollars for every day after a day to be named in the order that such carrier or other person shall fail to obey such injunction or other proper process, mandatory or otherwise; and such moneys shall be payable as the court shall direct, either to the party complaining, or into court to abide the ultimate decision of the court, or into the Treasury; and payment thereof may, without prejudice to any other mode of recovering the same, be enforced by attachment or order in the nature of a writ of execution, in like manner as if the same had been recovered by a final decree in personam in such court. When the subject in dispute shall be of the value of two thousand dollars or more, either party to such proceeding before said court may appeal to the Supreme Court of the United States, under the same regulations now provided by law in respect of security for such appeal; but such appeal shall not operate to stay or supersede the order of the court or the execution of any writ or process thereon; and such court may, in every such matter, order the payment of such costs and counsel fees as shall be deemed reasonable. Whenever any such petitions shall be filed or presented by the Commission it shall be the duty of the district attorney, under the direction of the Attorney-General of the United States, to prosecute the same; and the costs and expenses of such prosecution shall be paid out of the appropriation for the expenses of the courts of the United States. For the purposes of this act, excepting its penal provisions, the circuit courts of the United States shall be deemed to be always in session.

Sec. 17. That the Commission may conduct its proceedings in such manner as will best conduce to the proper dispatch of business and to the ends of justice. A majority of the Commission shall constitute a quorum for the transaction of business, but no Commissioner shall participate in any hearing or proceeding in which he has any pecuniary interest. Said Commission may, from time to time, make or amend such general rules or orders as may be requisite for the order and regulation of proceedings before it, including forms of notices and the service thereof, which shall conform, as nearly as may be, to those in use in the courts of the United

States. Any party may appear before said Commission and be heard, in person or by attorney. Every vote and official act of the Commission shall be entered of record, and its proceedings shall be public upon the request of either party interested. Said Commission shall have an official seal, which shall be judicially noticed. Either of the members of the Commission may administer oaths and affirmations.

Sec. 20. That the Commission is hereby authorized to require annual reports from all common carriers subject to the provisions of this act, to fix the time and prescribe the manner in which such reports shall be made, and to require from such carriers specific answers to all questions upon which the Commission may need information. Such annual reports shall show in detail the amount of capital stock issued, the amounts paid therefor, and the manner of payment for the same; the dividends paid, the surplus fund, if any, and the number of stock-holders; the funded and floating debts and the interest paid thereon; the cost and value of the carrier's property, franchises, and equipment; the number of employees and the salaries paid each class; the amounts expended for improvements each year, how expended, and the character of such improvements; the earnings and receipts from each branch of business and from all sources; the operating and other expenses; the balances of profit and loss; and a complete exhibit of the financial operations of the carrier each year, including an annual balance-sheet. Such reports shall also contain such information in relation to rates or regulations concerning fares or freights, or agreements, arrangements, or contracts with other common carriers, as the Commission may require; and the said Commission may, within its discretion, for the purpose of enabling it the better to carry out the purposes of this act; prescribe (if in the opinion of the Commission it is practicable to prescribe such uniformity and methods of keeping accounts) a period of time within which all common carriers subject to the provisions of this act shall have, as near as may be, a uniform system of accounts, and the manner in which such accounts shall be kept.

Sec. 21. That the Commission shall, on or before the first day of December in each year, make a report to the Secretary of the Interior, which shall be by him transmitted to Congress, and copies of which shall be distributed as are the other reports issued from the Interior Department. This report shall contain such information and data collected by the Commission as may be considered of value in the determination of questions connected with the regulation of commerce, together with such recommendations as to additional legislation relating thereto as the Commission may deem necessary.

Sec. 22. That nothing in this act shall apply to the carriage, storage, or handling of property free or at reduced rates for the United States, State, or municipal governments, or for charitable purposes, or to or from fairs and expositions for exhibition thereat, or the issuance of mileage, excursion, or commutation passenger tickets; nothing in this act shall be construed to prohibit any common carrier from giving reduced rates to ministers of religion; nothing in this act shall be construed to prevent railroads from giving free carriage to their own officers and employees, or to prevent the principal officers of any railroad company or companies from exchanging passes or tickets with other railroad companies for their officers and employees; and nothing in this act contained shall in any way abridge or alter the remedies now existing at common law or by statute, but the provisions of this act are in addition to such remedies; *Provided,* That no pending litigation shall in any way be affected by this act.

---

3. Establishment of the General Staff of the Army

a. Excerpt from the Report of the Secretary of War (Elihu Root, 1902)*

General Staff

The most important thing to be done now for the Regular Army is the creation of a general staff. I beg to call attention to the remarks made upon this subject under the head of "Improvement of Army organization" in the report for 1899 and under the head of "General Staff" in the report for 1901. Since the report for 1899 was made many of the important measures then recommended for the greater efficiency of the Army have been accomplished or are in course of accomplishment under authority conferred by legislation. Our military system, is, however, still exceedingly defective at the top. We have a personnel unsurpassed anywhere, and a population ready to respond to calls for the increase of the personnel in case of need, up to the full limit at which it is possible to

* U.S. Department of War, *Annual Reports of the Secretary of War, 1899-1903* (Washington, D.C.: Government Printing Office, 1904), pp. 292-300.

transport and subsist an army. We have wealth and a present willingness to expend it reasonably for the procurement of supplies and material of war as plentiful and as good as can be found in any country. We have the different branches of the military service well organized, each within itself, for the performance of its duties. Our administrative staff and supply departments, as a rule, have at their heads good and competent men, faithful to their duties, each attending assiduously to the business of his department.

But when we come to the coordination and direction of all these means and agencies of warfare, so that all parts of the machine shall work true together, we are weak. Our system makes no adequate provision for the directing brain which every army must have, to work successfully. Common experience has shown that this can not be furnished by any single man without assistants, and that it requires a body of officers working together under the direction of a chief and entirely separate from and independent of the administrative staff of an army (such as the adjutants, quartermasters, commissaries, etc., each of whom is engrossed in the duties of his own special department). This body of officers, in distinction from the administrative staff, has come to be called a general staff. There has been much misunderstanding as to the nature and duties of a general staff. Brig. Gen. Theodore Schwan, in his work on the organization of the German army, describes it as follows:

> In Prussia, at least, the term has been exclusively and distinctively applied, since about 1789, to a body of officers to whom, as assistants to the commander in chief and of his subordinate generals, is confided such work as is directly connected with the designing and execution of military operations. That in Germany, as elsewhere, chiefs of special arms, heads of supply departments, judge-advocates, etc., form an important branch of the higher commands, goes without saying, but they are not included in the term "general staff." Clausewitz's dictum that the general staff is intended to convert the ideas of the commanding general into orders, not only by communicating the former to the troops, but rather by working out all matters of detail, and thus relieving the general from a vast amount of unnecessary labor, is not a sufficient definition of general-staff duties, according to Von Schellendorf (upon this question certainly the better authority), as it fails to notice the important obligation of the general-staff officer of constantly watching over the effectiveness of the troops, which would be impaired by a lack of attention to their material welfare. Out of this obligation grows, he says, the further duty of furnishing to the heads of the supply departments and other officers attached to

headquarters such explanations touching the general military situation, or the effect of a sudden change therein, as will enable them to carry out intelligently what is expected of them. The general staff thus becomes a directing and explaining body, and its chief, therefore, is in some respects the head of the whole staff. It follows that of the two terms, staff and general staff, the Germans regard the former as the more comprehensive one and as embracing the latter.

It is conceded on all hands that the almost phenomenal success that has attended the German (Prussian) arms during the last thirty years is due in a large degree to the corps of highly trained general-staff officers which the German army possesses.

Neither our political nor our military system makes it suitable that we should have a general staff organized like the German general staff or like the French general staff; but the common experience of mankind is that the things which those general staffs do have to be done in every well-managed and well-directed army, and they have to be done by a body of men especially assigned to do them. We should have such a body of men selected and organized in our own way and in accordance with our own system to do those essential things. The most intelligible way to describe such a body of men, however selected and organized, is by calling it a general staff, because its duties are staff duties and are general in their character.

The duties of such a body of officers can be illustrated by taking for example an invasion of Cuba, such as we were all thinking about a few years ago. It is easy for a President, or a general acting under his direction, to order that 50,000 or 100,000 men proceed to Cuba and capture Havana. To make an order which has any reasonable chance of being executed he must do a great deal more than that. He must determine how many men shall be sent and how they shall be divided among the different arms of the service, and how they shall be armed and equipped, and to do that he must get all the information possible about the defenses of the place to be captured and the strength and character and armament of the forces to be met. He must determine at what points and by what routes the place shall be approached, and at what points his troops shall land in Cuba; and for this purpose he must be informed about the various harbors of the island and the depth of their channels; what classes of vessels can enter them; what the facilities for landing are; how they are defended; the character of the roads leading from them to the place to be attacked; the character of the intervening country; how far it is healthful or unhealthful; what the climate is liable to be at the season of the proposed movement; the temper and sympathies of the inhabitants; the quantity and kind of supplies that can be obtained from the country; the extent to which transportation can be obtained, and a great variety of other things which will go to determine whether it is better to make the approach from one point or from another, and to determine what it will be necessary for the Army to carry with it in order to succeed in moving and living and fighting.

All this information it is the business of a general staff to procure and present. It is probable that there would be in such case a number of alternative plans, each having certain advantages and disadvantages, and these should be worked out each by itself, with the reasons for and against it, and presented to the President or general for his determination. This the general staff should do. This can not be done in an hour. It requires that the staff shall have been at work for a long time collecting the information and arranging it and getting it in form to present. Then at home, where the preparation for the expedition is to be made, the order must be based upon a knowledge of the men and material available for its execution; how many men there are who can be devoted to that purpose, from what points they are to be drawn, what bodies of troops ought to be left or sent elsewhere, and what bodies may be included in the proposed expedition; whether there are ships enough to transport them; where they are to be obtained; whether they are properly fitted up; what more should be done to them; what are the available stocks of clothing, arms and ammunition, and engineers' material, and horses and wagons, and all the innumerable supplies and munitions necessary for a large expedition; how are the things to be supplied which are not ready, but which are necessary, and how long a time will be required to supply them.

All this and much more necessary information it is the business of a general staff to supply. When that has been done the order is made with all available knowledge of all the circumstances upon which the movement depends for its success. It is then the business of a general staff to see that every separate officer upon whose action the success of the movement depends understands his share in it and does not lag behind in the performance of that share; to see that troops and ships and animals and supplies of arms and ammunition and clothing and food, etc., from hundreds of sources, come together at the right times and places. It is a laborious, complicated, and difficult work, which requires a considerable number of men whose special business it is and who are charged with no other duties.

It was the lack of such a body of men doing that kind of work which led to the confusion attending the Santiago expedition in the summer of 1898. The confusion at Tampa and elsewhere was the necessary result of having a large number of men, each of them doing his own special work the best he could, but without any adequate force of officers engaged in seeing that they pulled together according to detailed plans made beforehand. Such a body of men doing general staff duty is just as necessary to prepare an army properly for war in time of peace as it is in time of war. It is not an executive body; it is not an administrative body; it acts only through the authority of others. It makes intelligent command possible by procuring and arranging information and working out plans in detail, and it makes intelligent and effective execution of commands possible by keeping all the separate agents advised of the parts they are to play in the general scheme.

In creating a general staff I think we should change the designation of the officer whom we have called the Commanding General of the Army to Chief of Staff, and at the same time enlarge his powers by giving him the immediate direction of the supply departments, which are now independent of the Commanding General of the Army and report directly to the Secretary of War. The position of the Commanding General of the Army is not created by statute. It depends entirely upon Executive order, and it could be abolished at any time by the President and the position of Chief of Staff could be created in its place. Legislative action, however, is desirable in two directions; one is to provide for the performance of duties of the president of the Board of Ordnance and Fortification and the president of the Board of Commissioners of the Soldiers' Home, both of which have been attached by statute to the position of the Commanding General of the Army. The other line of legislative action needed is to authorize the control of the Secretary of War over the supply departments to be exercised through the chief of staff. This probably could not be done except by Congress.

The change of title from "Commanding General of the Army" to "Chief of Staff" would be of little consequence were it not that the titles denote and imply in the officers bearing them the existence of widely different kinds of authority. When an officer is appointed to the position of "Commanding General of the Army" he naturally expects to command, himself, with a high degree of independence, following his own ideas rather than the ideas of others. We can not ordinarily expect an officer placed in such a position and thus endowed with what purports to be the right and title to command, not to stand up for his right to really command and not to regard any attempt to control his action or limit his power as unjustifiable interference.

The title of chief of staff, on the other hand, denotes a duty to advise, inform, and assist a superior officer who has command, and to represent him, acting in his name and by his authority, in carrying out his policies and securing the execution of his commands. The officer who accepts the position assumes the highest obligation to be perfectly loyal to his commander, to exclude all personal interest from his advice and representation, and to try, in the most whole-hearted way, to help him to right conclusions and to successful execution of his policies, even though his conclusions may not agree with the advice given. For the successful performance of his duties the chief of staff must have the entire confidence of his commander. In proportion as he merits that confidence, the chief of staff gradually comes to find his advice usually accepted, and to really exercise the authority of his commander, subject only to the most general directions, just as Von Moltke exercised the authority of King William of Prussia as his chief of staff.

Experience has shown that it is impossible for any officer to really exercise in this country, in time of peace, the powers which appear and are assumed to be conferred along with the title of "Commanding General of the Army." This follows from the constitution of our Government. The Constitution requires the President to be the commander of the Army, and a great variety of laws require the Secretary of War, who directly represents the President, to supervise and direct the expenditure of the vast sums of money appropriated annually by Congress for the support of the Army. As every important movement requires the use of money, so long as the Secretary of War performs this duty faithfully he must practically control the operations of the Army in time of peace, and there can not be any independent command of the Army, except that which the President himself exercises over the Secretary of War and everybody else in the military establishment. It is because Congress has always looked to the civilian Secretary as the head of the War Department to hold the purse strings that the laws require all the great departments which build the fortifications and furnish the arms, supplies, and munitions of war, and actually expend the money for those purposes, such as the Engineer, Ordnance, Quartermaster's, and Subsistence Departments, to act under the direction of the Secretary and withhold from the officer who is called "Commanding General of the Army" all control over those departments.

This way of treating the expenditure of money is an expression of the ingrained tendency of the American people to insist upon civilian control of the military arm. Our fathers inherited that from England and we have always held to it. It is not likely to be changed in substance. One result of the arrangement is that the officer who is called "Commanding General of the Army" can not in time of peace really exercise any substantial power at all unless he acts in conformity to the policy and views of the Secretary of War, acting under the direction of the President; that is to say, he can not exercise any independent command; and this must always be so as long as the Secretary of War performs the duties which are imposed upon him by law and which are essential to the maintenance of civilian control over the military establishment. It was the inability to exercise the power which the title of "Commanding General of the Army" appears to carry with it, but which does not really exist, that led General Scott to leave Washington and establish his headquarters in New York and General Sherman to remove to St. Louis, both of them abandoning the attempt to do anything in connection with the administration of the Army in Washington. And this difficulty has been the cause of almost constant conflict and bitter feeling in the administration of the Army for the past fifty years, to the very great injury of the service and very great loss of efficiency.

It does not follow, however, that the principal and most trusted general of the Army can not exercise a great and commanding influence in the control of the Army, and practically manage it in all military matters. What does follow is that he can do this only by abandoning the idea of independent command and by assuming the position and performing the functions which I have described as belonging to a chief of staff. General Schofield did this with entire success and rendered great service to the country by doing so. I quote his own words in describing the course he followed:

> Recent experience has served to confirm all the results of my life-long study and large experience that the proper position for the senior officer of the Army on duty at Washington is not that of commanding general, a position which is practically impossible, but that of general in chief, which means in fact chief of staff to the President. The title of general in chief was a permanent one during the entire history of the country up to the time when General Grant became Lieutenant-General.

> When I became the commanding general I addressed to the President a letter in which I pointed out to him what had been the result of my study and experience, and saying that the only way was to abandon entirely, which I did during my seven years of service, all pretense of being the commanding general and to content myself with acting as the chief of staff of the Army under the Secretary of War and the President. The result was that perfect harmony prevailed during my time, and I did exercise a legitimate influence in command of the Army, this because I did not claim to exercise anything which the law did not give me.

Everybody is not as self-restrained and sensible as General Schofield, and the best way to secure from others the same kind of good service that he rendered is to give the officer from whom it is expected a designation which indicates what he is really to do.

b. Act Creating the General Staff (1903)

AN ACT TO INCREASE THE EFFICIENCY OF THE
ARMY, FEBRUARY 14, 1903*

Be it enacted by the Senate and House of Representatives of the United States of America in Congress assembled, That there is hereby established a General Staff Corps, to be composed of officers detailed from the Army at large, under such rules as may be prescribed by the President.

Sec. 2. That the duties of the General Staff Corps shall be to prepare plans for the national defense and for the mobilization of the military forces in time of war; to investigate and report upon all questions affecting the efficiency of the Army and its state of preparation for military operation; to render professional aid and assistance to the Secretary of War and to general officers and other superior commanders, and to act as their agents in informing and coordinating the action of all the different officers who are subject, under the terms of this act, to the supervision of the Chief of Staff; and to perform such other military duties not otherwise assigned by law as may be from time to time prescribed by the President.

Sec. 3. That the General Staff Corps shall consist of one Chief of Staff and two general officers, all to be detailed by the President from officers of the Army at large not below the grade of brigadier-general; four colonels, six lieutenant-colonels, and twelve majors, to be detailed from the corresponding grades in the Army at large, under such rules for selection as the President may prescribe; twenty captains to be detailed from officers of the Army at large of the grades of captain or first lieutenant, who while so serving shall have the rank, pay, and allowances of captain mounted. All officers detailed in the General Staff Corps shall be detailed therein for periods of four years, unless sooner relieved. While serving in the General Staff Corps, officers may be temporarily assigned to duty with any branch of the Army. Upon being relieved from duty in the General Staff Corps, officers shall return to the branch of the Army in which they hold permanent commission, and no officer shall be eligible to a further detail in the General Staff Corps until he shall have served two years with the branch of the Army in which commissioned, except in case of emergency or in time of war.

Sec. 4. That the Chief of Staff, under the direction of the President or of the Secretary of War, under the direction of the President, shall have

* 32 Stat. 553 (1903).

supervision of all troops of the line and of the Adjutant-General's, Inspector-General's, Judge-Advocate's, Quartermaster's, Subsistence, Medical, Pay, and Ordnance departments, the Corps of Engineers, and the Signal Corps, and shall perform such other military duties not otherwise assigned by law as may be assigned to him by the President. Duties now prescribed by statute for the Commanding General of the Army as a member of the Board of Ordnance and Fortification and of the Board of Commissioners of the Soldiers' Home shall be performed by the Chief of Staff or other officer designated by the President. Acts and parts of acts authorizing aides-de-camp and military secretaries shall not apply to general officers of the General Staff Corps.

Sec. 5. That the Chief of Artillery shall hereafter serve as an additional member of the General Staff and by and with the advice and consent of the Senate shall have the rank, pay, and allowances of a brigadier-general and when the next vacancy occurs in the office of brigadier-general of the line, it shall not be filled, and thereafter the number of brigadier-generals of the line, exclusive of the Chief of Artillery, shall not exceed fourteen; and the provisions of the foregoing sections of this act shall take effect August fifteenth, nineteen hundred and three.

4. Report of the (Taft) Commission on Economy and Efficiency (1912)*

THE NEED FOR A NATIONAL BUDGET

June 19, 1912

The President:

The Commission on Economy and Efficiency has the honor to submit the following report on "The Need for a National Budget," and makes the following recommendations, each of which is fully discussed in Part II of this report.

Recommendations

The commission recommends:

1. That the President, as the constitutional head of the executive branch of the Government, shall each year submit to the Congress, not later than the first Monday after the beginning of the regular session, a budget.

2. That the budget so submitted shall contain:

(a) *A budgetary message,* setting forth in brief the significance of the proposals to which attention is invited.

(b) *A summary financial statement,* setting forth in very summary form: (1) the financial condition; (2) a statement of the condition of appropriations and other data pertaining to the "general fund" as well as to the other funds of the Government; (3) an account of revenues and expenditures for the last completed fiscal year; and (4) a statement showing the effect of past financial policy as well as of budget proposals on the general-fund surplus.

(c) *A summary of expenditures,* classified by objects, setting forth the contracting and purchasing relations of the Government.

(d) *Summaries of estimates,* setting forth: (1) the estimated revenues compared with actual revenues for a period of years; (2) estimated expenditures compared with actual expenditures for a period of years.

* U.S., Congress, House, H. Doc. 854, 62nd Cong., 2d sess., 1912, pp. 7-12.

(e) *A summary of changes in law,* setting forth what legislation it is thought should be enacted in order to enable the administration to transact public business with greater economy and efficiency, i.e., changes in organic law which, if enacted, would affect appropriations as well as the character of work to be done.

3. That the Secretary of the Treasury be required to submit to the Congress the following detailed reports supporting the general summaries and Executive conclusions or recommendations contained in the budget, as follows:

(a) *A book of estimates,* containing the supporting details to the summaries of estimates of expenditure contained in the budget.

(b) *A consolidated financial report,* containing a detailed statement of revenues and a consolidated statement of expenditures by departments and establishments for the last five fiscal years, with such explanatory matter as is necessary to give information with respect to increases or decreases in revenue or expenditure or other relations to which it is thought that the attention of the executive and legislative branches is to be given.

4. That the head of each department and independent establishment should be required to submit to the Secretary of the Treasury and to the Congress annual reports which, among other things, would contain detailed accounts of expenditures so classified as to show amounts expended by appropriations, as well as by classes of work, together with the amounts of increases or decreases in stores, equipment, property, etc., including lands, buildings, and other improvements, as well as such other data or operative statistics and comment in relation thereto as may be necessary to show results obtained and the economy and efficiency of doing Government work, as well as of contracting and of purchasing.

5. That the President and heads of departments issue orders which will require that such accounts be kept, such reports be made, and such estimates be prepared as will enable them to obtain the information needed to consider the different conditions, relations, and results above enumerated before the estimates are submitted; that the President recommend to the Congress the enactment of such laws as will enable the administration to comply with the requirements of the Congress.

6. That the President recommend for the consideration of the Congress such changes in the form of appropriation bills as will enable the Government to avail itself of the benefits of the exercise of discretion on

the part of the Executive in the transaction of current business in order
that the Government may do work and accomplish results with economy
and efficiency and as will definitely fix responsibility for failure so to
exercise such discretion.

Introduction

If we follow the accepted usage of most civilized nations, we must
conclude that a budget is a collection of documents assembled by an
officer who is at the head of or is responsible for the administration and
submitted to the legislative branch of the Government. Whatever else
such a budget contains, in every case it carries with it an estimate of
expenditures to be made by the Government during the coming financial
period. While each nation has a revenue policy, the lack of emphasis
which has been laid by nations in their budget upon the revenues and the
relation of expenditures thereto has probably been due to the fact that by
far the larger part of the revenues have come into the Public Treasury as
the result of the operation of permanent law. No regular periodical action
upon the part of the legislative authority has been necessary in order that
revenues might be collected. As a consequence, the budget has been
regarded primarily as an estimate of expenditures.

Inasmuch, however, as no nation can safely adopt for a long period a
policy of expenditures which has no regard to the amount of its revenues,
it has been usual in most national governments to fix the amount of the
expenditures in view of the expected revenue. Where, as is the case in this
country, the estimates have been a matter of legislative rather than executive responsibility, the legislature has imposed upon the Treasury the
duty of acquainting it with the estimated revenue for the coming budgetary period. It thus is the case that even in political systems in which
revenues are based on permanent law rather than on periodical legislative
action the demands of a conservative financial policy require that expenditures shall be estimated in view of revenue possibilities. We may say,
therefore, that a budget should consist of estimates of revenue as well as of
expenditures.

It has been said that a budget is primarily an estimate of the expenditures made necessary by the operations of the Government. That is, it is
assumed that a government already exists which operates in a given way.
A budget is based upon the theory that the Government for whose
operations expenditures must be made is already organized and dis-
charges certain activities whose number and extent have already been
determined. The purpose of a budget is thus to finance an existing
organization in order that it may successfully prosecute defined lines of
work. In case it is thought desirable to have changes made in organization

and in number and extent of activities, as compared with the organization and activities financed in the preceding budgetary period, these changes should be indicated at the time the budget is drawn up, and in any case, the changes must be determined before or at the time that appropriations are granted, since the appropriation is primarily a method of financing the existing organization and predefined activities.

Nevertheless since changes in organization and in number and extent of activities can hardly fail to affect expenditures, a budget, while primarily having to do with the expenditures made necessary by the defined operations of an existing governmental organization, must in the nature of things be concerned secondarily at any rate with questions of governmental organization and activities. It is, of course, to be borne in mind that other than financial considerations primarily control the decision of these questions, but it can not be forgotten that no State can enter upon an administrative program, however desirable, the expense of which its financial resources do not admit it to assume. Thus, a comprehensive naval program is entered upon for military and not for financial reasons. But if the resources of the country are insufficient the nation will have to forego the advantages of such a program, however marked they may be.

In this sense it may be said that a budget is in the nature of a prospectus and that its purpose is to present in summary form the facts necessary to the shaping of the policies of the Government so far as they affect its finances.

Budgetary practice has been influenced by the constitutional relations existing between the executive and legislative branches of government. Generally speaking, the executive authority (apart from the United States) has been conceived of as possessing powers of initiation and leadership while the legislative authority is regarded as possessing merely powers of final determination and control. In the United States, however, the legislature is usually regarded as the authority which initiates and determines a policy which it is the duty of the Executive to carry out. The effect of this conception of the relations of the Legislature to the Executive has been that the budget has been primarily an affair of the Congress rather than of the President. The Congress makes use of administrative officers in order to obtain the information which it must have to determine the important questions of policy devolved upon it by the American system. These administrative officers are acting as the ministerial agents of the Congress rather than as representatives of the President. The result is that while in most other countries the budget is in the nature of a proposal or program submitted on its responsibility by the executive to the legislature, in the United States the Book of Estimates, our nearest approach to a budget, is rather a more or less well-digested mass of information submitted by agents of the Legislature to the Legislature for the consideration of legislative committees to enable the Legislature both to originate and to determine the policy which is to be carried out by the Executive during the coming budgetary period.

Definition and purpose of the budget

As used in this report the budget is considered as a proposal to be prepared by the administration and submitted to the legislature. The use of a budget would require that there be a complete reversal of procedure by the Government—that the executive branch submit a statement to the Legislature which would be its account of stewardship as well as its proposals for the future. A national budget thus prepared and presented would serve the purposes of a prospectus. Its aim would be to present in summary form the facts necessary to shape the policy of the Government as well as to provide financial support. The summaries of fact included in the budget would also serve as a key or index to the details of transactions and of estimates which would be submitted with the budget or which would be contained in accounting records and reports.

An act of appropriation which follows a budget is a grant of money by the legislative branch to the executive branch of the Government. In the United States Government, in which the Congress habitually exercises the right to add to the estimates proposed by the Executive, and in which the President has no right to veto specific items in appropriation bills, items are usually found in appropriation acts which can hardly be said to have received Executive approval even where the appropriation acts containing them have been signed by the President. For, in many cases, formal Executive approval has been accorded to an appropriation act as a whole which contains items for which the Executive is not in any way responsible or to which he is positively opposed. In case the President has thus approved an appropriation act as a whole, he may, however, by instruction to his subordinates in the administration, prevent the expenditure of public money for many items of which he disapproves, since an appropriation act frequently is an authorization rather than a command.

The constitutional inhibition that "no money shall be drawn from the Treasury but in consequence of appropriations made by law" makes the budget an instrument of *legislative control* over the administration. The act of appropriation as the legal means of making funds available to the executive branch, also enables the Executive, or some officer directly responsible to the Executive, to exercise *administrative control* over liabilities incurred and over expenditures made by the many officers and agents employed by the Government in the conduct of its business.

Every branch of the business of the Government is necessarily highly complex and technical. One of the most important offices of a budget is to supply the need for an effective means whereby those who are responsible for direction and control over technical processes and who understand the technical needs of the service may formally present to the Legislature and through the Legislature to the people a well-defined plan or prospectus of work to be financed in order that the Government may make provision for the needs of the country as seen by those whose duty it is to serve these needs.

The Congress, as a deliberative body, while not in a position to know what are the technical service requirements, is by reason of its representative character best able to determine questions of policy involving the expenditure of money, i.e., decide what shall and what shall not be undertaken. An act of appropriation of public money should therefore be the result of the most careful consideration of both branches of the Government.

The financing of the Government calls into action both the "money raising" and the "appropriating" powers of the Congress—the one to provide funds, the other to authorize expenditures. The exercise of both of these powers affects immediately the welfare of the people. For the purpose of considering the relations of "revenue" and "borrowing" to welfare, a budget should present for the consideration of the Congress a definite financial program. For the purpose of considering the relation of expenditure authorizations to welfare, a budget should present a definite statement of the business to be done, or a work program.

The immediate relations of revenue raising to welfare have been a subject of constant national concern since the first year the Federal Government was organized. In fact, it reaches back through the Revolutionary period; it was one of the chief subjects of popular interest and agitation which culminated in the Declaration of Independence. During the entire national period a more or less definite revenue policy has been recognized. Though not presented in budgetary form, definite policies pertaining to the welfare relation of revenue raising have furnished a definite basis for appeal to the electorate for support. With respect to revenue, there has been a well-defined policy of government which may be traced from the beginning.

With respect to the relation of Government expenditure to welfare, there has been no conscious policy, nor has the subject of Government financing (the relation of revenues and borrowings to expenditures) been a matter of great public concern except in times of war, when the problem of defending our national integrity has depended on ability to finance the Government's needs. The result has been that the United States has had no definite financial program; appropriations have been regarded as special or local in their significance. It has only been within the last few years that what the Government does with its vast organization and resources has received the attention which it deserves. As was said by the President in a recent message:

> In political controversy it has been assumed generally that the individual citizen has little interest in what the Government spends. Now that population has become more dense, that large cities have developed, that people are required to live in congested centers, that the national resources frequently are the subject of private ownership and private control, and that transportation and other public-service facilities are held and operated by large corporations, what the Government does with nearly a thousand million dollars each year is of as much concern to the average citizen as is the manner of obtaining this amount of money for public use.

It is to the expenditure side of a budget that special attention is given in this report.

---

5. Model City Charter of the National Municipal League (1916)*

The Council

Sec. 3. *Powers of Council.* . . . Neither the council nor any of its committees or members shall dictate the appointment of any person to office or employment by the city manager, or in any manner interfere with the city manager or prevent him from exercising his own judgment in the appointment of officers and employes in the administrative service. Except for the purpose of inquiry the council and its members shall deal with the

---

* Officially entitled *A Model City Charter and Municipal Home Rule*, as prepared by the Committee on the Municipal Program of the National Municipal League, Philadelphia, 1916. Excluded from this presentation are the constitutional provisions for home rule and the charter provisions covering: the council, except for the sections limiting its powers in dealing with the administration, describing its appointive powers, and covering the powers of the mayor; nominations and elections; initiative; referendum; and recall; details about civil service rules and administration; details about financial administration and accounts; public utilities; report and staffing of city planning board; certain miscellaneous matters; and footnotes.

administrative service solely through the city manager, and neither the council nor any member thereof shall give orders to any of the subordinates of the city manager, either publicly or privately. Any such dictation, prevention, orders or other interference on the part of a member of council with the administration of the city shall be deemed to be a misdemeanor, and upon conviction any member so convicted shall be subject to a fine not exceeding $ or imprisonment for a term not exceeding   months, or both, and to removal from office in the discretion of the court.

Sec. 4. *Election by Councils. Rules. Quorum.* The council shall elect one of its members as chairman, who shall be entitled mayor; also a city manager, a clerk and a civil service board, but no member of the council shall be chosen as manager, or as a member of the civil service commission. . . .

Sec. 6. *Powers of Mayor.* The mayor shall preside at meetings of the council and perform such other duties consistent with his office as may be imposed by the council. He shall be recognized as the official head of the city for all ceremonial purposes, by the courts for the purpose of serving civil processes, and by the governor for military purposes. In time of public danger or emergency he may, with the consent of the council, take command of the police and maintain order and enforce the laws. During his absence or disability his duties shall be performed by another member appointed by the council.

Administrative Service: The City Manager

Sec. 34.*The City Manager.* The city manager shall be the chief executive officer of the city. He shall be chosen by the council solely on the basis of his executive and administrative qualifications. The choice shall not be limited to inhabitants of the city or state.

The city manager shall receive a compensation of not less than   a year. He shall be appointed for an indefinite period. He shall be removable by the council. If removed at any time after six months he may demand written charges and a public hearing on the same before the council prior to the date on which his final removal shall take effect, but during such hearing the council may suspend him from office. During the absence or disability of the city manager the council shall designate some properly qualified person to perform the duties of the office.

Sec. 35. *Powers and Duties of the City Manager.* The city manager shall be responsible to the council for the proper administration of all affairs of the city, and to that end shall make all appointments, except as otherwise provided in this charter. Except when the council is considering his removal, he shall be entitled to be present at all meetings of the council and of its committees and to take part in their discussion.

Sec. 36. *Annual Budget.* The city manager shall prepare and submit to the council the annual budget after receiving estimates made by the directors of the departments.

Administrative Departments

Sec. 37. *Administrative Departments Created.* There shall be six administrative departments as follows: Law, health, works and utilities, safety and welfare, education and finance, the functions of which shall be prescribed by the council except as herein otherwise provided. The council shall fix all salaries, which in the classified service shall be uniform for each grade, as established by the civil service commission, and the council may, by a three-fourths vote of its entire membership, create new departments, combine or abolish existing departments or establish temporary departments for special work.

Sec. 38. *Duties of Directors of Departments.* At the head of each department there shall be a director. Each director shall be chosen on the basis of his general executive and administrative experience and ability and of his education, training and experience in the class of work which he is to administer. The director of the department of law shall be a lawyer; of health, a sanitary engineer or a member of the medical profession; of works, an engineer; of education, a teacher by profession; of safety, and welfare, a man who has had administrative experience; and of finance, a man who has had experience in banking, accounting or other financial matters; or in each case the man must have rendered active service in the same department in this or some other city.

Each director shall be appointed by the city manager and may be removed by him at any time; but in case of such removal, if the director so demands, written charges must be preferred by the city manager, and the director shall be given a public hearing before the order of removal is made final. The charges and the director's reply thereto shall be filed with the clerk of council.

Sec. 39. *Responsibility of Directors of Departments.* The directors of departments shall be immediately responsible to the city manager for the administration of their departments and their advice in writing may be required by him on all matters affecting their departments. They shall prepare departmental estimates, which shall be open to public inspection, and they shall make all other reports and recommendations concerning their departments at stated intervals or when requested by the city manager.

Civil Service Board

Sec. 41. *Creation of Civil Service Board.* A civil service board shall be appointed by the council to consist of three members. The terms of the members when the first appointments are made shall be so arranged as to expire one every two years, and each appointment made thereafter upon the expiration of any term shall be for six years. The council shall also fill any vacancy for an unexpired term. A member of the board shall be removable for neglect, incapacity or malfeasance in office by a four-fifths vote of the council, after written charges upon at least ten days' notice and after a public hearing.

The board shall employ a secretary and a chief examiner (but the same person may perform the duties of both offices) and such further examiners and such clerical and other assistance as may be necessary, and shall determine the compensation of all persons so employed. Provision shall be made in the annual budget and appropriation bill for the expenses of the board.

Sec. 42. *Power to Make Rules and What the Rules Shall Provide.* The board shall, after public notice and hearing, make, promulgate and, when necessary, amend rules for the appointment, promotion, transfer, lay off, reinstatement, suspension and removal of city officials and employes, reporting its proceedings to the council and to the city manager when required. Such rules shall, among other things, provide:

(a) For the standardization and classification of all positions and employments in the civil service of the city. . . .

(b) For open competitive tests, to ascertain the relative fitness of all applicants for appointment to the classified civil service of said city, including mechanics and laborers—skilled and unskilled. Such tests shall be practical and relate to matters which will fairly measure the relative fitness of the candidates to discharge the duties of the positions to which they seek to be appointed. . . .

(c) For the creation of eligible lists upon which shall be entered the names of successful candidates in the order of their standing in examination, and for the filling of places in the civil service of the city by selection from not more than the three candidates graded highest on such eligible lists. Eligible lists shall remain in force not longer than two years. . . .

(d) For a period of probation not exceeding six months before an appointment or employment is made permanent.

(e) For reinstatement on the eligible lists of persons who without fault or delinquency are separated from the service.

(f) For promotion from the lower grades to the higher, based upon competitive records of efficiency and seniority to be furnished by the departments in which the person is employed and kept by said civil service board, or upon competitive promotion tests, or both. . . .

Sec. 43. *Supervisory Powers of Civil Service Board.* It shall be the duty of the civil service board to supervise the execution of the civil service sections and the rules made thereunder, and it shall be the duty of all persons in the public service of said city to comply with said rules and aid in their enforcement. . . .

Sec. 44. *Power of Removal and Suspension.* Any officer or employe in the classified service may be removed, suspended, laid off, or reduced in grade by the city manager or by the head of the department in which he is employed, for any cause which will promote the efficiency of the service; but he must first be furnished with a written statement of the reasons therefor and be allowed a reasonable time for answering such reasons in writing, which answer, if he so request, shall (so far as the same is relevant and pertinent) be made a part of the records of the board; and he may be suspended from the date when such written statement of reasons is furnished him. No trial or examination of witnesses shall be required in such case except in the discretion of the officer making the removal. In all cases provided for in this paragraph the action of the city manager or head of the department shall be final.

The civil service board shall also have the right to remove or reduce any official or employe upon written charges of misconduct preferred by any citizen, but only after reasonable notice to the accused and full hearing. It shall also be the duty of the board to fix a minimum standard of conduct and efficiency for each grade in the service, and whenever it shall appear from the reports of efficiency made to said board, for a period of three months, that the conduct and efficiency of any employe has fallen below this minimum, such employe shall be called before the board to show cause why he should not be removed, and if upon hearing no reason is shown satisfactory to the board he shall be removed, suspended or reduced in grade as the board shall determine.

Sec. 45. *Restrictions on Civil Service Appointees and Forbidden Practices.* No person shall willfully or corruptly make any false statement, certificate, mark, grading or report in regard to any examination or appointment held or made under this article, or in any other manner attempt to commit any fraud upon the impartial execution of this article or of the civil service rules and regulations.

No person in the classified service shall directly or indirectly give, solicit or receive or be in any manner concerned in giving, soliciting or receiving any assessment, subscription or contribution for any political party or purpose whatever. No person whosoever shall orally or by letter solicit or be in any manner concerned in soliciting any assessment, subscription or contribution for any political party from any person holding a position in the classified service. No person shall use or promise to use his influence or official authority to secure any appointment or prospect of appointment to any position classified and graded under this charter as a reward or return for personal or partisan political service. No person about to be appointed to any position classified and graded under this charter shall sign or execute a resignation dated or undated in advance of such appointment. No person in the service of the city shall discharge, suspend, lay off, degrade, or promote, or in any manner change the official rank or compensation of any other person in said service, or promise or threaten to do so for withholding or neglecting to make any contribution of money or service or any other valuable thing for any political purpose.

No person shall take part in preparing any political assessment, subscription or contribution with the intent that the same shall be sent or presented to or collected from any person in the classified service of the city; and no person shall knowingly send or present, directly or indirectly, in person or by letter, any political assessment, subscription or contribution to, or request its payment by any person in the classified service.

No person in the service of the city shall use his official authority or influence to coerce the political action of any person or body, or to interfere with any nomination or election to public office.

No person holding office or place classified and graded under the provisions of this article shall act as an officer of a political organization or take any active part in a political campaign or serve as a member of a committee of any such organization or circulate or seek signatures to any petition provided for by any primary or election laws, other than an initiative or referendum petition, or act as a worker at the polls in favor of or opposed to any candidate for election or nomination to a public office, whether federal, state, county or municipal.

Sec. 46. *Politics and Religion Excluded.* No question in any examination held hereunder shall relate to political or religious opinions, affiliations or service, and no appointment, transfer, lay off, promotion, reduction, suspension or removal shall be affected or influenced by such opinions, affiliations or service.

Sec. 47. *Violations of Civil Service Rules and Regulations.* Any person who shall willfully, or through culpable negligence, violate any of the provisions of this article or of the rules of the board made in pursuance thereof shall be guilty of a misdemeanor, and shall, on conviction, be punished by a fine of not less than $50 nor more than $1000. . . .

Financial Provisions

Sec. 49. *The Director of Finance.* The director of finance shall have direct supervision over the department of finance and the administration of the financial affairs of the city, including the keeping of accounts and financial records; the levy, assessment and collection of taxes, special assessments and other revenues (except as otherwise provided by general law); the custody and disbursement of city funds and moneys; the control over expenditures; and such other duties as the council may, by ordinance, provide.

Sec. 51. *Annual Budget.* Not later than one month before the end of each fiscal year, the city manager shall prepare and submit to the council an annual budget for the ensuing fiscal year, based upon detailed estimates furnished by the several departments and other divisions of the city government, according to a classification as nearly uniform as possible. The budget shall present the following information:

(a) An itemized statement of the appropriations recommended by the city manager for current expenses and for permanent improvements for each department and each division thereof for the ensuing fiscal year, with comparative statements in parallel columns of the appropriations and expenditures for the current and next preceding fiscal year, and the increases or decreases in the appropriations recommended;

(b) An itemized statement of the taxes required and of the estimated revenues of the city from all other sources for the ensuing fiscal year, with comparative statements in parallel columns of the taxes and other revenues for the current and next preceding fiscal year, and of the increases or decreases estimated or proposed;

(c) A statement of the financial condition of the city; and

(d) Such other information as may be required by the council.

Copies of such budget shall be printed and available for distribution not later than two weeks after its submission to the council; and a public hearing shall be given thereon by the council or a committee thereof before action by the council.

City Planning

Sec. 73. *Creation of a City Planning Board.* There shall be a city planning board of three members, consisting of the director of public works and utilities and two citizen members chosen because of their knowledge of city planning. It shall be the duty of the board to keep itself informed of the progress of city planning in this and other countries, to make studies and recommendations for the improvement of the plan of the city with a view to the present and future movement of traffic, the convenience, amenity, health, recreation, general welfare and other needs of the city dependent on the city plan; to consider and report upon the designs and their relations to the city plan of all new public ways, lands, buildings, bridges and all other public places and structures, of additions to and alterations in those already existing, and of the layout or plotting of new subdivisions of the city, or of territory adjacent to or near the city.

Sec. 74. *Power of Board.* All acts of the council or of any other branch of the city government affecting the city plan shall be submitted to the board for report and recommendations. The council may at any time call upon the board to report with recommendations, and the board of its own volition may also report to the council with recommendations on any matter which, in the opinion of either body, affects the plan of the city.

Any matter referred by the council to the board shall be acted upon by the board within thirty days of the date of reference, unless a longer or shorter period is specified. No action by the council involving any points hereinbefore set forth shall be legal or binding until it has been referred to the board and until the recommendations of the board thereon have been accepted or rejected by the council.

6. Budget and Accounting Act (1921)*

Title I—Definitions

Section 1. This Act may be cited as the "Budget and Accounting Act, 1921."

Sec. 2. When used in this Act—

The terms "department and establishment" and "department or establishment" mean any executive department, independent commission, board, bureau, office, agency, or other establishment of the Government,

* 42 Stat. 18 (1921). Excluded are: sections 208 and 217, which contain details on the internal administration and initial funding of the Bureau of the Budget; the second paragraph of section 304, which established a Bureau of Accounts in the Post Office Department; and sections 311, and 314-318, which provide details on internal administration and funding of the General Accounting Office.

including the municipal government of the District of Columbia, but do not include the Legislative Branch of the Government or the Supreme Court of the United States;

The term "the Budget" means the Budget required by section 201 to be transmitted to Congress;

The term "Bureau" means the Bureau of the Budget;

The term "Director" means the Director of the Bureau of the Budget; and

The term "Assistant Director" means the Assistant Director of the Bureau of the Budget.

Title II—The Budget

Sec. 201. The President shall transmit to Congress on the first day of each regular session, the Budget, which shall set forth in summary and in detail:

(a) Estimates of the expenditures and appropriations necessary in his judgment for the support of the Government for the ensuing fiscal year; except that the estimates for such year for the Legislative Branch of the Government and the Supreme Court of the United States shall be transmitted to the President on or before October 15th of each year, and shall be included by him in the Budget without revision;

(b) His estimates of the receipts of the Government during the ensuing fiscal year, under (1) laws existing at the time the Budget is transmitted and also (2) under the revenue proposals, if any, contained in the Budget;

(c) The expenditures and receipts of the Government during the last completed fiscal year;

(d) Estimates of the expenditures and receipts of the Government during the fiscal year in progress;

(e) The amount of annual, permanent, or other appropriations, including balances of appropriations for prior fiscal years, available for expenditure during the fiscal year in progress, as of November 1 of such year;

(f) Balanced statements of (1) the condition of the Treasury at the end of the last completed fiscal year, (2) the estimated condition of the Treasury at the end of the fiscal year in progress, and (3) the estimated condition of the Treasury at the end of the ensuing fiscal year if the financial proposals contained in the Budget are adopted;

(g) All essential facts regarding the bonded and other indebtedness of the Government; and

(h) Such other financial statements and data as in his opinion are necessary or desirable in order to make known in all practicable detail the financial conditions of the Government.

Sec. 202. (a) If the estimated receipts for the ensuing fiscal year contained in the Budget, on the basis of laws existing at the time the Budget is transmitted, plus the estimated amounts in the Treasury at the close of the fiscal year in progress, available for expenditure in the ensuing fiscal year, are less than the estimated expenditures for the ensuing fiscal year contained in the Budget, the President in the Budget shall make recommendations to Congress for new taxes, loans, or other appropriate action to meet the estimated deficiency.

(b) If the aggregate of such estimated receipts and such estimated amounts in the Treasury is greater than such estimated expenditures for the ensuing fiscal year, he shall make such recommendations as in his opinion the public interests require.

Sec. 203. (a) The President from time to time may transmit to Congress supplemental or deficiency estimates for such appropriations or expenditures as in his judgment (1) are necessary on account of laws enacted after the transmission of the Budget, or (2) are otherwise in the public interest. He shall accompany such estimates with a statement of the reasons therefor, including the reasons for their omission from the Budget.

(b) Whenever such supplemental or deficiency estimates reach an aggregate which, if they had been contained in the Budget, would have required the President to make a recommendation under subdivision (a) of section 202, he shall thereupon make such recommendation.

Sec. 204. (a) Except as otherwise provided in this Act, the contents, order, and arrangement of the estimates of appropriations and the statements of expenditures and estimated expenditures contained in the Budget or transmitted under section 203, and the notes and other data submitted therewith, shall conform to the requirements of existing law

(b) Estimates for lump-sum appropriations contained in the Budget or transmitted under section 203 shall be accompanied by statements showing, in such detail and form as may be necessary to inform Congress, the manner of expenditure of such appropriations and of the corresponding appropriations for the fiscal year in progress and the last completed fiscal year. Such statements shall be in lieu of statements of like character now required by law.

Sec. 205. The President, in addition to the Budget, shall transmit to Congress on the first Monday in December, 1921, for the service of the fiscal year ending June 30, 1923, only, an alternative budget, which shall be prepared in such form and amounts and according to such system of classification and itemization as is, in his opinion, most appropriate, with such explanatory notes and tables as may be necessary to show where the various items embraced in the Budget are contained in such alternative budget.

Sec. 206. No estimate or request for an appropriation and no request for an increase in an item of any such estimate or request, and no recommendation as to how the revenue needs of the Government should be met, shall be submitted to Congress or any committee thereof by any officer or employee of any department or establishment, unless at the request of either House of Congress.

Sec. 207. There is hereby created in the Treasury Department a Bureau to be known as the Bureau of the Budget. There shall be in the Bureau a Director and an Assistant Director, who shall be appointed by the President and receive salaries of $10,000 and $7,500 a year, respectively. The Assistant Director shall perform such duties as the Director may designate, and during the absence or incapacity of the Director or during a vacancy in the office of Director he shall act as Director. The Bureau, under such rules and regulations as the President may prescribe, shall prepare for him the Budget, the alternative Budget, and any supplemental or deficiency estimates, and to this end shall have authority to assemble, correlate, revise, reduce, or increase the estimates of the several departments or establishments.

Sec. 209. The Bureau, when directed by the President, shall make a detailed study of the departments and establishments for the purpose of enabling the President to determine what changes (with a view of securing greater economy and efficiency in the conduct of the public service) should be made in (1) the existing organization, activities, and methods of business of such departments or establishments, (2) the appropriations therefor, (3) the assignment of particular activities to particular services, or (4) the regrouping of services. The results of such study shall be embodied in a report or reports to the President, who may transmit to Congress such report or reports or any part thereof with his recommendations on the matters covered thereby.

Sec. 210. The Bureau shall prepare for the President a codification of all laws or parts of laws relating to the preparation and transmission to Congress of statements of receipts and expenditures of the Government and of estimates of appropriations. The President shall transmit the same to Congress on or before the first Monday in December, 1921, with a recommendation as to the changes which, in his opinion, should be made in such laws or parts of laws.

Sec. 211. The powers and duties relating to the compiling of estimates now conferred and imposed upon the Division of Bookkeeping and

Warrants of the office of the Secretary of the Treasury are transferred to the Bureau.

Sec. 212. The Bureau shall have at the request of any committee of either House of Congress having jurisdiction over revenue or appropriations, furnish the committee such aid and information as it may request.

Sec. 213. Under such regulations as the President may prescribe, (1) every department and establishment shall furnish to the Bureau such information as the Bureau may from time to time require, and (2) the Director and the Assistant Director, or any employee of the Bureau, when duly authorized, shall, for the purpose of securing such information, have access to, and the right to examine, any books, documents, papers, or records of any such department or establishment.

Sec. 214. (a) The head of each department and establishment shall designate an official thereof as budget officer therefor, who, in each year under his direction and on or before a date fixed by him, shall prepare the departmental estimates.

(b) Such budget officer shall also prepare, under the direction of the head of the department or establishment, such supplemental and deficiency estimates as may be required for its work.

Sec. 215. The head of each department and establishment shall revise the departmental estimates and submit them to the Bureau on or before September 15 of each year. In case of his failure so to do, the President shall cause to be prepared such estimates and data as are necessary to enable him to include in the Budget estimates and statements in respect to the work of such department or establishment.

Sec. 216. The departmental estimates and any supplemental or deficiency estimates submitted to the Bureau by the head of any department or establishment shall be prepared and submitted in such form, manner, and detail as the President may prescribe.

Title III—General Accounting Office

Sec. 301. There is created an establishment of the Government to be known as the General Accounting Office, which shall be independent of the executive departments and under the control and direction of the Comptroller General of the United States. The offices of Comptroller of the Treasury and Assistant Comptroller of the Treasury are abolished, to take effect July 1, 1921. All other officers and employees of the office of the Comptroller of the Treasury shall become officers and employees in the General Accounting Office at their grades and salaries on July 1, 1921, and all books, records, documents, papers, furniture, office equipment and other property of the office of the Comptroller of the Treasury shall become the property of the General Accounting Office. The Comptroller General is authorized to adopt a seal for the General Accounting Office.

Sec. 302. There shall be in the General Accounting Office a Comptroller General of the United States and an Assistant Comptroller General of the United States, who shall be appointed by the President with the advice and consent of the Senate, and shall receive salaries of $10,000 and $7,500 a year, respectively. The Assistant Comptroller General shall perform such duties as may be assigned to him by the Comptroller General, and during the absence or incapacity of the Comptroller General, or during a vacancy in that office, shall act as Comptroller General.

Sec. 303. Except as hereinafter provided in this section, the Comptroller General and the Assistant Comptroller General shall hold office for fifteen years. The Comptroller General shall not be eligible for reappointment. The Comptroller General or the Assistant Comptroller General may be removed at any time by joint resolution of Congress after notice and hearing, when, in the judgment of Congress, the Comptroller General or Assistant Comptroller General has become permanently incapacitated or has been inefficient, or guilty of neglect of duty, or of malfeasance in office, or of any felony or conduct involving moral turpitude, and for no other cause and in no other manner except by impeachment. Any Comptroller General or Assistant Comptroller General removed in the manner herein provided shall be ineligible for reappointment to that office. When a Comptroller General or Assistant Comptroller General attains the age of seventy years, he shall be retired from his office.

Sec. 304. All powers and duties now conferred or imposed by law upon the Comptroller of the Treasury or the six auditors of the Treasury Department, and the duties of the Division of Bookkeeping and Warrants of the Office of the Secretary of the Treasury relating to keeping the personal ledger accounts of disbursing and collecting officers, shall, so far as not inconsistent with this Act, be vested in and imposed upon the General Accounting Office and be exercised without direction from any other officer. The balances certified by the Comptroller General shall be final and conclusive upon the executive branch of the Government. The revision by the Comptroller General of settlements made by the six auditors shall be discontinued, except as to settlements made before July 1, 1921.

Sec. 305. Section 236 of the Revised Statutes is amended to read as follows:

"Sec. 236. All claims and demands whatever by the Government of the United States or against it, and all accounts whatever in which the Government of the United States is concerned, either as debtor or creditor, shall be settled and adjusted in the General Accounting Office."

Sec. 306. All laws relating generally to the administration of the departments and establishments, shall, so far as applicable, govern the General Accounting Office. Copies of any books, records, papers, or documents, and transcripts from the books and proceedings of the General Accounting Office, when certified by the Comptroller General or the Assistant Comptroller General under its seal, shall be admitted as evidence with the same effect as the copies and transcripts referred to in sections 882 and 886 of the Revised Statutes.

Sec. 307. The Comptroller General may provide for the payment of accounts or claims adjusted and settled in the General Accounting Office, through disbursing officers of the several departments and establishments, instead of by warrant.

Sec. 308. The duties now appertaining to the Division of Public Moneys of the Office of the Secretary of the Treasury, so far as they relate to the covering of revenues and repayments into the Treasury, the issue of duplicate checks and warrants, and the certification of outstanding liabilities for payment, shall be performed by the Division of Bookkeeping and Warrants of the Office of the Secretary of the Treasury.

Sec. 309. The Comptroller General shall prescribe the forms, systems, and procedure for administrative appropriation and fund accounting in the several departments and establishments, and for the administrative examination of fiscal officers' accounts and claims against the United States.

Sec. 310. The offices of the six auditors shall be abolished, to take effect July 1, 1921. All other officers and employees of these offices except as otherwise provided herein shall become officers and employees of the General Accounting Office at their grades and salaries on July 1, 1921. All books, records, documents, papers, furniture, office equipment, and other property of these offices, and of the Division of Bookkeeping and Warrants, so far as they relate to the work of such division transferred by section 304, shall become the property of the General Accounting Office. The General Accounting Office shall occupy temporarily the rooms now occupied by the office of the Comptroller of the Treasury and the six auditors.

Sec. 312. (a)The Comptroller General shall investigate, at the seat of government or elsewhere, all matters relating to the receipt, disbursement, and application of public funds, and shall make to the President when requested by him, and to Congress at the beginning of each regular session, a report in writing of the work of the General Accounting Office, containing recommendations concerning the legislation he may deem necessary to facilitate the prompt and accurate rendition and settlement of accounts and concerning such other matters relating to the receipt, disbursement, and application of public funds as he may think advisable. In such regular report, or in special reports at any time when Congress is in session, he shall make recommendations looking to greater economy or efficiency in public expenditures.

(b) He shall make such investigations and reports as shall be ordered by either House of Congress or by any committee of either House having jurisdiction over revenue, appropriations, or expenditures. The Comptroller General shall also, at the request of any such committee, direct assistants from his office to furnish the committee such aid and information as it may request.

(c) The Comptroller General shall specially report to Congress every expenditure or contract made by any department or establishment in any year in violation of law.

(d) He shall submit to Congress reports upon the adequacy and effectiveness of the administrative examination of accounts and claims in the respective departments and establishments and upon the adequacy and effectiveness of departmental inspection of the offices and accounts of fiscal officers.

(e) He shall furnish such information relating to expenditures and accounting to the Bureau of the Budget as it may request from time to time.

Sec. 313. All departments and establishments shall furnish to the Comptroller General such information regarding the powers, duties, activities, organization, financial transactions, and methods of business of their respective offices as he may from time to time require of them; and the Comptroller General, or any of his assistants or employees, when duly authorized by him, shall, for the purpose of securing such information, have access to and the right to examine any books, documents, papers, or records of any such department or establishment. The authority contained in this section shall not be applicable to expenditures made under the provisions of section 291 of the Revised Statutes.

7. Classification Act (1923)*

Be it enacted by the Senate and the House of Representatives of the United States of America in Congress assembled, That this Act may be cited as "The Classification Act of 1923."

Sec. 2. That the term "compensation schedules" means the schedules of positions, grades, and salaries, as contained in section 13 of this Act.

The term "department" means an executive department of the United States Government, a governmental establishment in the executive branch of the United States Government which is not a part of an executive department, the municipal government of the District of Columbia, the Botanic Garden, Library of Congress, Library Building and Grounds, Government Printing Office, and the Smithsonian Institution.

The term "the head of the department" means the officer or group of officers in the department who are not subordinate or responsible to any other officer of the department.

The term "board" means the Personnel Classification Board established by section 3 hereof.

The term "position" means a specific civilian office or employment, whether occupied or vacant, in a department other then the following: offices or employments in the Postal Service; teachers, librarians, school attendance officers, and employees of the community center department under the Board of Education of the District of Columbia; officers and members of the Metropolitan police, the fire department of the District of Columbia, and the United States park police; and the commissioned personnel of the Coast Guard, the Public Health Service, and the Coast and Geodetic Survey.

The term "employee" means any person temporarily or permanently in a position.

The term "service" means the broadest division of related offices and employments.

The term "grade" means a subdivision of a service, including one or more positions for which approximately the same basic qualifications and compensation are prescribed, the distinction between grades being based upon differences in the importance, difficulty, responsibility, and value of the work.

---

* 42 Stat. 265 (1923). Excluded are the extensive descriptions of duties and compensation for the grades of each service in section 13, and all of section 14, which provides for implementation of the Act in the upcoming budget.

The term "class" means a group of positions to be established under this Act sufficiently similar in respect to the duties and responsibilities thereof that the same requirements as to education, experience, knowledge, and ability are demanded of incumbents, the same tests of fitness are used to choose qualified appointees, and the same schedule of compensation is made to apply with equity.

The term "compensation" means any salary, wage, fee, allowance, or other emolument paid to an employee for service in a position.

Sec. 3. That there is hereby established an ex officio board, to be known as the Personnel Classification Board, to consist of the Director of the Bureau of the Budget or an alternate from that Bureau, designated by the Director, a member of the Civil Service Commission or an alternate from that commission designated by the commission, and the Chief of the United States Bureau of Efficiency or an alternate from that bureau designated by the chief of the bureau. The Director of the Bureau of the Budget or his alternate shall be chairman of the board.

Subject to the approval of the President, the heads of the departments shall detail to the board, at its request, for temporary service under its direction, officers or employees possessed of special knowledge, ability, or experience required in the classification and allocation of positions. The Civil Service Commission, the Bureau of the Budget, and the Bureau of Efficiency shall render the board such cooperation and assistance as the board may require for the performance of its duties under this Act.

The board shall make all necessary rules and regulations not inconsistent with the provisions of this Act and provide such subdivisions of the grades contained in section 13 hereof and such titles and definitions as it may deem necessary according to the kind and difficulty of the work. Its regulations shall provide for ascertaining and recording the duties of positions and the qualifications required of incumbents, and it shall prepare and publish an adequate statement giving (1) the duties and responsibilities involved in the classes to be established within the several grades, illustrated where necessary by examples of typical tasks, (2) the minimum qualifications required for the satisfactory performance of such duties and tasks, and (3) the titles given to said classes. In performing the foregoing duties, the board shall follow as nearly as practicable the classification made pursuant to the Executive order of October 24, 1921. The board may from time to time designate additional classes within the several grades and may combine, divide, alter, or abolish existing classes. Department heads shall promptly report the duties and responsibilities of new positions to the board. The board shall make necessary adjustments in compensation for positions carrying maintenance and for positions requiring only part-time service.

Sec. 4. That after consultation with the board, and in accordance with a uniform procedure prescribed by it, the head of each department shall allocate all positions in his department in the District of Columbia to their appropriate grades in the compensation schedules and shall fix the rate of compensation of each employee thereunder, in accordance with the rules prescribed in section 6 herein. Such allocations shall be reviewed and may be revised by the board and shall become final upon their approval by said board. Whenever an existing position or a position hereafter created by law shall not fairly and reasonably be allocable to one of the grades of the several services described in the compensation schedules, the board shall adopt for such position the range of compensation prescribed for a grade, or a class thereof, comparable therewith as to qualifications and duties.

In determining the rate of compensation which an employee shall receive, the principle of equal compensation for equal work irrespective of sex shall be followed.

Sec. 5. That the compensation schedule shall apply only to civilian employees in the departments within the District of Columbia and shall not apply to employees in positions the duties of which are to perform or assist in apprentice, helper, or journeyman work in a recognized trade or craft and skilled and semiskilled laborers, except such as are under the direction and control of the custodian of a public building or perform work which is subordinate, incidental, or preparatory to work of a professional, scientific, or technical character. The board shall make a survey of the field services and shall report to Congress at its first regular session following the passage of this Act schedules of positions, grades, and salaries for such services, which shall follow the principles and rules of the compensation schedules herein contained in so far as these are applicable to the field services. This report shall include a list prepared by the head of each department, after consultation with the board and in accordance with a uniform procedure prescribed by it, allocating all field positions in his department to their approximate grades in said schedules and fixing the proposed rate of compensation of each employee thereunder in accordance with the rules prescribed in section 6 herein.

Sec. 6. That in determining the compensation to be established initially for the several employees the following rules shall govern:

1. In computing the existing compensation of an employee, any bonus which the employee receives shall be included.

2. If the employee is receiving compensation less than the minimum rate of the grade or class thereof in which his duties fall, the compensation shall be increased to that minimum rate.

3. If the employee is receiving compensation within the range of salary prescribed for the appropriate grade at one of the rates fixed therein, no change shall be made in the existing compensation.

4. If the employee is receiving compensation within the range of salary prescribed for the appropriate grade, but not at one of the rates fixed therein, the compensation shall be increased to the next higher rate.

5. If the employee is not a veteran of the Civil War, or a widow of such veteran, and is receiving compensation in excess of the range of salary prescribed for the appropriate grade, the compensation shall be reduced to the rate within the grade nearest the present compensation.

6. All new appointments shall be made at the minimum rate of the appropriate grade or class thereof.

Sec. 7. Increases in compensation shall be allowed upon the attainment and maintenance of the appropriate efficiency ratings, to the next higher rate within the salary range of the grade: *Provided, however,* That in no case shall the compensation of any employee be increased unless Congress has appropriated money from which the increase may lawfully be paid, nor shall the rate for any employee be increased beyond the maximum rate for the grade to which his position is allocated. Nothing herein contained shall be construed to prevent the promotion of an employee from one class to a vacant position in a higher class at any time in accordance with civil service rules, and when so promoted the employee shall receive compensation according to the schedule established for the class to which he is promoted.

Sec. 8. That nothing in this Act shall modify or repeal any existing preference in appointment or reduction in the service of honorably discharged soldiers, sailors, or marines under any existing law or any Executive order now in force.

Sec. 9. That the board shall review and may revise uniform systems of efficiency rating established or to be established for the various grades or classes thereof, which shall set forth the degree of efficiency which shall constitute ground for (a) increase in the rate of compensation for employees who have not attained the maximum rate of the class to which their positions are allocated, (b) continuance at the existing rate of compensation without increase or decrease, (c) decrease in the rate of compensation for employees who at the time are above the minimum rate for the class to which their positions are allocated, and (d) dismissal.

The head of each department shall rate in accordance with such systems the efficiency of each employee under his control or direction. The current ratings for each grade or class thereof shall be open to inspection by the representatives of the board and by the employees of the department under conditions to be determined by the board after consultation with the department heads.

Reductions in compensation and dismissals for inefficiency shall be made by heads of departments in all cases whenever the efficiency ratings warrant, as provided herein, subject to the approval of the board.

The board may require that one copy of such current ratings shall be transmitted to and kept on file with the board.

Sec. 10. That, subject to such rules and regulations as the President may from time to time prescribe, and regardless of the department or independent establishment in which the position is located, an employee may be transferred from a position in one grade to a vacant position within the same grade at the same rate of compensation, or promoted to a vacant position in a higher grade at a higher rate of compensation, in accordance with civil service rules, any provision of existing statutes to the contrary notwithstanding: *Provided,* That nothing herein shall be construed to authorize or permit the transfer of any employee of the United States to a position under the municipal government of the District of Columbia, or any employee of the municipal government of the District of Columbia to a position under the United States.

Sec. 11. That nothing contained in this Act shall be construed to make permanent any temporary appointments under existing law.

Sec. 12. That it shall be the duty of the board to make a study of the rates of compensation provided in this Act for the various services and grades with a view to any readjustment deemed by said board to be just and reasonable. Said board shall, after such study and at such subsequent times as it may deem necessary, report its conclusions to Congress with any recommendations it may deem advisable.

Sec. 13. That the compensation schedules be as follows:

Professional and Scientific Service

The professional and scientific service shall include all classes of positions the duties of which are to perform routine, advisory, administrative, or research work which is based upon the established principles of a profession or science, and which requires professional, scientific, or technical training equivalent to that represented by graduation from a college or university of recognized standing. . . .

Subprofessional Service

The subprofessional service shall include all classes of positions the duties of which are to perform work which is incident, subordinate, or preparatory to the work required of employees holding positions in the professional and scientific service, and which requires or involves professional, scientific, or technical training of any degree inferior to that represented by graduation from a college or university of recognized standing. . . .

Clerical, Administrative, and Fiscal Service

The clerical, administrative, and fiscal service shall include all classes of positions the duties of which are to perform clerical, administrative, or accounting work, or any other work commonly associated with office, business, or fiscal administration. . . .

Custodial Service

The custodial service shall include all classes of positions the duties of which are to supervise or to perform manual work involved in the custody, maintenance, and protection of public buildings, premises, and equipment, the transportation of public officers, employees or property, and the transmission of official papers. . . .

Clerical-Mechanical Service

The clerical-mechanical service shall include all classes of positions which are not in a recognized trade or craft and which are located in the Government Printing Office, the Bureau of Engraving and Printing, the Mail Equipment Shop, the duties of which are to perform or to direct manual or machine operations requiring special skill or experience, or to perform or direct the counting, examining, sorting, or other verification of the product of manual or machine operations. . . .

PART III

Depression
and
New Deal

Depression and New Deal

For American society and government and for public administration, the New Deal was revolutionary. It involved the assumption of massive responsibilities by government, unprecedented in peacetime, particularly in the social and economic realms. It occasioned the transfer to the national level of programs and responsibilities theretofore carried on at state and local levels insofar as they were recognized at all. Yet at the same time that it made state and local governments far more dependent upon the national government, it greatly enlarged the responsibilities of the former and thus changed the whole tone of federalism. The national government became the recourse of last resort at a time when there were virtually no other resorts. Leadership in society, in government, and in public administration moved to Washington.

In the famous first hundred days of the Roosevelt Administration, and for some years after that, the government invented, extended, or adapted a great variety of administrative devices to meet pragmatically the problems which confronted it. In fact, most of these devices had some precedent in the United States or elsewhere. They included, for example, among many others: governmental social insurance; a tax credit system to force state participation in unemployment compensation; work projects as a substitute for welfare; regulation of financial markets; government participation and regulation in labor-management disputes; the beginning of fiscal policy, including deliberate deficit financing; a vast proliferation of grant programs to state and local governments; a government corporation for general regional development (TVA); and governmental payments for non-production in agriculture. It is not feasible in these pages to reproduce the legislation and other documents which legitimated the New Deal, even though many of them have survived and continue to have profound impact upon American public administration.

The early or "first" New Deal violated almost every doctrine in the gospel of the disciples of the management movement. New agencies were established for new programs independent of established departments and agencies already operating in the same fields. Personnel for the new agencies were employed without reference to the established civil service. Funds for the new programs were appropriated quite outside the regular budget process in what became known as a "double budget" system. The time-honored division between policy and administration was repeatedly violated, since most policy initiatives came from the Administration. For orthodox students of public administration, the "first" New Deal was chaos.

The second Roosevelt term, 1937 to 1941, lying between the trauma of the "first" New Deal and the exigencies of full-scale involvement in World War II, offered an opportunity to reexamine, rearrange, and consolidate the national structures and mechanisms in a more orderly way. The main directions of administrative change were set during that period. Some of them were implemented then; others were delayed until the period following the war; still others persisted for decades thereafter. In the main, the principles and the doctrines enumerated in the late nineteen-thirties reflected and were logical culminations of the management movement. It is probably fair to observe that they remained the dominating ethos of American public administration for at least the third of a century which followed.

1. REPORT OF THE PRESIDENT'S COMMITTEE ON ADMINISTRATIVE MANAGEMENT (The Brownlow Committee, 1937)

Early in the last year of his first term (March 22, 1936), President Franklin D. Roosevelt appointed a three-man Committee on Administrative Management to study and make recommendations on the over-all management of the Executive Branch. That Committee, which came to be known as the Brownlow Committee for its chairman, Louis Brownlow, was paralleled by select committees in both the Senate and House which followed different paths and sought different objectives. Their reports were divergent in significant respects, and the Brownlow Report has proved, over subsequent years, by far the most significant. Its basic theme was that the President should be the manager of the Executive Branch and accordingly that his office should be empowered, staffed, organized, and otherwise equipped to manage in a positive and continuing manner. This would involve the development of tools of a staff nature, responsible to the President, in the areas of budget, personnel, and planning; the integration of diverse programs and agencies under a limited number of departments; the extension of the civil service; and the vesting in the Presidency of powers to reorganize. For a number of political reasons, most of the Committee's proposals were not immediately heeded. But over the years, its underlying philosophy became the base point for administrative reforms at all levels of government, and its influence persisted for many decades. As one knowledgeable scholar observed, almost four decades later, "It was the first comprehensive reconsideration of the Presidency and the President's control of the executive branch since 1787, and is probably the most important constitutional document of our time."*

2. REORGANIZATION ACT OF 1939

Legislation to effectuate much of the Brownlow Report failed of passage in 1937 and 1938, partly because of the storm raised by President Roosevelt's proposal to "pack" the Supreme Court and its popular association with his reorganization bill, which was publicly blasted as the "dictator" bill. A modified version was subsequently enacted as the Reorganization Act of 1939, which authorized two of the more important Brownlow proposals and made possible a great many more. One of these was the authorization of administrative assistants to the President. Another was the temporary provision of Presidential initiative to prepare reorganization plans, subject to Congressional veto. The basic idea for the latter was from the Brownlow Report; the mechanism was a Congressional invention. The reorganization plan machinery in that first act expired in 1941, but, with occasional lapses, it has been renewed by temporary legislation through most of the succeeding decades.

* Rowland Egger, "The Period of Crisis: 1933 to 1945," in Frederick C. Mosher, ed., *American Public Administration: Past, Present, Future* (University of Alabama Press, 1975), p. 71.

3. Reorganization Plan No. 1, 1939

The first Reorganization Plan under the Reorganization Act of 1939 remains perhaps the most important of all such plans. It established the Executive Office of the President and transferred to it the Bureau of the Budget, the Central Statistical Board, and the National Resources Planning Board (which was abolished by Congress a few years later). It also created the Federal Security Agency, which by the first Eisenhower Reorganization Plan in 1953 became the Department of Health, Education, and Welfare, and still later, the largest domestic department of the government.

4. Executive Order No. 8248 (1939)

A few weeks after Reorganization Plan No. 1 became effective, the President, on September 8, 1939, issued Executive Order No. 8248, which defined the responsibilities and limitations of the White House Office and the other elements of the Executive Office of the President. Drafted in the Bureau of the Budget with the assistance of Louis Brownlow, this Order was, and remains, one of the most significant documents in American administrative history. Many years later, Clinton Rossiter, a preeminent scholar of the American presidency, wrote: "For some years now, it has been popular, even among his friends, to write off Mr. Roosevelt as a second-rate administrator. In the light of Executive Order 8248, an accomplishment in public administration superior to that of any other President, this familiar judgment seems a trifle musty."*

5. Act to Prevent Pernicious Political Activities (1939) as Amended (1940), (Hatch Acts)

During the same period that witnessed the development of mechanisms for executive reorganization, there was growing concern and argument about the political activities of public employees. Such activities were narrowly restricted for regular civil service personnel by the Pendleton Act and the rules of the Civil

---

* Clinton Rossiter,*The American Presidency* (Harcourt, Brace, and World Inc., revised edition, 1960), p. 130.

Service Commission. But most of those in the New Deal agencies, particularly those in welfare and work relief, were not covered in the civil service, and by the late nineteen-thirties, these constituted nearly forty per cent of federal employees. In reaction to the alleged political activities of many of these on the public payroll, to President Roosevelt's efforts to purge dissident Democratic Congressmen in the 1938 elections, and to fears of a Roosevelt third term, legislation was developed to assure the political purification of public employees whether or not under civil service. First introduced in 1938 and subsequently enacted in August, 1939, was the (Hatch) Act to Prevent Pernicious Political Activities. It is of some interest that the 1939 Hatch Act included, in Section 9A, the first peacetime federal prohibition against its employees belonging to subversive political organizations. It was introduced as an amendment from the floor.

A year later, the Act was amended to apply its restrictions to employees of state and local governments who worked on programs supported fully or partly by federal funds. The 1940 amendments in some respects liberalized the original prohibitions, in others made them more specific; and they made the U.S. Civil Service Commission the investigatory and enforcing agency. For the thirty-six years since 1940, the amended Hatch Act has been a festering center of controversy, the focus for a conflict between, on the one hand, the full rights of public employees to participate in the political system and, on the other, the conduct of public employment on the basis of merit rather than political favoritism. The reproduction of the Hatch Acts which follows incorporates the principal amendments of 1940 but does not include some provisions, including the extended procedures for enforcement which are principally charged to the U.S. Civil Service Commission.

1. Report of the President's Committee on Administrative Management

The Brownlow Committee (1937)*

Introduction

The government of the United States is the largest and most difficult task undertaken by the American people, and at the same time the most important and the noblest. Our Government does more for men, women, and children than any other institution; it employs more persons in its work than any other employer. It covers a wider range of aims and activities than any other enterprise; it sustains the frame of our national and our community life, our economic system, our individual rights and liberties. Moreover, it is a government of, by, and for the people—a democracy that has survived for a century and a half and flourished among competing forms of government of many different types and colors, old and new.

From time to time the decay, destruction, and death of democracy has been gloomily predicted by false prophets who mocked at us, but our American system has matched its massive strength successfully against all the forces of destruction through parts of three centuries.

Our American Government rests on the truth that the general interest

---

* The President's Committee on Administrative Management, *Report of the Committee* (Washington, D.C.: Government Printing Office, 1937). Reproduced herein are: Introduction; Chapter I, The White House Staff; recommendations only of Chapter II, Personnel Management; recommendations only of Chapter III, Fiscal Management; recommendations only of Chapter IV, Planning Management; recommendations only of Chapter V, Administrative Reorganization of the Government of the United States; Chapter VI, Accountability of the Executive to the Congress; and Conclusion.

is superior to and has priority over any special or private interest, and that final decision in matters of common interest to the Nation should be made by free choice of the people of the Nation, expressed in such manner as they shall from time to time provide, and enforced by such agencies as they may from time to time set up. Our goal is the constant raising of the level of the happiness and dignity of human life, the steady sharing of the gains of our Nation, whether material or spiritual, among those who make the Nation what it is.

We are too practical a people to be satisfied by merely looking forward to glittering goals or with mere plans, talk, and pledges. By democracy we mean getting things done that we, the American people, want done in the general interest. Without results we know that democracy means nothing and ceases to be alive in the minds and hearts of men. With us the people's will is not merely an empty phrase; it denotes a grave and stern determination in the major affairs of our Nation—a determination which we propose to make good as promptly and firmly as may be necessary and appropriate—a determination which does not intend to be baffled in its basic plans and purposes by any cluttering or confusion in the machinery for doing what it has been deliberately decided to do.

After the people's judgment has been expressed in due form, after the representatives of the Nation have made the necessary laws, we intend that these decisions shall be promptly, effectively, and economically put into action.

The American Executive

The need for action in realizing democracy was as great in 1789 as it is today. It was thus not by accident but by deliberate design that the founding fathers set the American Executive in the Constitution on a solid foundation. Sad experience under the Articles of Confederation, with an almost headless Government and committee management, had brought the American Republic to the edge of ruin. Our forefathers had broken away from hereditary government and pinned their faith on democratic rule, but they had not found a way to equip the new democracy for action. Consequently, there was grim purpose in resolutely providing for a Presidency which was to be a national office. The President is indeed the one and only national officer representative of the entire Nation. There was hesitation on the part of some timid souls in providing the President with an election independent of the Congress; with a longer term than most governors of that day; with the duty of informing the Congress as to the state of the Union and of recommending to its consideration "such Measures as he shall judge necessary and expedient"; with a two-thirds veto; with a wide power of appointment; and with military and diplomatic authority. But this reluctance was overcome in the face of need and a democratic executive established.

Equipped with these broad constitutional powers, reenforced by statute, by custom, by general consent, the American Executive must be regarded as one of the very greatest contributions made by our Nation to the development of modern democracy—a unique institution the value of which is as evident in times of stress and strain as in periods of quiet.

As an instrument for carrying out the judgment and will of the people of a nation, the American Executive occupies an enviable position among the executives of the states of the world, combining as it does the elements of popular control and the means for vigorous action and leadership—uniting stability and flexibility. The American Executive as an institution stands across the path of those who mistakenly assert that democracy must fail because it can neither decide promptly nor act vigorously.

Our Presidency unites at least three important functions. From one point of view the President is a political leader—leader of a party, leader of the Congress, leader of a people. From another point of view he is head of the Nation in the ceremonial sense of the term, the symbol of our American national solidarity. From still another point of view the President is the Chief Executive and administrator within the Federal system and service. In many types of government these duties are divided or only in part combined, but in the United States they have always been united in one and the same person whose duty it is to perform all of these tasks.

Your Committee on Administrative Management has been asked to investigate and report particularly upon the last function; namely, that of administrative management—the organization for the performance of the duties imposed upon the President in exercising the executive power vested in him by the Constitution of the United States.

Improving the Machinery of Government

Throughout our history we have paused now and then to see how well the spirit and purpose of our Nation is working out in the machinery of everyday government with a view to making such modifications and improvements as prudence and the spirit of progress might suggest. Our Government was the first to set up in its formal Constitution a method of amendment, and the spirit of America has been from the beginning of our history the spirit of progressive changes to meet conditions shifting perhaps more rapidly here than elsewhere in the world.

Since the Civil War, as the tasks and responsibilities of our Government have grown with the growth of the Nation in sweep and power, some notable attempts have been made to keep our administrative system abreast of the new times. The assassination of President Garfield by a disappointed office seeker aroused the Nation against the spoils system and led to the enactment of the civil-service law of 1883. We have struggled to make the principle of this law effective for half a century. The confusion in fiscal management led to the establishment of the Bureau of the Budget and the budgetary system in 1921. We still strive to realize the goal set for the Nation at that time. And, indeed, many other important forward steps have been taken.

Now we face again the problem of governmental readjustment, in part as the result of the activities of the Nation during the desperate years of the industrial depression, in part because of the very growth of the Nation, and in part because of the vexing social problems of our times. There is room for vast increase in our national productivity and there is much bitter wrong to set right in neglected ways of human life. There is need for improvement of our governmental machinery to meet new conditions and to make us ready for the problems just ahead.

Facing one of the most troubled periods in all the troubled history of mankind, we wish to set our affairs in the very best possible order to make the best use of all of our national resources and to make good our democratic claims. If America fails, the hopes and dreams of democracy over all the world go down. We shall not fail in our task and our responsibility, but we cannot live upon our laurels alone.

We seek modern types of management in National Government best fitted for the stern situations we are bound to meet, both at home and elsewhere. As to ways and means of improvement, there are naturally sincere differences of judgment and opinion, but only a treasonable design could oppose careful attention to the best and soundest practices of government available for the American Nation in the conduct of its heavy responsibilities.

The Foundations of Governmental Efficiency

The efficiency of government rests upon two factors: the consent of the governed and good management. In a democracy consent may be achieved readily, though not without some effort, as it is the cornerstone of the Constitution. Efficient management in a democracy is a factor of peculiar significance.

Administrative efficiency is not merely a matter of paper clips, time clocks, and standardized economies of motion. These are but minor gadgets. Real efficiency goes much deeper down. It must be built into the structure of a government just as it is built into a piece of machinery.

Fortunately the foundations of effective management in public affairs, no less than in private, are well known. They have emerged universally wherever men have worked together for some common purpose, whether through the state, the church, the private association, or the commercial enterprise. They have been written into constitutions, charters, and articles of incorporation, and exist as habits of work in the daily life of all organized peoples. Stated in simple terms these canons of efficiency require the establishment of a responsible and effective chief executive as the center of energy, direction, and administrative management; the systematic organization of all activities in the hands of a qualified personnel under the direction of the chief executive; and to aid him in this, the establishment of appropriate managerial and staff agencies. There must also be provision for planning, a complete fiscal system, and means for holding the Executive accountable for his program.

Taken together, these principles, drawn from the experience of mankind in carrying on large-scale enterprises, may be considered as the first requirement of good management. They comprehend the subject matter of administrative management as it is dealt with in this report. Administrative management concerns itself in a democracy with the executive and his duties, with managerial and staff aides, with organization, with personnel, and with the fiscal system because these are the indispensable means of making good the popular will in a people's government.

Modernizing Our Governmental Management

In the light of these canons of efficiency, what must be said of the Government of the United States today? Speaking in the broadest terms at this point, and in detail later on, we find in the American Government at the present time that the effectiveness of the Chief Executive is limited and restricted, in spite of the clear intent of the Constitution to the contrary; that the work of the Executive Branch is badly organized; that the managerial agencies are weak and out of date; that the public service does not include its share of men and women of outstanding capacity and character; and that the fiscal and auditing systems are inadequate. These weaknesses are found at the center of our Government and involve the office of the Chief Executive itself.

While in general principle our organization of the Presidency challenges the admiration of the world, yet in equipment for administrative management our Executive Office is not fully abreast of the trend of our American times, either in business or in government. Where, for example, can there be found an executive in any way comparable upon whom so much petty work is thrown? Or who is forced to see so many persons on unrelated matters and to make so many decisions on the basis of what may be, because of the very press of work, incomplete information? How is it humanly possible to know fully the affairs and problems of over 100 separate major agencies, to say nothing of being responsible for their general direction and coordination?

These facts have been known for many years and are so well appreciated that it is not necessary for us to prove again that the President's administrative equipment is far less developed than his responsibilities, and that a major task before the American Government is to remedy this dangerous situation. What we need is not a new principle, but a modernizing of our managerial equipment.

This is not a difficult problem in itself. In fact, we have already dealt with it successfully in State governments, in city governments, and in large-scale private industry. Gov. Frank O. Lowden in Illinois, Gov. Alfred E. Smith in New York, Gov. Harry F. Byrd in Virginia, and Gov. William Tudor Gardiner in Maine, among others, have all shown how similar problems can be dealt with in large governmental units. The Federal Government is more extensive and more complicated, but the principles of reorganization are the same. On the basis of this experience and our examination of the Executive Branch, we conclude that the following steps should now be taken:

1. To deal with the greatly increased duties of executive management falling upon the President, the White House staff should be expanded.

2. The managerial agencies of the Government, particularly those dealing with the budget, efficiency research, personnel, and planning, should be greatly strengthened and developed as arms of the Chief Executive.

3. The merit system should be extended upward, outward, and downward to cover all non-policy-determining posts, and the civil service system should be reorganized and opportunities established for a career system attractive to the best talent of the Nation.

4. The whole Executive Branch of the Government should be overhauled and the present 100 agencies reorganized under a few large departments in which every executive activity would find its place.

5. The fiscal system should be extensively revised in the light of the best governmental and private practice, particularly with reference to financial records, audit, and accountability of the Executive to the Congress.

These recommendations are explained and discussed in the following sections of this report.

The Purpose of Reorganization

In proceeding to the reorganization of the Government it is important to keep prominently before us the ends of reorganization. Too close a view of machinery must not cut off from sight the true purpose of efficient management. Economy is not the only objective, though reorganization is the first step to savings; the elimination of duplication and contradictory policies is not the only objective, though this will follow; a simple and symmetrical organization is not the only objective, though the new organization will be simple and symmetrical; higher salaries and better jobs are not the only objectives, though these are necessary; better business methods and fiscal controls are not the only objectives, though these too are demanded. There is but one grand purpose, namely, to make democracy work today in our National Government; that is, to make our Government an up-to-date, efficient, and effective instrument for carrying out the will of the Nation. It is for this purpose that the Government needs thoroughly modern tools of management.

As a people we congratulate ourselves justly on our skill as managers—in the home, on the farm, in business big and little—and we properly expect that management in government shall be of the best American model. We do not always get these results, and we must modestly say "we count not ourselves to have attained," but there is a steady purpose in America to press forward until the practices of our governmental administration are as high as the purpose and standards of our people. We know that bad management may spoil good purposes, and that without good management, democracy itself cannot achieve its highest goals.

I. The White House Staff

In this broad program of administrative reorganization the White House itself is involved. The President needs help. His immediate staff assistance is entirely inadequate. He should be given a small number of executive assistants who would be his direct aides in dealing with the managerial agencies and administrative departments of the Government. These assistants, probably not exceeding six in number, would be in addition to his present secretaries, who deal with the public, with the Congress, and with the press and the radio. These aides would have no power to make decisions or issue instructions in their own right. They would not be interposed between the President and the heads of his departments. They would not be assistant presidents in any sense. Their function would be, when any matter was presented to the President for action affecting any part of the administrative work of the Government, to assist him in obtaining quickly and without delay all pertinent information possessed by any of the executive departments so as to guide him in making his responsible decisions; and then when decisions have been made, to assist him in seeing to it that every administrative department and agency affected is promptly informed. Their effectiveness in assisting the President will, we think, be directly proportional to their ability to discharge their functions with restraint. They would remain in the background, issue no orders, make no decisions, emit no public statements. Men for these positions should be carefully chosen by the President from within and without the Government. They should be men in whom the President has personal confidence and whose character and attitude is such that they would not attempt to exercise power on their own account. They should be possessed of high competence, great physical vigor, and a passion for anonymity. They should be installed in the White House itself, directly accessible to the President. In the selection of these aides the President should be free to call on departments from time to time for the assignment of persons who, after a tour of duty as his aides, might be restored to their old positions.

This recommendation arises from the growing complexity and magnitude of the work of the President's office. Special assistance is needed to insure that all matters coming to the attention of the President have been examined from the over-all managerial point of view, as well as from all standpoints that would bear on policy and operation. It also would facilitate the flow upward to the President of information upon which he is to base his decisions and the flow downward from the President of the decisions once taken for execution by the department or departments affected. Thus such a staff would not only aid the President but would also be of great assistance to the several executive departments and to the managerial agencies in simplifying executive contacts, clearance, and guidance.

The President should also have at his command a contingent fund to enable him to bring in from time to time particular persons possessed of particular competency for a particular purpose and whose services he might usefully employ for short periods of time.

The President in his regular office staff should be given a greater number of positions so that he will not be compelled, as he has been compelled in the past, to use for his own necessary work persons carried on the payrolls of other departments.

If the President be thus equipped he will have but the ordinary assistance that any executive of a large establishment is afforded as a matter of course.

In addition to this assistance in his own office the President must be given direct control over and be charged with immediate responsibility for the great managerial functions of the Government which affect all of the administrative departments, as is outlined in the following sections of this report. These functions are personnel management, fiscal and organizational management, and planning management. Within these three groups may be comprehended all of the essential elements of business management.

The development of administrative management in the Federal Government requires the improvement of the administration of these managerial activities, not only by the central agencies in charge, but also by the departments and bureaus. The central agencies need to be strengthened and developed as managerial arms of the Chief Executive, better equipped to perform their central responsibilities and to provide the necessary leadership in bringing about improved practices throughout the Government.

The three managerial agencies, the Civil Service Administration, the Bureau of the Budget, and the National Resources Board, should be a part and parcel of the Executive Office. Thus the President would have reporting to him directly the three managerial institutions whose work and activities would affect all of the administrative departments.

The budgets for the managerial agencies should be submitted to the Congress by the President as a part of the budget for the Executive Office. This would distinguish these agencies from the operating administrative departments of the Government, which should report to the President through the heads of departments who collectively compose his Cabinet. Such an arrangement would materially aid the President in his work of supervising the administrative agencies and would enable the Congress and the people to hold him to strict accountability for their conduct.

The following three sections deal with these managerial functions, namely, personnel management, fiscal management, and planning management, and contain recommendations for their development.

II. Personnel Management

A. *Extension of the Merit System*

In order to extend the merit system we recommend that:

1. The merit system should be extended to positions in new and emergency agencies whose activities are to continue, and the President should be authorized to place such positions, including those in governmental corporations, in the classified civil service.

2. The merit system should be extended to permanent high posts and all other civilian positions in the regular departments and establishments. Exceptions should be made only in the case of such of the highest positions as the President may find to be principally policy-determining in character.

3. The merit system should be extended to the lowest positions in the regular establishments including those filled by skilled workmen and laborers.

4. The incumbent of any position which is placed within the classified civil service should receive civil-service status only after passing a special noncompetitive examination, following certification by the head of his agency that he has served with merit.

5. All civilian positions in regular departments and establishments now filled by Presidential appointment should be filled by the heads of such departments or establishments, without fixed term, except under secretaries and officers who report directly to the President or whose appointment by the President is required by the Constitution.

B. Reorganization and Improvement of Personnel Administration

In order to effect the reorganization of the civil service administration of the United States, we recommend that:

1. A United States Civil Service Administration should be established to serve as the central personnel agency of the Federal Government. The officers of the Administration should consist of a single executive officer to be known as the Civil Service Administrator and a nonsalaried Civil Service Board of seven members, with the powers and duties outlined below.

2. The Administrator should be highly competent, should possess a broad knowledge of personnel administration, and should be a qualified and experienced executive. He should be appointed by the President, with the advice and consent of the Senate, on the basis of an open competitive examination conducted by a special board of examiners appointed by the Civil Service Board. He should be responsible to and hold office at the pleasure of the President.

3. The duties, powers, functions, and authority now vested in the Civil Service Commission should be transferred to the Administrator. Authority should be given to the Administrator to develop and perform the additional functions which should be performed by an adequate central personnel agency. He should be authorized to participate in employee training programs; to make, or to cooperate with other groups in making, studies or investigations of personnel policies, practices, procedures, and methods in other governmental jurisdictions and in industry; and to cooperate with State and local personnel agencies and with independent agencies and corporations of the Federal Government. The Civil Service Administration should be authorized to render services to outside governmental units under suitable provision for reimbursement for the actual cost of such services.

4. The Civil Service Board should consist of seven members, appointed by the President, with the advice and consent of the Senate, for overlapping terms of 7 years. This Board should be composed of outstanding men and women drawn from private business, education, labor, agriculture, public administration, and professional life. No person should be eligible for membership if at any time within 5 years preceding the date of his appointment he has been a member or officer of any local,

State, or national political party committee or has held, or been a candidate for, any elective public office. Members of the Board should receive no salaries, but they should be reimbursed for their actual time and expenses, plus the cost of transportation.

5. The Board should meet not less than four times a year upon call by the President, the chairman of the Board, or any four members of the Board. It should have authority and funds to employ temporary personnel for special investigations in addition to secretarial, clerical, and other necessary services provided by assignment from the staff of the Administrator.

6. The functions of the Civil Service Board should be:

   a. To act as watchdog of the merit system and to represent the public interest in the improvement of personnel administration in the Federal service.

   b. To appoint a special board of qualified examiners whenever there is a vacancy in the office of the Civil Service Administrator in order to conduct a new open competitive examination for the office, and to certify to the President the names of the three highest candidates.

   c. To advise the President as to plans and procedures for dealing with Federal employment questions which cannot be handled satisfactorily through established channels.

   d. To propose to the President or to the Administrator amendments to the rules for the administration of the Federal Civil Service and to review and comment upon amendments proposed by the Administrator.

   e. To make annual and special reports to the President and the Congress on the quality and status of the personnel administration of the Federal Government and to make recommendations on possible improvements in the laws or the administration of matters affecting Federal personnel. In this connection, the Board should have powers to undertake special investigations.

   f. To act in an advisory capacity upon the request of the President or the Administrator on matters concerning personnel administration.

   g. To study and report from time to time upon the relations of the Federal Civil Service to the merit system in State and local jurisdictions, particularly with reference to State and local activities in which there is Federal participation through grants-in-aid.

h. To advise and assist the Administrator in fostering the interest of institutions of learning, civic and professional organizations, and labor and employee organizations in the improvement of personnel standards in the Federal Service. . . .

C. Compensation and Classification

In order to make needed improvements in the salary policy of the Government, we recommend that:

1. The annual salaries of heads of executive departments, under secretaries, and assistant secretaries should be fixed by law at $20,000, $15,000, and $12,000 respectively. Salaries of heads of independent establishments and of members of regulatory commissions should be fixed by the President at amounts not to exceed the maximum rate of the appropriate classification grades in which their respective positions are placed.

2. Compensation in the highest grades of the career service should be increased by appropriate amendment of the Classification Act; permanent officials in the highest civil-service positions, who are charged with the continuous conduct of the Government's work and who have no opportunities to enjoy the honor and prestige of Cabinet and sub-Cabinet posts, should receive annual salaries ranging from $12,000 to $15,000. Career officials in the next lower grade should receive annual salaries ranging from $8,000 to $10,000.

3. The Classification Act should be extended to the field service and to exempted positions in the departmental service and in some of the governmental corporations. The President should be authorized to define suitable services and grades when positions cannot be fairly and reasonably allocated to existing services in the Classification Act and to prescribe schedules of standardized compensation which shall not exceed rates fixed therein for positions of similar responsibility. At the same time governmental corporations and temporary agencies, whether or not they are subject to civil-service rules, should be required to apply the merit principle of appointment and promotion to their personnel.

III. Fiscal Management

A. Budgeting and Administrative Control

Our recommendations regarding budgeting and administrative control may be briefly summarized as follows:

1. The Director of the Bureau of the Budget should be relieved from routine duties and thus enabled to devote himself to problems of fiscal

policy and planning. Provision should be made for an adequate permanent staff of the highest competence, implemented by special assistants on
assignment from the operating agencies and by temporary consultants
and specialists recruited from business and industry for special assign-
ments.

2. The execution, as well as the preparation, of the budget should be
supervised by the Bureau of the Budget and should be closely correlated
with fiscal programs and plans.

3. The administrative research function of the Bureau of the Budget
should be adequately developed to aid the President in his duties as head
of the executive establishment. The Bureau should carry on constructive
studies in public administration for the constant improvement of Government organization and procedure and should also stimulate continuous study of these problems by departments and bureaus.

4. The information function of the Bureau of the Budget should be
developed and improved. The United States Information Service should
be transferred to it, as should other appropriate activities in the coordination of the field services of the Government.

5. The Bureau of the Budget should serve in various ways as an agency
of the President. Improvement should be made in its facilities for the
clearance of Executive orders and the establishment of uniform codes of
management in the Government. It should assist the departments in their
regulations governing internal organization. It could render important
service to the President and to the Congress in coordinating and clearing
legislative recommendations which originate in the Executive Branch.

B. *Direction and Control of Accounting and Expenditures*

Our recommendations regarding the direction and control of accounting and expenditures are as follows:

1. For the purpose of providing the Chief Executive with the essential
vehicles for current financial management and administrative control,
the authority to prescribe and supervise accounting systems, forms, and
procedures in the Federal establishments should be transferred to and
vested in the Secretary of the Treasury. This recommendation is not new.
In 1932 President Hoover recommended to the Congress that the power
to prescribe accounting systems be transferred to the Executive Branch,
stating:

> It is not, however, a proper function of an establishment
> created primarily for the purpose of auditing Government
> accounts to make the necessary studies and to develop and
> prescribe accounting systems involving the entire field of Gov-
> ernment accounting. Neither is it a proper function of such an
> establishment to prescribe the procedure for nor to determine
> the effectiveness of the administrative examination of ac-

counts. Accounting is an essential element of effective administration, and it should be developed with the primary objective of serving this purpose.

In 1934 a special committee of the United States Chamber of Commerce on Federal expenditures, headed by Mr. Matthew S. Sloan, recommended that all accounting activities be removed from the Comptroller General and placed in a General Accounting Office directly responsible to the President. This committee stated in its report:

> Since the Comptroller General is not under Executive Control, as he reports to Congress and is responsible only to that body, the Executive is deprived of one of the most essential means of establishing effective supervision over expenditures, namely, a satisfactory accounting system directly under Executive control. Moreover, the Comptroller General is now in the anomalous position of auditing his own accounting.

> The Committee is convinced that accounting should be segregated from auditing, and that accounting should be centralized in an agency under the control of the President. Such a system would provide the administration with machinery necessary to establish control over expenditures and also afford Congress an independent agency for checking the fiscal operations of the administration.

2. For the purpose of fixing responsibility for the fiscal management of the Government establishment on the Chief Executive in conformity with the constitutional principle that the President "Shall take Care that the Laws be faithfully executed," claims and demands by the Government of the United States or against it and accounts in which the Government of the United States is concerned, either as debtor or as creditor, should be settled and adjusted in the Treasury Department.

3. To avoid conflict and dispute between the Secretary of the Treasury and the departments as to the jurisdiction of the Secretary to settle public accounts, which conflicts and disputes have so marred the relationship between the Comptroller General and the departments in the past, and to make it impossible for the Secretary of the Treasury to usurp any of the powers vested in the heads of departments by the Congress, the Attorney General should be authorized to render opinions on such questions of jurisdiction (but not on the merits of the case) upon the request of the head of the department or upon the request of the Secretary of the Treasury, and the opinion of the Attorney General on such questions of jurisdiction should be final and binding.

4. In order to conform to the limitations in the functions remaining within the jurisdiction of the Comptroller General, the titles of the Comptroller General and the Assistant Comptroller General should be changed

to Auditor General and Assistant Auditor General, respectively, and the name of the General Accounting Office should be changed to the General Auditing Office.

5. The Auditor General should be authorized and required to assign representatives of his office to such stations in the District of Columbia and the field as will enable them currently to audit the accounts of the accountable officers, and they should be required to certify forthwith such exceptions as may be taken to the transactions involved (a) to the officer whose account is involved; (b) to the Auditor General; and (c) to the Secretary of the Treasury.

The auditing work would thus proceed in a decentralized manner independent of, but practically simultaneous with, disbursement. Duplication of effort and delays due to centralization in Washington could be reduced to a minimum. It would not be necessary for the Treasury Department to duplicate the field audit of the General Auditing Office. Exceptions would be promptly reported to the Treasury. Prompt, efficient service could be afforded in the scrutiny of questioned vouchers and in the review of accounts of disbursing officers.

6. In the event of the failure of the Secretary of the Treasury and the Auditor General to reach an agreement with respect to any exception reported by representatives of the Auditor General concerning any expenditure, it should be the duty of the Auditor General to report such exception to the Congress through such committees or joint committees as the Congress may choose to designate.

IV. Planning Management

1. It is recommended that a National Resources Board, consisting of five members appointed by the President, without salary and with indefinite terms, be created to serve as a central planning agency under the President.

2. It is further recommended that there be a director appointed by the Board, in general charge of the staff, and an executive officer, in the classified service; and that the further organization of divisions of the work be left to the determination of the Board.

3. It would be necessary for the Board to have ample provision for the maintenance of a staff equal to the performance of the heavy tasks imposed upon it. In general, the equipment of such a Board as is proposed would consist of:

a. A permanent skeleton staff of career men of undoubted competence, with their assistants.

b. Other governmental personnel with special skills detailed from time to time for the work of the Board.

c. Experts and assistants brought in from time to time to deal with special problems as they arise. A contingent fund for this purpose should be available, but inevitably the amounts required would vary widely from one period to another, as different types of assistance were required.

In support of the proposed indefinite term of office for members of the Board, it may be pointed out that a long term of office is no adequate protection against an unfriendly or indifferent Executive and Congress; and in any case a deadlock between the Board and the authorities would make the success of the Board very dubious. A board may be swept out of existence by the Congress at any time, or it may be ignored by the Executive and the Administration.

Life tenure for such a Board, even if it were possible to obtain, would not be desirable, for it would tend to widen gaps between the Government and the Board, or between the public and the Board. In a rapidly changing situation, a Board of this type must be responsive to the broad sweep of national interest and judgment.

The personnel of the Board should bring together insight, experience, and judgment in the analysis and interpretation of national planning policies, skill in the invention of ways and means of utilizing our national resources, and social vision in the fusion of American interests, techniques, and ideals into sounder and more satisfactory modes of conserving and expanding our national resources and facilitating their equitable award.

The Board should be provided with an annual appropriation, a considerable part of which should be used for aiding the several States in the maintenance of their State planning boards; another part should be budgeted for stated projects of research; and another portion be reserved for other inquiries undertaken at the request of the President for some special purpose, in cooperation with some of the several departments or with local agencies.

V. Administrative Reorganization of the Government of the United States

A. Plan of Reorganization

To meet these conditions and make and keep the Government thoroughly up-to-date, we make four principal recommendations, as follows:

1. Provide for 12 major executive departments, by the addition to the existing 10 of a Department of Social Welfare and a Department of Public Works.

2. Require and authorize the President to determine the appropriate assignment to the 12 executive departments of all operating administrative agencies and fix upon the Executive continuing responsibility and power for the maintenance of the effective division of duties among the departments.

3. Equip the President with the essential modern arms of management in budgeting, efficiency research, personnel, and planning.

4. Revive and extend the principle of Executive accountability to the Congress through the development of an effective independent audit and report on fiscal transactions and through the simplification of the confusing structure of the Government.

It is the purpose of these recommendations to make effective management possible by restoring the President to his proper place as Chief Executive and giving him both a governmental structure that can be managed and modern managerial agencies, and by restoring to the Congress effective legislative control over the Executive. One element of this program, that dealing with managerial agencies, has been discussed above. As a part of other phases of this program, many minor changes will be required. These are discussed in the following pages in connection with a fuller statement of our principal recommendations concerning departmental reorganization.

Twelve Major Departments

Any large industrial or commercial enterprise with plants, stores, or services scattered over a continent would, for the sake of good management, organize the business on the basis of the separate services, plants or areas. Each one of these divisions would then have a manager, and there would be over all a president or general manager who would direct the whole enterprise, working through 8 to 10 executive assistants in accordance with the policies determined by the stockholders and the board of directors. This is in general what we propose for the Government of the United States, making allowance for the differences in method and purpose of the Government as a servant of the Nation.

No man can manage, coordinate, or control more than 100 separate agencies, particularly when in some of them responsibility to the Chief Executive is not definitely placed. The number of immediate subordinates with whom an executive can deal effectively is limited. Just as the hand can cover but a few keys on the piano, so there is for management a limited span of control. In the Army this has been said to be 3 subordinates, in business it has frequently been set at 5 or 6; and some students of government have placed the limit at 10 or 12. Obviously the number is not the same for all work or for all men, nor can it be determined mathematically. But one thing is clear: It should be the smallest possible number without bringing together in any department activities which are unrelated or in conflict with each other.

It is thus necessary to determine what are the new major fields of activity of the National Government and to make a place for them. These are disclosed in the multitude of new agencies and laws of the past 25 years. As we view them they seem to fall in five great categories: Public welfare, public works, public lending, conservation, and business controls. These are the great thrusts which have come to the surface in the last generation, not only in this country, but in all countries, though in different ways. Certain phases of these activities may not be permanent, but the major purposes are apparently here to stay, and deserve appropriate departmental homes.

An examination of the existing executive departments shows that there is no adequate place in the present structure for two of these new developments: Public welfare and public works. We therefore recommend that new departments be set up by law to cover these two fields, and that there be assigned to these departments by the President not only the appropriate new activities in these fields but also the old activities closely related thereto. The remainder of the new activities, which have to do with lending, regulating, and conservation, may be assigned to existing departments without altering their fundamental purposes.

In the case of conservation, however, it would seem desirable to establish a Department of Conservation, which would take over most of the activities of the present Department of Interior. The name "conservation" should be among the departmental titles because it represents a major purpose of our Government today. We therefore recommend that the name of the Department of the Interior be changed to Department of Conservation.

In accordance with these recommendations, the operating divisions of the Executive Branch of the Federal Government would be as follows:

Department of State.	Department of Conservation.
Department of the Treasury.	Department of Agriculture.
Department of War.	Department of Commerce.
Department of Justice.	Department of Labor.
Post Office Department.	Department of Social Welfare.
Department of the Navy.	Department of Public Works.

The establishment of these 12 great departments directly responsible in administration to the Chief Executive in place of the present multitude of independent, and at times conflicting departments, boards, commissions, administrations, authorities, corporations, committees, and agencies will make possible the more simple, more effective, more efficient, more economical, and more democratically controlled management of public affairs.

B. Continuing Executive Responsibility for Efficient Organization

The division of work for its effective performance is a part of the task of doing that work. Under changing conditions, and conditions are always changing, public policy and efficiency require a continual change in the division of work of government, that is, in its organization. Under the circumstances it seems clear that the Executive should always be held responsible not alone for the management of the executive departments, but also for the division of work among the major departments. To render the Executive truly responsible for administration and its efficiency, he must be required to accept the responsibility for the continuous reorganization of the Government.

[Section C., Departmental Organization, has been omitted.]

D. The Independent Regulatory Commissions

The following proposal is put forward as a possible solution of the independent commission problem, present, and future. Under this proposed plan the regulatory agency would be set up, not in a governmental vacuum outside the executive departments, but within a department. There it would be divided into an administrative section and a judicial section. The administrative section would be a regular bureau or division in the department, headed by a chief with career tenure and staffed under civil-service regulations. It would be directly responsible to the Secretary and through him to the President. The judicial section, on the other hand, would be "in" the department only for purposes of "administrative housekeeping," such as the budget, general personnel administration, and materiel. It would be wholly independent of the department and the President with respect to its work and its decisions. Its members would be appointed by the President with the approval of the Senate for long, staggered terms and would be removable only for causes stated in the statute.

The division of work between the two sections would be relatively simple. The first procedural steps in the regulatory process as now carried on by the independent commissions would go to the administrative section. It would formulate rules, initiate action, investigate complaints, hold preliminary hearings, and by a process of sifting and selection prepare the formal record of cases which is now prepared in practice by the staffs of the commissions. It would, of course, do all the purely administrative or sublegislative work now done by the commissions—in short all the work which is not essentially judicial in nature. The judicial section would sit as an impartial, independent body to make decisions affecting the public interest and private rights upon the basis of the records and findings presented to it by the administrative section. In certain types of cases where the volume of business is large and quick and routine action is necessary, the administrative section itself should in the first instance decide the cases and issue orders, and the judicial section should sit as an appellate body to which such decisions could be appealed on questions of law.

This proposed plan meets squarely the problems presented by the independent commissions. It creates effective responsibility for the administrative and policy-determining aspects of the regulatory job and, at the same time, guarantees the complete independence and neutrality for that part of the work which must be performed after the manner of a court. It facilitates and strengthens administrative management without lessening judicial independence.

E. Government Corporations

Federal "business corporations" is the term used here to designate corporations which are federally chartered and in which private rights are represented by stock ownership and board representation. . . .

Federal "governmental corporation" is the term used here to designate corporations (whether incorporated under Federal or State charter) which are federally owned and controlled. In these organizations a majority of the stock is owned by the United States and no member of the board of directors is elected or appointed by private interests. . . .

Our recommendations on Federal corporations may be summarized as follows:

1. "Business corporations" should be placed under special supervisory agencies to be set up in appropriate departments of the Government to give continuous and careful scrutiny to their affairs. These agencies should be provided with the special equipment and staff necessary to supervise competently the particular field in which the corporations operate.

2. Each "governmental corporation" should also be placed under a supervisory agency in an appropriate department. In addition, there should be continuing authority in the President to place such corporations under civil service, under other rules regarding personnel, and to apply such over-all governmental controls as may be found advisable in each case in the fields of budgeting, accounting, audit, and the issuance of obligations.

3. Where it is desirable to preserve the independence of the supervisory agency, it should be given semi-autonomous status in a department.

The single responsible administrator at the head of a supervisory agency is preferable to the board form. The head of the supervisory agency should appoint the boards of directors of corporations in the case of boards which have government representation. If heads of supervisory agencies are to exercise an independent review of corporate activities, they should not be directors of corporations they supervise.

4. The boards of directors of corporations in turn should not attempt to divide management work among themselves, but should assign the task of corporate administration to a president or general manager who reports to them. Interdepartmental committees in charge of corporate activities have not been successful and should be avoided. Responsibility is either assumed by one department or is entirely diffused. Ex-officio designation of specific public officers as board members is undesirable and should be discontinued.

With these safeguards we are convinced that the corporate form can continue to be used as a valuable instrument in effectuating public policy.

Reorganization and Administrative Management

Modern management under responsible leadership is the keynote of the reorganization herein recommended. This is to be achieved through placing all administrative agencies under 12 major departments. These departments may be set up by the Congress and all of the administrative work of the various agencies of the Government brought into them or into the three managerial agencies of the President by Executive order, after careful examination of their work, their needs, and their personnel. The responsibility for maintaining continuously an efficient and manageable organization within the framework of the broad policies outlined by the Congress is to be placed directly upon the President, since it is a continuing Executive function. The Executive should be given the essential tools for modern administrative management and at the same time should be made more effectively accountable to the Congress.

In this reorganization of the Government every administrative activity should be set up with a single responsible head. Boards should not be burdened with administration, but should be continued for advisory, corporate, and quasi-judicial purposes. This would require the separation of the administrative and judicial functions of the independent regulatory agencies. Their administrative work would be transferred to a regular department and the board or commission would be continued within the department to deal with the judicial work.

All Government corporations should likewise be brought under supervision and control through transfer into regular departments. They should be established therein as semi-autonomous divisions, with extension to them of such budgetary, financial, and personnel supervision or control as may be appropriate in any given case.

With the entrance into the departments of the multitude of agencies now floating around or loosely independent, the departments themselves will require internal reorganization. It is suggested that the departments should follow the general pattern recommended for the Government as a whole. Each department should have at its head a Member of the Cabinet. Working under him in policy posts there would be a small number of men of his own selection, and a group of technical advisers. The operation of the department would be carried on through bureaus and semi-autonomous agencies, manned throughout by civil servants, and under the administrative supervision of a career executive officer.

By such a reorganization the heads of the 12 great departments will of necessity rise higher above the level of administrative detail than they have in the past, will be more responsibly engaged in the formulation of policy as they delegate their administrative work to their subordinates, and collectively the department heads may act more and more as a council of state upon whom the President may rely for advice and whose jurisdictional differences of opinion he will himself have the power and the authority to compose.

Such a reorganization of the administrative agencies of the Executive Branch will reduce the number of agencies reporting to the President to a manageable compass and will bring the machinery of our Federal Government up to date and enable it to deal economically, effectively, and democratically with modern problems.

VI. Accountability of the Executive
to the Congress

Under the American system the Executive power is balanced and made safe by freedom of speech, by elections, by the protection of civil rights under an independent judiciary, by the making of laws which determine policies including especially appropriations and tax measures, by an independent elective Congress, and by the establishment of Executive accountability.

The preservation of the principle of the full accountability of the Executive to the Congress is an essential part of our republican system. In actual practice the effectiveness of this accountability is often obstructed and obscured, and sometimes is defeated by the processes of diffusion, processes which are at work not only in the Executive Branch but in the Congress itself.

If the reorganization of the administrative departments and the establishment of the managerial agencies that we have recommended be carried out, then we believe that the country may confidently look forward to an improvement in coordination of administrative work. Contradictory administrative policies which are so irritating to the Congress and so confounding to the people would be minimized. Thus the accountability of the Executive Branch may be made sharp, distinct, and effective.

There is, we believe, too little appreciation among the people of the country of the day-to-day work of the Congress. Although it is generally understood that the Members of Congress spend many days and weeks in the preparation, perfection, and adoption of legislative measures, the extent of their work is not generally known. They serve on committees which not only prepare legislative measures for submission to their respective Houses, but conduct hearings and investigations which throw light upon the problems of the country and the processes of government through which the people are enabled to see and understand their Government.

Nothing should be done that would diminish the importance of the work of the congressional committees in conducting hearings and pursuing investigations. Time and time again in our history, investigations conducted by congressional committees have illumined dark places in the Government and in the affairs of the Nation and have resulted in the correction of abuses that otherwise might have been undetected for years and years. It is with full realization of the necessity of continuing and preserving this important function of the Congress and its committees that we suggest the necessity for improving the machinery of holding the Executive Branch more effectively accountable to the Congress.

This accountability often is obscured by the Congress itself in imposing upon the Executive in too great detail minute requirements for the organization and operation of the administrative machinery. Faced by such mandatory and detailed legislative requirements (whether in general law or in a rider on an appropriation bill), first the bureau chief, then the Secretary of the department, and then the President is absolved from part of his executive responsibility, and in consequence the Congress is foreclosed from adequately criticizing the conduct of the business.

We have called attention to this difficulty with respect to fiscal accountability. We hold that once the Congress has made an appropriation, an appropriation which it is free to withhold, the responsibility for the administration of the expenditures under that appropriation is and should be solely upon the Executive.

The Executive then should be held to account through an independent audit made by an independent auditor who will report promptly to the Congress his criticisms and exceptions of the actions of the Executive. Based upon these reports the appropriate committees of the Congress may call upon an executive officer to explain his conduct and if it has been characterized by illegality or impropriety, the Congress can take the necessary corrective steps and safeguard the future.

With respect to the accountability of the Executive Branch to the Legislative Branch for fiscal and other activities, the difficulty now is that the diffusion and dispersion of activities in the uncoordinated organization of the Executive Branch is twinned by a similar diffusion and dispersion in the Congress. Separate committees of the Congress must of necessity be set up to pursue investigatorial activities, hold hearings, and consider legislation and appropriations. But the Congress has not in either House adequate machinery for the collection and coordination of the information which it requires if it is to hold the President effectively accountable for the conduct of the Executive Branch as a whole.

With respect to fiscal affairs this need might be met by the organization by each House of special committees or by both Houses of a joint committee on fiscal control to receive the reports of its Auditor General.

With respect to nonfiscal affairs, the creation of similar special committees or of a joint committee to keep currently informed of the activities of the three managerial agencies dealing with budget, personnel, and planning, which we recommend should be set up directly under the President, would go far toward lessening the evil effects of the present lack of coordination.

Thus the principle of the accountability of the Executive to the Congress might be made effective in action.

Conclusion

Your Committee has no illusions about setting up a perfect system of administrative management, for we realize fully that any substantial improvement is a task which will require time for its achievement and that other problems will always be emerging. To revive the drooping merit system, to straighten out warped lines of responsibility, to simplify a topsy-turvy organizational growth—these are by no means simple advances.

Moreover, these changes cannot be adopted and maintained unless the American public itself fully appreciates the advantages of good management and insists upon getting them. The need for reorganization rests not alone on the idea of savings, considerable as they will be, but upon better service to society. While good management is important to those who have much, it is still more important to those who have not or have little; for they need the help of government in their struggle for justice, security, steadier employment, better living and working conditions, and a growing share of the gains of civilization.

In order to avoid any misunderstandings, it must be made perfectly clear that it was not the task of this Committee to determine whether particular activities of the Government should or should not continue in operation or upon what scale of magnitude. This is an important question of policy determination which fell outside the field of our undertaking. It has been our problem to consider what forms of administrative management are most suitable, given such governmental activities as there are. As the work of the Government changes, the form of management will also alter somewhat, although not greatly unless the changes are considerable.

It will be noted that we have made no estimate of the amount of money that will be saved by such a rearrangement and reorganization of the Executive Branch as we have suggested. We have not made such an estimate for two reasons, despite the fact that we are convinced that the establishment of the managerial agencies and the reorganization of the administrative departments that we have recommended will result in large savings, not only of money, but of time and effort.

The two reasons that we have not made such an estimate are as follows:

First, the scope of our inquiry was limited to the realm of administrative management and excluded the realm of policy. It would have been easy to say that so much might be saved by utterly abolishing this, that, or the other activity of the Government. But this was not our task. We have been charged with the duty of suggesting means of making more effective, more efficient, and more economical the machinery for administering whatever activities have been decided upon by the people, the Congress, and the President.

Second, it has been demonstrated over and over again in large organizations of every type in business and in government that genuine savings in operation and true economies are to be achieved only by the provision of adequate managerial machinery which will afford an opportunity for central executive direction to pursue day after day and year after year, in season and out of season, the task of cutting costs, of improving the service, and of raising the standards of performance. It cannot be done by arbitrary percentage cuts, arbitrary dismissal of employees, arbitrary consolidation of agencies. It is an operation that must be performed, but for its successful performance, we must requisition the skill of the surgeon and his scalpel and not be tempted to call in the butcher with his cleaver.

To equip the Executive Branch with better means of managerial direction, better personnel, better fiscal controls, better machinery for planning; to simplify its organization and reduce the number of its agencies; and to sharpen its accountability to the Congress will result in savings— savings in money, in time, in energy. To estimate these savings in terms of dollars and cents would be but to guess in a situation where not guessing but intensive scientific research is the means, and the firm and courageous application of the results of the research is the method, if the aim is to be achieved.

The paramount purpose of your Committee has been throughout to find modern methods of carrying out the national aims and programs of America as far as this duty is imposed upon our Executive by our Constitution. We have not been concerned with strengthening the Executive alone and as such, but with the larger aim of strengthening the American system as a whole in its practical operations.

We should be the first, moreover, to recognize that there is wide room for differences in the details of any program, but we believe that there should be no division upon the soundness of the broad principle that the managerial powers and equipment of the President should be equal to his responsibilities under the Constitution.

With the program here suggested, your Committee believes that this may be accomplished, and that administrative management in the office of the President will work more smoothly and effectively in the task of executing the judgment and decisions of the Nation and carrying out the general policies of the Congress.

The proposals of the Committee may be summarized as follows:

1. Expand the White House staff so that the President may have a sufficient group of able assistants in his own office to keep him in closer and easier touch with the widespread affairs of administration and to make a speedier clearance of the knowledge needed for executive decision;

2. Strengthen and develop the managerial agencies of the Government, particularly those dealing with the Budget, efficiency research, personnel, and planning, as management arms of the Chief Executive;

3. Extend the merit system upward, outward, and downward to cover all nonpolicy-determining posts; reorganize the civil-service system as a part of management under a single responsible Administrator, strengthening the Civil Service Commission as a citizen Civil Service Board to serve as the watchdog of the merit system; and increase the salaries of key posts throughout the service so that the Government may attract and hold in a career service men and women of the highest ability and character;

4. Overhaul the 100 independent agencies, administrations, authorities, boards, and commissions, and place them by Executive order within one or the other of the following 12 major executive departments: State, Treasury, War, Justice, Post Office, Navy, Conservation, Agriculture, Commerce, Labor, Social Welfare, and Public Works; and place upon the Executive continuing responsibility for the maintenance of effective organization;

5. Establish accountability of the Executive to the Congress by provid-

ing a genuine independent postaudit of all fiscal transactions by an Auditor General, and restore to the Executive complete responsibility for accounts and current financial transactions.

These proposals have the merit, we believe, of eliminating the evils of the patronage system; of opening out our civil service more fully and completely as a sound career service, permanent, nonpartisan, competent, fairly compensated, and affording promotion to posts of eminence: of unifying the responsible direction of personnel activities while at the same time providing for disinterested citizen supervision of the whole program.

These plans are designed to make possible a more responsible and effective supervision and direction of fiscal management than hitherto, first, by strengthening the Bureau of the Budget, particularly through the development of efficiency research; second, by returning to the Executive the powers inappropriately exercised by the Comptroller General; and third, by departmental reorganization. This opens the way for genuine Executive direction and for efficiency and economy.

At the same time, provision is made for what is equally essential. namely, genuine accountability of the Executive Office to the Congress through adequate audit and through general supervision of broad policies of fiscal and other administration.

The proposed arrangements provide for the organization of planning management through a National Resources Board with an advisory function of overhead consideration of the conservation and utilization of our national resources, both natural and human. Department reorganization, also, will increase the scope and effectiveness of planning.

These changes taken together will give to the Executive agencies of fiscal management, personnel management, and planning management. Under the plans proposed, these three arms of management are knit together in the White House, under the immediate direction of the President.

The drastic reduction in the number of departments, commissions boards, authorities, agencies, and activities from over 100 to 12 will have many implications. It will take us back to the Constitution in that it ties in the wandering independencies and abolishes the irresponsible and headless "fourth branch" of the Government which has grown up unnoticed. It will reestablish a single Executive Branch, with the President as its responsible head, as provided by the Constitution. Moreover, it will make it humanly possible for a President to do his job, and to coordinate the activities for which he is constitutionally, legally, and popularly responsible, by greatly lessening the contacts and detail which now engulf him. It will make of the Government a businesslike organization for effective and efficient service, and, finally, will render the whole Government more easily understood and controllable by the people, and thus a more faithful servant of the people.

At the same time, sharper lines of accountability to the Congress are traced, and forms of decentralization, both geographical and departmental, outlined.

Your Committee fully appreciates that there is no magic in management alone. Management is a servant, not a master—a means, not an end, a tool in the hands and for the purposes of the Nation. Public service is the service of the common good in peace or war and will be judged by this standard. Not merely lower unit costs but higher human happiness and values are the supreme ends of our national life, and by these terms this and every other system must finally be tested. Good management will promote in the fullest measure the conservation and utilization of our national resources, and spell this out plainly in social justice, security, order, liberty, prosperity, in material benefits, and in higher values of life. The adjustments and arrangements we suggest have no other purpose or justification than better public service for our people through better administrative management.

It may be said that there is danger that management itself will grow too great and forget where it came from or what it is for—in the old and recurring insolence of office. But in the judgment of your Committee, based upon broad observation of the bewildering sweep of recent events here and elsewhere, the really imminent danger now is that our democracy and perhaps others may be led by false or mistaken guides to place their trust in weak and faltering inaction, which in the bitter end runs to futility and defeat. In the late war, democracies showed vast strength and tenacity in times of strain that racked every fiber of the ship of state. And now we face and will master the critical tasks of reorganization and readjustment of many tangled parts of our national life on many new frontiers. The injustice and oppression intertwined with solid good in our American system will not always yield without a firm display of our national constitutional powers. Our national will must be expressed not merely in a brief, exultant moment of electoral decision, but in persistent, determined, competent day-by-day administration of what the Nation has decided to do.

Honesty and courage alone are not enough for victory, either in peace or in war. Intelligence, vision, fairness, firmness, and flexibility are required in an assembled, competent, strong organization of democracy. To falter at this point is fatal. A weak administration can neither advance nor retreat successfully—it can merely muddle. Those who waiver at the sight of needed power are false friends of modern democracy. Strong executive leadership is essential to democratic government today. Our choice is not between power and no power, but between responsible but capable popular government and irresponsible autocracy.

The forward march of American democracy at this point of our history depends more upon effective management than upon any other single factor. The times demand better governmental organization, staffed with more competent public servants, more free to do their best, and coordinated by an Executive accountable to the Congress and fully equipped with modern tools of management. Thus the President will have effective managerial authority over the Executive Branch commensurate with his responsibility under the Constitution of the United States.

2. Reorganization Act of 1939*

Title I—Reorganization

Part 1

Section 1. (a) The Congress hereby declares that by reason of continued national deficits beginning in 1931 it is desirable to reduce substantially Government expenditures and that such reduction may be accomplished in some measure by proceeding immediately under the provisions of this Act. The President shall investigate the organization of all agencies of the Government and shall determine what changes therein are necessary to accomplish the following purposes:

(1) To reduce expenditures to the fullest extent consistent with the efficient operation of the Government;

(2) To increase the efficiency of the operations of the Government to the fullest extent practicable within the revenues;

(3) To group, coordinate, and consolidate agencies of the Government, as nearly as may be, according to major purposes;

* 53 Stat. 36 (1939). Not included here are: part 2 of Title I, which modified House and Senate rules for handling reorganization plans; and Title II, which was a minor amendment of an earlier law.

(4) To reduce the number of agencies by consolidating those having similar functions under a single head, and to abolish such agencies as may not be necessary for the efficient conduct of the Government; and

(5) To eliminate overlapping and duplication of effort.

(b) The Congress declares that the public interest demands the carrying out of the purposes specified in subsection (a) and that such purposes may be accomplished in great measure by proceeding immediately under the provisions of this title, and can be accomplished more speedily thereby than by the enactment of specific legislation.

Sec. 2. When used in this title, the term "agency" means any executive department, commission, independent establishment, corporation owned or controlled by the United States, board, bureau, division, service, office, authority, or administration, in the executive branch of the Government.

Sec. 3. No reorganization plan under section 4 shall provide—

(a) For the abolition or transfer of an executive department or all the functions thereof or for the establishment of any new executive department;

(b) In the case of the following agencies, for the transfer, consolidation, or abolition of the whole or any part of such agency or of its head, or of all or any of the functions of such agency or of its head: Civil Service Commission, Coast Guard, Engineer Corps of the United States Army, Mississippi River Commission, Federal Communications Commission, Federal Power Commission, Federal Trade Commission, General Accounting Office, Interstate Commerce Commission, National Labor Relations Board, Securities and Exchange Commission, Board of Tax Appeals, United States Employees' Compensation Commission, United States Maritime Commission, United States Tariff Commission, Veterans' Administration, National Mediation Board, National Railroad Adjustment Board, Railroad Retirement Board, the Federal Deposit Insurance Corporation, or the Board of Governors of the Federal Reserve System; or

(c) For changing the name of any executive department or the title of its head, or for designating any agency as "Department" or its head as "Secretary"; or

(d) For the continuation of any agency beyond the period authorized by law for the existence of such agency; or

(e) For the continuation of any function of any agency beyond the period authorized by law for the exercise of such function; or

(f) For authorizing any agency to exercise any function which is not expressly authorized by law.

Sec. 4. Whenever the President, after investigation, finds that—

(a) the transfer of the whole or any part of any agency or the functions thereof to the jurisdiction and control of any other agency; or

(b) the consolidation of the functions vested in any agency; or

(c) the abolition of the whole or any part of any agency which agency or part (by reason of transfers under this Act or otherwise, or by reason of termination of its functions in any manner) does not have, or upon the taking effect of the reorganizations specified in the reorganization plan will not have, any functions,

is necessary to accomplish one or more of the purposes of section 1 (a), he shall—

(d) prepare a reorganization plan for the making of the transfers, consolidations, and abolitions, as to which he has made findings and which he includes in the plan. Such plan shall also—

> (1) designate, in such cases as he deems necessary, the name of any agency affected by a reorganization and the title of its head;
>
> (2) make provision for the transfer or other disposition of the records, property (including office equipment), and personnel affected by such transfer, consolidation, or abolition;
>
> (3) make provision for the transfer of such unexpended balances of appropriations available for use in connection with the function or agency transferred or consolidated, as he deems necessary by reason of the transfer or consolidation for use in connection with the transferred or consolidated functions, or for the use of the agency to which the transfer is made, but such unexpended balances so transferred shall be used only for the purposes for which such appropriation is originally made;
>
> (4) make provision for winding up the affairs of the agency abolished; and

(e) transmit such plan (bearing an identifying number) to the Congress, together with a declaration that, with respect to each transfer, consolidation, or abolition referred to in paragraph (a), (b), or (c) of this section and specified in the plan, he has found that such transfer, consolidation, or abolition is necessary to accomplish one or more of the purposes of section 1 (a). The delivery to both Houses shall be on the same day and shall be made to each House while it is in session.

The President, in his message transmitting a reorganization plan, shall state the reduction of expenditures which it is probable will be brought about by the taking effect of the reorganizations specified in the plan.

Sec. 5. The reorganizations specified in the plan shall take effect in accordance with the plan:

(a) Upon the expiration of sixty calendar days after the date on which the plan is transmitted to the Congress, but only if during such sixty-day period there has not been passed by the two Houses a concurrent resolution stating in substance that the Congress does not favor the reorganization plan.

(b) If the Congress adjourns sine die before the expiration of the sixty-day period, a new sixty-day period shall begin on the opening day of the next succeeding regular or special session. A similar rule shall be applicable in the case of subsequent adjournments sine die before the expiration of sixty days.

Sec. 6. No reorganization under this title shall have the effect—

(a) of continuing any agency or function beyond the time when it would have terminated if the reorganization had not been made; or

(b) of continuing any function beyond the time when the agency in which it was vested before the reorganization would have terminated if the reorganization had not been made; or

(c) of authorizing any agency to exercise any function which is not expressly authorized by law.

Sec. 7. For the purposes of this title any transfer, consolidation, abolition, designation, disposition, or winding up of affairs, referred to in section 4 (d), shall be deemed a "reorganization."

Sec. 8. (a) All orders, rules, regulations, permits, or other privileges made, issued, or granted by or in respect of any agency or function transferred to, or consolidated with, any other agency or function under the provisions of this title, and in effect at the time of the transfer or consolidation, shall continue in effect to the same extent as if such transfer or consolidation had not occurred, until modified, superseded, or repealed.

(b) No suit, action, or other proceeding lawfully commenced by or against the head of any agency or other officer of the United States, in his official capacity or in relation to the discharge of his official duties, shall abate by reason of any transfer of authority, power, and duties from one officer or agency of the Government to another under the provisions of this title, but the court, on motion or supplemental petition filed at any time within twelve months after such transfer takes effect, showing a necessity for a survival of such suit, action, or other proceeding to obtain a settlement of the questions involved, may allow the same to be maintained by or against the head of the agency or other officer of the United States to whom the authority, powers, and duties are transferred.

(c) All laws relating to any agency or function transferred to, or consolidated with, any other agency or function under the provisions of this title, shall, insofar as such laws are not inapplicable, remain in full force and effect.

Sec. 9. The appropriations or portions of appropriations unexpended by reason of the operation of this title shall not be used for any purpose, but shall be impounded and returned to the Treasury.

Sec. 10. (a) Whenever the employment of any person is terminated by a reduction of personnel as a result of a reorganization effected under this title, such person shall thereafter be given preference, when qualified, whenever an appointment is made in the executive branch of the Government, but such preference shall not be effective for a period longer than twelve months from the date the employment of such person is so terminated.

(b) Any transfer of personnel under this title shall be without change in classification or compensation, except that this requirement shall not operate after the end of the fiscal year during which the transfer is made to prevent the adjustment of classification or compensation to conform to the duties to which such transferred personnel may be assigned.

Sec. 11. If the reorganizations specified in a reorganization plan take effect, the reorganization plan shall be printed in the Statutes at Large in the same volume as the public laws, and shall be printed in the Federal Register.

Sec. 12. No reorganization specified in a reorganization plan shall take effect unless the plan is transmitted to the Congress before January 21, 1941.

Title III—Administrative Assistants

Sec. 301. The President is authorized to appoint not to exceed six administrative assistants and to fix the compensation of each at the rate of not more than $10,000 per annum. Each such administrative assistant shall perform such duties as the President may prescribe.

3. Reorganization Plan No. 1, 1939*

Part 1.—Executive Office of the President

Section 1. *Bureau of the Budget.*—The Bureau of the Budget and all of its functions and personnel (including the Director and Assistant Director) are hereby transferred from the Treasury Department to the Executive Office of the President; and the functions of the Bureau of the Budget shall be administered by the Director thereof under the direction and supervision of the President.

Section 2. *Central Statistical Board.*—The Central Statistical Board and all of its functions and personnel (including the Chairman and the members of the Board) are hereby transferred to the Bureau of the Budget in the Executive Office of the President. The Chairman of the Board shall perform such administrative duties as the Director of the Bureau of the Budget shall direct.

Section 3. *Central Statistical Committee Abolished and Functions Transferred.*—The Central Statistical Committee is hereby abolished, and its functions are transferred to the Director of the Bureau of the Budget to be administered by him under the direction and supervision of the President. The Director of the Bureau of the Budget shall promptly wind up any outstanding affairs of the Central Statistical Committee.

Section 4. *National Resources Planning Board.*—(a) The functions of the National Resources Committee, established by Executive Order No. 7065 of June 7, 1935, and its personnel (except the members of the Committee) and all of the functions of the Federal Employment Stabilization Office in the Department of Commerce and its personnel are hereby transferred to the Executive Office of the President. The functions transferred by this section are hereby consolidated, and they shall be administered under the direction and supervision of the President by the National Resources Planning Board (hereafter referred to as the Board), which shall be composed of five members to be appointed by the President. The President shall designate one of the members of the Board as Chairman and

* 53 Stat. Reorganization Plan No. 1 (1939). Not included are sections 7 through 9 of part 1, which provided technical authority for the transfers of records, property, funds, and personnel, and parts 2, 3, and 4, which established, respectively, the Federal Security Agency (forerunner of the Department of Health, Education, and Welfare, which was later established by Reorganization Plan No. 1 of 1953), the Federal Works Agency, and the Federal Loan Agency. Both of the latter were subsequently abolished.

another as Vice Chairman. The Vice Chairman shall act as Chairman in the absence of the Chairman or in the event of a vacancy in that office. The members of the Board shall be compensated at the rate of $50.00 per day for time spent in attending and traveling to and from meetings, or in otherwise exercising the functions and duties of the Board, plus the actual cost of transportation: *Provided,* That in no case shall a member be entitled to receive compensation for more than thirty days' service in two consecutive months.

(b) The Board shall determine the rules of its own proceedings, and a majority of its members in office shall constitute a quorum for the transaction of business, but the Board may function notwithstanding vacancies.

(c) The Board may appoint necessary officers and employees and may delegate to such officers authority to perform such duties and make such expenditures as may be necessary.

Sec. 5. *National Resources Committee Abolished.*—The National Resources Committee is hereby abolished, and its outstanding affairs shall be wound up by the National Resources Planning Board.

Sec. 6. *Federal Employment Stabilization Office Abolished.*—The Federal Employment Stabilization Office is hereby abolished, and the Secretary of Commerce shall promptly wind up its affairs.

---

4. Executive Order No. 8248
Establishing the Divisions of the Executive Office of the President and Defining their Functions and Duties (1939)

By virtue of the authority vested in me by the Constitution and Statutes, and in order to effectuate the purposes of the Reorganization Act of 1939, Public No. 19, Seventy-sixth Congress, approved April 3, 1939, and of Reorganization Plans Nos. I and II [4 F.R. 2727, 2733 DI] submitted to the Congress by the President and made effective as of July 1, 1939 by Public Resolution No. 2, Seventy-sixth Congress, approved June 7, 1939, by organizing the Executive Office of the President with functions and duties so prescribed and responsibilities so fixed that the President will have adequate machinery for the administrative management of the Executive branch of the Government, it is hereby ordered as follows:

I

There shall be within the Executive Office of the President the following principal divisions, namely: (1) The White House Office, (2) the Bureau of the Budget, (3) the National Resources Planning Board, (4) the Liaison Office for Personnel Management, (5) the Office of Government Reports, and (6) in the event of a national emergency, or threat of a national emergency, such office for emergency management as the President shall determine.

II

The functions and duties of the divisions of the Executive Office of the President are hereby defined as follows:

1.*The White House Office.* In general, to serve the President in an intimate capacity in the performance of the many detailed activities incident to his immediate office. To that end, The White House Office shall be composed of the following principal subdivisions, with particular functions and duties as indicated:

(a)*The Secretaries to the President.* To facilitate and maintain quick and easy communication with the Congress, the individual members of the Congress, the heads of executive departments and agencies, the press, the radio, and the general public.

(b)*The Executive Clerk.* To provide for the orderly handling of documents and correspondence within The White House Office, and to organize and supervise all clerical services and procedure relating thereto.

(c)*The Administrative Assistants to the President.* To assist the President in such matters as he may direct, and at the specific request of the President, to get information and to condense and summarize it for his use. These Administrative Assistants shall be personal aides to the President and shall have no authority over anyone in any department or agency, including the Executive Office of the President, other than the personnel assigned to their immediate offices. In no event shall the Administrative Assistants be interposed between the President and the head of any department or agency, or between the President and any one of the divisions in the Executive Office of the President.

2.*The Bureau of the Budget.* (a) To assist the President in the preparation of the Budget and the formulation of the fiscal program of the Government.

(b) To supervise and control the administration of the Budget.

(c) To conduct research in the development of improved plans of administrative management, and to advise the executive departments and agencies of the Government with respect to improved administrative organization and practice.

(d) To aid the President to bring about more efficient and economical conduct of Government service.

(e) To assist the President by clearing and coordinating departmental advice on proposed legislation and by making recommendations as to Presidential action on legislative enactments, in accordance with past practice.

(f) To assist in the consideration and clearance and, where necessary, in the preparation of proposed Executive orders and proclamations, in accordance with the provisions of Executive Order No. 7298 of February 18, 1936.

(g) To plan and promote the improvement, development, and coordination of Federal and other statistical services.

(h) To keep the President informed of the progress of activities by agencies of the Government with respect to work proposed, work actually initiated, and work completed, together with the relative timing of work between the several agencies of the Government; all to the end that the work programs of the several agencies of the Executive branch of the Government may be coordinated and that the monies appropriated by the Congress may be expended in the most economical manner possible with the least possible overlapping and duplication of effort.

3.*The National Resources Planning Board.* (a) To survey, collect data on, and analyze problems pertaining to national resources, both natural and human, and to recommend to the President and the Congress long-time plans and programs for the wise use and fullest development of such resources.

(b) To consult with Federal, regional, state, local, and private agencies in developing orderly programs of public works and to list for the President and the Congress all proposed public works in the order of their relative importance with respect to (1) the greatest good to the greatest number of people, (2) the emergency necessities of the Nation, and (3) the social, economic, and cultural advancement of the people of the United States.

(c) To inform the President of the general trend of economic conditions and to recommend measures leading to their improvement or stabilization.

(d) To act as a clearing house and means of coordination for planning activities, linking together various levels and fields of planning.

4.*The Liaison Office for Personnel Management.* In accordance with the statement of purpose made in the Message to Congress of April 25, 1939, accompanying Reorganization Plan No. I, one of the Administrative Assistants to the President, authorized in the Reorganization Act of 1939, shall be designated by the President as Liaison Officer for Personnel Management and shall be in charge of the Liaison Office for Personnel Management. The functions of this office shall be:

(a) To assist the President in the better execution of the duties imposed upon him by the Provisions of the Constitution and the laws with respect to personnel management, especially the Civil Service Act of 1883, as amended, and the rules promulgated by the President under authority of that Act.

(b) To assist the President in maintaining closer contact with all agencies dealing with personnel matters insofar as they affect or tend to determine the personnel management policies of the Executive branch of the Government.

5.*The Office of Government Reports.* (a) To provide a central clearing house through which individual citizens, organizations of citizens, state or local governmental bodies, and, where appropriate, agencies of the Federal Government, may transmit inquiries and complaints and receive advice and information.

(b) To assist the President in dealing with special problems requiring the clearance of information between the Federal Government and state and local governments and private institutions.

(c) To collect and distribute information concerning the purposes and activities of executive departments and agencies for the use of the Congress, administrative officials, and the public.

(d) To keep the President currently informed of the opinions, desires, and complaints of citizens and groups of citizens and of state and local governments with respect to the work of Federal agencies.

(e) To report to the President on the basis of the information it has obtained possible ways and means for reducing the cost of the operation of the Government.

III

The Bureau of the Budget, the National Resources Planning Board, and the Liaison Office for Personnel Management shall constitute the three principal management arms of the Government for the (1) preparation and administration of the Budget and improvement of administrative management and organization, (2) planning for conservation and utilization of the resources of the Nation, and (3) coordination of the administration of personnel, none of which belongs in any department but which are necessary for the over-all management of the Executive branch of the Government, so that the President will be enabled the better to carry out his Constitutional duties of informing the Congress with respect to the state of the Union, of recommending appropriate and expedient measures, and of seeing that the laws are faithfully executed.

IV

To facilitate the orderly transaction of business within each of the five divisions herein defined and to clarify the relations of these divisions with each other and with the President, I direct that the Bureau of the Budget, the National Resources Planning Board, the Liaison Office for Personnel Management, and the Office of Government Reports shall respectively prepare regulations for the governance of their internal organizations and procedures. Such regulations shall be in effect when approved by the President and shall remain in force until changed by new regulations approved by him. The President will prescribe regulations governing the conduct of the business of the division of The White House Office.

V

The Director of the Bureau of the Budget shall prepare a consolidated budget for the Executive Office of the President for submission by the President to the Congress. Annually, pursuant to the regular request issued by the Bureau of the Budget, each division of the Executive Office of the President shall prepare and submit to the Bureau estimates of proposed appropriations for the succeeding fiscal year. The form of the estimates and the manner of their consideration for incorporation in the Budget shall be the same as prescribed for other Executive departments and agencies.

The Bureau of the Budget shall likewise perform with respect to the several divisions of the Executive Office of the President such functions and duties relating to supplemental estimates, apportionments, and budget administration as are exercised by it for other agencies of the Federal Government.

VI

Space already has been assigned in the State, War and Navy Building, adjacent to The White House, sufficient to accommodate the Bureau of the Budget with its various divisions (including the Central Statistical Board), the central office of the National Resources Planning Board, the Liaison Office for Personnel Management, and the Administrative Assistants to the President, and although for the time being, a considerable portion of the work of the National Resources Planning Board and all of that of the Office of Government Reports will have to be conducted in other quarters, if and when the Congress makes provision for the housing of the Department of State in a building appropriate to its function and dignity and provision is made for the other agencies now accommodated in the State, War and Navy Building, it then will be possible to bring into this building, close to The White House, all of the personnel of the Executive Office of the President except The White House Office.

This Order shall take effect on September 11th 1939.

---

5. Act to Prevent Pernicious Political Activities (1939) as Amended (1940)*
Hatch Acts

Be it enacted by the Senate and House of Representatives of the United States of America in Congress assembled, That it shall be unlawful for any person to intimidate, threaten, or coerce, or to attempt to intimidate, threaten, or coerce, any other person for the purpose of interfering with the right of such other person to vote or to vote as he may choose, or of causing such other person to vote for, or not to vote for, any candidate for the office of President, Vice President, Presidential elector, Member of the Senate, or Member of the House of Representatives at any election held solely or in part for the purpose of selecting a President, a Vice President, a Presidential elector, or any Member of the Senate or any Member of the House of Representatives, Delegates or Commissioners from the Territories and insular possessions.

---

* 53 Stat. 410 (1939), as amended by 54 Stat. 640 (1940). The original act consisted of 11 sections, and the amendments to these sections are indicated by quotation marks. Sections 12 through 20 were all new additions in the 1940 amendments. Of these, the following are omitted from this presentation: sections 12 b, c, d, e, f, which provide for enforcement by the United States Civil Service Commission and, in great detail, the procedures and protections in such enforcement; section 13, which limits political contributions in Presidential campaigns; section 20, which limits the amounts of political contributions a political committee may receive.

"Sec. 2. It shall be unlawful for (1) any person employed in any administrative position by the United States, or by any department, independent agency, or other agency of the United States (including any corporation controlled by the United States or any agency thereof, and any corporation all of the capital stock of which is owned by the United States or any agency thereof), or (2) any person employed in any administrative position by any State, by any political subdivision or municipality of any State, or by any agency of any State or any of its political subdivisions or municipalities (including any corporation controlled by any State or by any such political subdivision, municipality, or agency, and any corporation all of the capital stock of which is owned by any State or by any such political subdivision, municipality, or agency), in connection with any activity which is financed in whole or in part by loans or grants made by the United States, or by any such department, independent agency, or other agency of the United States, to use his official authority for the purpose of interfering with, or affecting, the election or the nomination of any candidate for the office of President, Vice President, Presidential elector, Member of the Senate, Member of the House of Representatives, or Delegate or Resident Commissioner from any Territory or insular possession."

Sec. 3. It shall be unlawful for any person, directly or indirectly, to promise any employment, position, work, compensation, or other benefit, provided for or made possible in whole or in part by any Act of Congress, to any person as consideration, favor, or reward for any political activity or for the support of or opposition to any candidate or any political party in any election.

Sec. 4. Except as may be required by the provisions of subsection (b), section 9 of this Act, it shall be unlawful for any person to deprive, attempt to deprive, or threaten to deprive, by any means, any person of any employment, position, work, compensation, or other benefit provided for or made possible by any Act of Congress appropriating funds for work relief or relief purposes, on account of race, creed, color, or any political activity, support of, or opposition to any candidate or any political party in any election.

Sec. 5. It shall be unlawful for any person to solicit or receive or be in any manner concerned in soliciting or receiving any assessment, subscription, or contribution for any political purpose whatever from any person known by him to be entitled to or receiving compensation, employment, or other benefit provided for or made possible by any Act of Congress appropriating funds for work relief or relief purposes.

Sec. 6. It shall be unlawful for any person for political purposes to furnish or to disclose, or to aid or assist in furnishing or disclosing, any list or names of persons receiving compensation, employment, or benefits provided for or made possible by any Act of Congress appropriating, or authorizing the appropriation of, funds for work relief or relief purposes, to a political candidate, committee, campaign manager, or to any person for delivery to a political candidate, committee, or campaign manager, and it shall be unlawful for any person to receive any such list or names for political purposes.

Sec. 7. No part of any appropriation made by any Act, heretofore or hereafter enacted, making appropriations for work relief, relief, or otherwise to increase employment by providing loans and grants for public-works projects, shall be used for the purpose of, and no authority conferred by any such Act upon any person shall be exercised or administered for the purpose of, interfering with, restraining, or coercing any individual in the exercise of his right to vote at any election.

Sec. 8. Any person who violates any of the foregoing provisions of this Act upon conviction thereof shall be fined not more than $1,000 or imprisoned for not more than one year, or both.

Sec. 9. (a) It shall be unlawful for any person employed in the executive branch of the Federal Government, or any agency or department thereof, to use his official authority or influence for the purpose of interfering with an election or affecting the result thereof. No officer or employee in the executive branch of the Federal Government, or any agency or department thereof, shall take any active part in political management or in political campaigns. "All such persons shall retain the right to vote as they may choose and to express their opinions on all political subjects and candidates." For the purposes of this section the term "officer" or "employee" shall not be construed to include (1) the President and Vice President of the United States; (2) persons whose compensation is paid from the appropriation for the office of the President; (3) heads and assistant heads of executive departments; (4) officers who are appointed by the President, by and with the advice and consent of the Senate, and who determine policies to be pursued by the United States in its relations with foreign powers or in the Nation-wide administration of Federal laws.

(b) Any person violating the provisions of this section shall be immediately removed from the position or office held by him, and thereafter no part of the funds appropriated by any Act of Congress for such position or office shall be used to pay the compensation of such person.

Sec. 9A. (1) It shall be unlawful for any person employed in any capacity by any agency of the Federal Government, whose compensation, or any part thereof, is paid from funds authorized or appropriated by any Act of Congress, to have membership in any political party or organization which advocates the overthrow of our constitutional form of government in the United States.

(2) Any person violating the provisions of this section shall be immediately removed from the position or office held by him, and thereafter no part of the funds appropriated by any Act of Congress for such position or office shall be used to pay the compensation of such person.

"Sec. 10. The provisions of this Act shall be in addition to and not in substitution for any other provision of law."

Sec. 11. If any provision of this Act, or the application of such provision to any person or circumstance, is held invalid, the remainder of the Act, and the application of such provision to other persons or circumstances, shall not be affected thereby.

"Sec. 12. (a) No officer or employee of any State or local agency whose principal employment is in connection with any activity which is financed in whole or in part by loans or grants made by the United States or by any Federal agency shall (1) use his official authority or influence for the purpose of interfering with an election or a nomination for office, or affecting the result thereof, or (2) directly or indirectly coerce, attempt to coerce, command, or advise any other such officer or employee to pay, lend, or contribute any part of his salary or compensation or anything else of value to any party, committee, organization, agency, or person for political purposes. No such officer or employee shall take any active part in political management or in political campaigns. All such persons shall retain the right to vote as they may choose and to express their opinions on all political subjects and candidates. For the purposes of the second sentence of this subsection, the term 'officer or employee' shall not be construed to include (1) the Governor or the Lieutenant Governor of any State or any person who is authorized by law to act as Governor, or the mayor of any city; (2) duly elected heads of executive departments of any State or municipality who are not classified under a State or municipal merit or civil-service system; (3) officers holding elective offices.

"Sec. 14. For the purposes of this Act, persons employed in the government of the District of Columbia shall be deemed to be employed in the executive branch of the Government of the United States, except that for the purposes of the second sentence of section 9(a) the Commissioners and the Recorder of Deeds of the District of Columbia shall not be deemed to be officers or employees.

"Sec. 15. The provisions of this Act which prohibit persons to whom such provisions apply from taking any active part in political management or in political campaigns shall be deemed to prohibit the same activities on the part of such persons as the United States Civil Service Commission has heretofore determined are at the time this section takes effect prohibited on the part of employees in the classified civil service of the United States by the provisions of the civil-service rules prohibiting such employees from taking any active part in political management or in political campaigns.

"Sec. 16. Whenever the United States Civil Service Commission determines that, by reason of special or unusual circumstances which exist in any municipality or other political subdivision, in the immediate vicinity of the National Capital in the States of Maryland and Virginia or in municipalities the majority of whose voters are employed by the Government of the United States, it is in the domestic interest of persons to whom the provisions of this Act are applicable, and who reside in such municipality or political subdivision, to permit such persons to take an active part in political management or in political campaigns involving such municipality or political subdivision, the Commission is authorized to promulgate regulations permitting such persons to take an active part in such political management and political campaigns to the extent the Commission deems to be in the domestic interest of such persons.

"Sec. 17. Nothing in the second sentence of section 12 (a) of this Act shall be construed to prevent or prohibit any officer or employee of a State or local agency (as defined in section 12 (f)), from continuing, until the election in connection with which he was nominated, to be a bona fide candidate for election to any public office and from engaging in any political activity in furtherance of his candidacy for such public office, if (1) he was nominated before the date of the enactment of this Act, and (2) upon his election to such public office he resigns from the office or employment in which he was employed prior to his election, in a State or local agency (as defined in section 12 (f)).

"Sec. 18. Nothing in the second sentence of section 9 (a) or in the second sentence of section 12 (a) of this Act shall be construed to prevent or prohibit any person subject to the provisions of this Act from engaging in any political activity (1) in connection with any election and the preceding campaign if none of the candidates is to be nominated or elected at such election as representing a party any of whose candidates for presidential elector received votes in the last preceding election at which presidential electors were selected, or (2) in connection with any question which is not specifically identified with any National or State political party. For the purposes of this section, questions relating to constitutional amendments, referendums, approval of municipal ordinances, and others of a similar character, shall not be deemed to be specifically identified with any National or State political party.

"Sec. 19. As used in this Act, the term 'State' means any State, Territory, or possession of the United States."

PART IV

The Post-War Period

The Post-War Period

Every major war in America's history has required enormous adjustments in the nation's governance and administration. In this respect, the Second World War probably exceeded most of its predecessors, for it required the virtually total dedication of all the nation's resources and energies. Empowered by its singleness and unanimity of purpose, the nation could effectively allocate resources and productive capacities, develop and direct the utilization of manpower, control prices and ration consumer goods, systematize transportation and communications, limit inflation, and virtually eliminate unemployment. Through the trauma of all-out war, American elections and the other attributes of democracy survived, as did the philosophy of its public administration.

The consensus which had made victory possible in World War II evaporated following the peace in 1945, and many of the Administration's initiatives in such fields as labor relations, price stabilization, health, and education were defeated in Congress. As in earlier post-war periods, there was a push toward "normalcy," the status quo ante. For a good many, "ante" meant not only "ante bellum" but also "ante New Deal." Such a reversion was hardly realistic following World War II, given, on the one hand, the emerging cold war with Russia and, on the other, the rising expectations of the American people. The emergent international position of the United States during those early post-war years, which is not documented here, is best depicted by Secretary of State Dean Acheson, who was "present at the creation"* of the strategy which was to guide United States foreign policy for the succeeding quarter-century. On the domestic front, President Truman and other Democratic leaders undertook to revive the activist, people-

---

* Dean Acheson, *Present at the Creation: My Years in the State Department* (Norton, 1969).

oriented spirit of the New Deal through a variety of proposals, many of which had earlier been discussed in the thirties: federal aid to education, national health insurance, a comprehensive civil rights program, and others. Most of these failed of passage by a conservative Congress, but they provided a preliminary agenda for the avalanche of new domestic programs pushed through in the nineteen-sixties by Presidents Kennedy and Johnson.

The legacy of New Deal thinking carried over also to the fields of public administration and organization. There were a great many changes and developments during the Truman years, some of them of major importance. Yet few reflected significant advances in thinking and philosophy about administration. The Brownlow Report still provided the dominant motifs; and the majority of specific actions taken after the war had been proposed before it.

This reversion to "tried and true"doctrines of administration is somewhat surprising, if only because so many intelligent persons, participant-observers during the war *and* the New Deal, had seen that many such doctrines had not been tried and that others, if tried, had not proven true. An impressive array of books and articles during the early post-war period attested to the widely felt skepticism toward, if not outright repudiation of, some of the oldest of administrative principles (a word which itself fell into disrepute): the policy-administration dichotomy; unity of command and, indeed, the idea of command itself; hierarchy; specific delineation of duties; specialization; even the civil service system.*
The Hawthorne experiments, then more than a decade old, had been widely described and publicized, and the human relations movement was in full flourish. The sociologists had discovered, translated, and even read and challenged Max Weber's analysis of bureaucracy and launched with full force into their study in that field. Some economists, fresh from their triumphs in macro fiscal policy and recently experienced in the planning of controlled materials during the war, were delving into the analysis of public policies and expenditure programs. Virtually all the social sciences, including public administration, were being awakened to the na-

---

* See, for example, the works during that period of Paul Appleby, Robert Dahl, Herbert Simon, Victor Thompson, Dwight Waldo, and, indeed, virtually all the authors who contributed to the remarkable collection, edited by Fritz Morstein Marx, *Elements of Public Administration* (Prentice-Hall, 1946).

tures of foreign cultures, the problems of change away from home (as well as at home), and the cultural relativism of their disciplines.

The documents reproduced below reflect rather little of these changing foci of interest and approach. They are in the main orthodox, in an orthodoxy matured before World War II. This is not to suggest that these documents were not important, nor indeed that they were not correct. They provided the administrative framework for much of what has happened since 1950, and at this writing (1976), they are all still significant. Except in foreign affairs, most of them were efforts to institutionalize, regularize, refine, and hopefully improve on activities and practices which had been initiated some years before. The "new public administration," whatever it might later prove to be, was not yet embraced by the operative authorities in American government.

With the single exception of the Veterans' Preference Act of 1944, all of the documents reproduced below were adopted and issued in the period between the end of World War II and 1950. The Veterans' Preference Act was not in strict chronological terms a post-war measure, having been passed more than a year before the end of hostilities; but its intent as well as its major impact was clearly to influence federal employment policies during the post-war years.

1. Veterans' Preference Act of 1944

Employment preference for some or all war veterans has been an informal or formal federal policy since the founding of the Republic. Its first Congressional authorization was a rather pious joint resolution at the end of the Civil War in 1865 in behalf of disabled veterans only. In the absence of a formal system of appointment, it was unenforceable, depending totally on the good will of the appointing officers. It was reaffirmed in the Civil Service Act of 1883 and given teeth through subsequent executive orders and rules of the Civil Service Commission. Following World War I, in 1919, Congress extended preference to non-disabled as well as disabled veterans, their widows, and the wives of those who were disabled. Subsequent orders and rules specified preference in appointments substantially as they remain today. The law of 1944 was the product of several years of effort by the major veterans' organizations, working in close collaboration with the Civil Service Commission and the appropriate committees of Congress. It gave statutory sanction to the detailed provisions already expressed in the Civil Service rules and extended and elaborated upon them in a number of ways. In addition to specifics about examinations, certification, appointments, and appeals, it listed the points to be considered, including veterans' preference, in the event of staff reductions. These were confounded by the implementing rules of the Civil Service Commission to the point that reductions in force, which were frequent in the years following the war, became a procedural nightmare. One rather little advertised sentence of the Act (in Section 5), applicable to veterans and non-veterans alike, prohibited any "minimum educational requirement" for civil service examinations (i.e., credentials) except where the Civil Service Commission found the scientific, technical, or professional requirements of the position demanded it. Since that time, the Commission has pretty largely negated this provision by excepting the majority of recognized professions and disciplines from the prohibition.

The 1944 Act was amended frequently in succeeding years, usually to extend its coverage and its preferences. Comparable legislation has been adopted by many state and local governments; in some cases this has been more rigid than the federal legislation (as, for example, in the application of preference to promotions, which are not covered in the federal legislation). For better or worse, veterans' preference remains a pervasive fact and condition of life and work in American government.

2. GOVERNMENT CORPORATION CONTROL ACT (1945)

The United States Government first "got into business" at its outset with the Post Office. In 1904, it acquired the Panama Railroad Company. During World War I, the Depression, and World War II, its business-type operations expanded greatly in a wide variety of fields of activity. Most of the so-called government corporations—all of those created since 1945—were established by acts of Congress, and there were rather few common denominators in terms of structure, lines of responsibility, degrees of autonomy, employment practices, and financial control. Most were, and are, distinguished from other agencies by the fact that most or all of their revenues derive from their own operations, like private businesses, and they are therefore relatively or totally independent of the federal budget and the budget process. In the words of Harold Seidman, the preeminent authority in this field: "The Government corporation is essentially an empirical response to problems posed by increasing reliance on Government-created business enterprises and business-type operations to accomplish public purposes."* At the close of World War II, there were about forty wholly owned government corporations and a handful of such corporations with mixed public-private ownership. Almost all of the mixed variety were involved in banking. The majority of the corporations were assigned to, and more or less under the jurisdiction of, departments of the national government. A very few, but among the most important, were independent of the established departments and under the presumed jurisdiction and authority of the President: the Federal Deposit Insurance Corporation; the Export-Import Bank; the Tennessee Valley Authority. The Corporation Control Act of 1945 was the first legislation to regularize and control the financial activities of the government corporations and to require appraisal and audit of their activities according to the commercial standards of private business. Curiously, the oldest and by far the largest business-type enterprise in the government, the U.S. Postal Service, is not covered by the Government Corporation Control Act.

3. EMPLOYMENT ACT OF 1946

The economic, political, organizational, and intellectual antecedents of the Employment Act go back at least to the early months of the New Deal. Behind the Act lay the acknowledgment of a federal responsibility for the economic and social welfare of the nation, and also a vigorous, even bitter controversy over the nature and degree of that responsibility and the appropriate actions for carrying it out. Behind it too was a widening acceptance of the theses of John Maynard Keynes concerning governmental intervention in the

---

* Harold Seidman, *Politics, Position, and Power: The Dynamics of Federal Organization* (Oxford University Press, 2nd edition, 1975), p. 254.

economy, and the accompanying development of sophisticated tools whereby the condition of the economy could be measured, analyzed, predicted, and manipulated. A principal motivating factor was the fear of widespread unemployment and even a major depression during the reconversion from a wartime to a peacetime economy. The Council of Economic Advisers, which was established by the Employment Act of 1946, was not without predecessors going back many years. The National Resources Planning Board, the last incarnation of a series of planning organizations created during the New Deal years, had produced, in 1943, an enormous report on post-war economic problems and policies which contemplated wide-scale federal action on a variety of fronts. For its efforts, Congress abolished the Board within three months. The Bureau of the Budget meanwhile was concerning itself more and more with the condition of the economy and the impact of actual or potential federal actions upon it. During the war, its Fiscal Division employed some of the nation's outstanding macro-economists, some of whom later staffed the Council of Economic Advisers.

The original bill leading to the Employment Act was drafted by committee staff in the Senate during 1944 and was entitled the Full Employment Bill; it would have committed the government to assuring full employment. Later, after passage by the Senate, a conservative House Sub-Committee rewrote it, very substantially weakened it, and renamed it the Employment and Production Act. Among other things, it removed the federal commitment on full employment. The Employment Act, which finally emerged from the Conference Committee, was passed and signed into law in February, 1946. It was the product of eighteen months of drafting, revision, argument (often bitter), interest group pressure, negotiation, and compromise. The tale of the development and passage of that Act by Stephen Kemp Bailey* is a classic description of the conception, pregnancy, labor, and birth of a highly controversial piece of legislation. The Act, by virtue of its very existence and through the machinery for economic assessment and planning which it prescribed, has had a major impact upon the conduct of American government ever since its passage.

* *Congress Makes a Law: The Story Behind the Employment Act of 1946* (Vintage Books, 1964; copyright 1950 by Columbia University Press).

4. ADMINISTRATIVE PROCEDURE ACT (1946)

Only a few months after the President signed the Employment Act into law, he received and signed the Administrative Procedure Act, which had experienced a comparably tortuous history over the course of more than a decade. Over the years federal agencies, and particularly the regulatory commissions, had produced a growing body of rules and other decisions which had the force of law. Each such agency operated on the basis of its own authority from Congress and according to standards and procedures which it had built up. During the nineteen-thirties and forties, there was increasing dissatisfaction and criticism, principally on two grounds: (1) that the regulatory process was "secret, mysterious, unstandardized, and unknowable"; and (2) that agencies' procedures in many instances did not "guarantee the minimum fundamentals of fairness and justice."* Passage of the Federal Register Act of 1935 had been intended to correct the former problem, but it proved less than totally satisfactory.

As early as 1933, the American Bar Association (ABA), through various committees, scrutinized and criticized the regulatory process. Later the Brownlow Committee alluded to it, and in 1938, hearings before the Senate Judiciary Committee highlighted the problems. The ABA-sponsored legislation in 1939 (the Walter-Logan Bill) passed the Congress but was vetoed by the President. Roosevelt vetoed the bill because he preferred to await the report then being prepared by a Committee on Administrative Procedure designated by Attorney General Frank Murphy. That group reported in 1941 with recommended legislation, but despite considerable debate and redrafting, nothing was passed before American entry into World War II. Ultimately, agreement was reached on a measure introduced in 1945 as the McCarran-Summers Bill, which eventually became the Administrative Procedure Act.

The Act was intended to standardize, legalize, and judicialize a significant segment of governmental decision-making. It undertook to assure what Emmette S. Redford has described as the four basic protections of citizens before their government: "notice, op-

---

* Vincent M. Barnett, Jr., "Judicialization of the Administrative Process," *Public Administration Review*, VIII, 2 (1948), p. 126.

portunity to be heard, decision without bias, and independent review."* Its effectiveness in these regards and its alleged drawbacks have been objects of debate for many years since 1946. But the main features of the Act continue in force.

5. ORGANIZATION FOR NATIONAL SECURITY (1947 AND 1949)

The need for more effective coordination and unity between the military departments, then the Departments of War and Navy, was evident well before World War II. It became strikingly and disastrously clear at the time of Pearl Harbor and in the months and years that followed. Coordinating machinery, formal and informal, evolved during the course of the war with the development of unified commands in the field, the Joint Chiefs of Staff with its own Joint Staff, the Office of Strategic Services, and a number of other mechanisms. At the same time, with the growth in importance and muscle of air power, the old Air Corps became the Army Air Forces, and its commander participated as a member of the Joint Chiefs of Staff. Before conclusion of the war, competing plans, negotiations, and arguments were well underway for consolidating or otherwise relating the services with an air force coequal with the Army and Navy. In general, the leadership of the War Department and the Army and Army Air Forces sought a unified single department to consist primarily of the three services—Army, Navy, and Air Force; the Navy leaders argued for preservation of the two departments essentially as they were, with an overlay of interdepartmental committees to coordinate plans and operations.

The Department of Defense and associated agencies in the security area were created in two statutory stages following World War II. The first Act in 1947 set up the National Military Establishment, to consist of the Departments of Army, Navy, and Air Force. It was to be headed by a Secretary of Defense, but his authority was defined in the most general and equivocal terms. That Act also established (or gave legislative sanction to) the National Security Council, the Central Intelligence Agency, the National Security Resources Board, the Joint Chiefs of Staff, and a

---

* *Democracy in the Administrative State* (Oxford University Press, 1969), p. 136.

number of other bodies. The 1947 Act was clearly a compromise between the opposing positions of the War and Navy Departments.

Weakness and frustration in the office of Secretary of Defense contributed to pressures to modify the provisions in the direction of a more integrated and centralized organization. Accordingly, the amendments of 1949 changed the National Military Establishment to the Department of Defense, amplified the authority of the Secretary of Defense (especially in the fiscal realm), and reduced the service departments from the status of Executive Departments with Cabinet rank to Military Departments under Defense. The new Department of Defense thus became the first "super-department" in the national government. The 1949 amendments also added a new Title IV, which specified the full authority of the Secretary of Defense over budget and fiscal matters, established an office of Comptroller in each of the departments, and gave legislative recognition to the "performance budget," which the Hoover Commission had vigorously recommended for the entire government a few months earlier (see below).

6. CONCLUDING REPORT OF THE COMMISSION ON ORGANIZATION
OF THE EXECUTIVE BRANCH OF THE GOVERNMENT
(First Hoover Commission, 1949)

The formation of the First Hoover Commission was stimulated in great part by the perceived need to rationalize the structure of the administration in the wake of war, to reduce the multiplicity of agencies created in earlier years, and to facilitate an orderly demobilization. The conservative Congress of the period was doubtless also motivated by the hopes of reducing expenditures and debt *and* reducing taxes. The nature of the Commission was nearly a miracle of compromise: twelve members, divided equally between the two parties and divided equally between private citizens and public officials; four to be appointed by the President, four by the Presiding Officer of the Senate, four by the Speaker of the House. The mixed membership of the Commission coupled with the leadership of its Chairman, ex-President Herbert Hoover, and the continuing support of Democratic President Truman and his aides probably all contributed to its success. Few, if any, Presidential commissions have achieved so high a batting average in terms of implementation of their proposals.

In its administrative philosophy, the First Hoover Commission was not innovative. In the words of Herman Finer, "The Hoover Commission and many of its collaborators are Mr. Brownlow's children. . . ."* It accepted and added emphasis to the Brownlow proposals on Presidential leadership in executive management, but its major concerns were with the management at departmental and sub-departmental levels. With the aid of a considerable number of specialized task forces, it delved into and made recommendations upon federal programs in considerable detail. Its many reports, along with the voluminous reports of its task forces, very nearly comprise a five-foot shelf on the executive branch. It is possible herein to include only an abbreviated version of its *Concluding Report,* which summarizes the main thrusts and recommendations.

The First Hoover Report was very probably the most ambitious and comprehensive study of administrative operations in American history. It was consistent in its philosophy and represented a capstone of the "management movement." It provided the model for "little Hoover Commissions" in states and some local governments across the country. In short, its direct and indirect practical influence on American public administration through the years that followed it was tremendous. It therefore seems a particularly appropriate piece with which to close this compendium.

---

* Herman Finer, "The Hoover Commission Reports," *Political Science Quarterly* (September 1949), p. 412.

1. Veterans' Preference Act of 1944*

Be it enacted by the Senate and House of Representatives of the United States of America in Congress assembled, That this Act may be cited as the "Veterans' Preference Act of 1944."

Sec. 2. In certification for appointment, in appointment, in reinstatement, in reemployment, and in retention in civilian positions in all establishments, agencies, bureaus, administrations, projects, and departments of the Government, permanent or temporary, and in either (a) the classified civil service; (b) the unclassified civil service; (c) any temporary or emergency establishment, agency, bureau, administration, project, and department created by Acts of Congress or Presidential Executive order; and (d) the civil service of the District of Columbia, preference shall be given to (1) those ex-service men and women who have served on active duty in any branch of the armed forces of the United States and have been separated therefrom under honorable conditions and who have established the present existence of a service-connected disability or who are receiving compensation, disability retirement benefits, or pension by reason of public laws administered by the Veterans' Administration, the War Department or the Navy Department; (2) the wives of such service-connected disabled ex-servicemen as have themselves been unable to qualify for any civil-service appointment; (3) the unmarried widows of deceased ex-servicemen who served on active duty in any branch of the armed forces of the United States during any war, or in any campaign or expedition (for which a campaign badge has been authorized), and who were separated therefrom under honorable conditions; and (4) those ex-servicemen and women who have served on active duty in any branch

---

* 58 Stat. 33 (1944).

of the armed forces of the United States, during any war, or any campaign or expedition (for which a campaign badge has been authorized), and have been separated therefrom under honorable conditions.

Sec. 3. In all examinations to determine the qualifications of applicants for entrance into the service ten points shall be added to the earned ratings of those persons included under section 2 (1), (2), and (3), and five points shall be added to the earned ratings of those persons included under section 2 (4) of this Act: *Provided,* That in examinations for the positions of guards, elevator operators, messengers, and custodians competition shall be restricted to persons entitled to preference under this Act as long as persons entitled to preference are available and during the present war and for a period of five years following the termination of the present war as proclaimed by the President or by a concurrent resolution of the Congress for such other positions as may from time to time be determined by the President.

Sec. 4. In examinations where experience is an element of qualification, time spent in the military or naval service of the United States shall be credited in a veteran's rating where his or her actual employment in a similar vocation to that for which he or she is examined was interrupted by such military or naval service. In all examinations to determine the qualifications of a veteran applicant, credit shall be given for all valuable experience, including experience gained in religious, civic, welfare, service, and organizational activities, regardless of whether any compensation was received therefor.

Sec. 5. In determining qualifications for examination, appointment, promotion, retention, transfer, or reinstatement, with respect to preference eligibles, the Civil Service Commission or other examining agency shall waive requirements as to age, height, and weight, provided any such requirement is not essential to the performance of the duties of the position for which examination is given. The Civil Service Commission or other examining agency, after giving due consideration to the recommendation of any accredited physician, shall waive the physical requirements in the case of any veteran, provided such veteran is, in the opinion of the Civil Service Commission, or other examining agency physically able to discharge efficiently the duties of the position for which the examination is given. No minimum educational requirement will be prescribed in any civil-service examination except for such scientific, technical, or professional positions the duties of which the Civil Service Commission decides cannot be performed by a person who does not have such education. The Commission shall make a part of its public records its reasons for such decision.

Sec. 6. Preference eligibles shall not be subject to the provisions of section 9 of the Civil Service Act concerning two or more members of a family in the service, or to the provisions of section 2 of that Act concerning apportionment of appointments in the Government departments in the District of Columbia among the several States and Territories according to population, but may be required to furnish evidence of residence and domicile.

Sec. 7. The names of preference eligibles shall be entered on the appropriate registers or lists of eligibles in accordance with their respective augmented ratings, and the name of a preference eligible shall be entered ahead of all others having the same rating: *Provided,* That, except for positions in the professional and scientific services for which the entrance salary is over $3,000 per annum, the names of all qualified preference eligibles, entitled to ten points in addition to their earned ratings shall be placed at the top of the appropriate civil-service register or employment list, in accordance with their respective augmented ratings.

Sec. 8. When, in accordance with civil-service laws and rules, a nominating or appointing officer shall request certification of eligibles for appointment purposes, the Civil Service Commission shall certify, from the top of the appropriate register of eligibles, a number of names sufficient to permit the nominating or appointing officer to consider at least three names in connection with each vacancy. The nominating or appointing officer shall make selection for each vacancy from not more than the highest three names available for appointment on such certification, unless objection shall be made, and sustained by the Commission, to one or more of the persons certified, for any proper and adequate reason, as may be prescribed in the rules promulgated by the Civil Service Commission: *Provided,* That an appointing officer who passes over a veteran eligible and selects a nonveteran shall file with the Civil Service Commission his reasons in writing for so doing, which shall become a part of the record of such veteran eligible, and shall be made available upon request to the veteran or his designated representative; the Civil Service Commission is directed to determine the sufficiency of such submitted reasons and, if found insufficient, shall require such appointing officer to submit more detailed information in support thereof; the findings of the Civil Service Commission as to the sufficiency or insufficiency of such reasons shall be transmitted to and considered by such appointing officer, and a copy thereof shall be sent to the veteran eligible or to his designated representative upon request therefor: *Provided, further,* That if, upon certification, reasons deemed sufficient by the Civil Service Commission for passing over his name shall three times have been given by an appointing officer, certification of his name for appointment may thereafter be discontinued, prior notice of which shall be sent to the veteran eligible. Whenever in the Postal Service two or more substitutes are appointed on the same day, they shall be promoted to the regular force in the order in which their names appeared on the civil-service register from which they were originally appointed, whenever there are substitutes of the required sex who are eligible and will accept, unless such vacancies are filled by transfer or reinstatement.

Sec. 9. In the unclassified Federal, and District of Columbia, civil service, and in all other positions and employment hereinbefore referred to in (c) of section 2 hereof, the nominating or appointing officer or employing official shall make selection from the qualified applicants in accordance with the provisions of this Act.

Sec. 10. The Civil Service Commission is authorized and directed to hold an examination, during the next succeeding quarterly period, for any position to which any appointment has been made within the preceding three years, for any person included under section 2 (1), (2), and (3) of this Act upon application for examination for any such position.

Sec. 11. The Civil Service Commission is hereby authorized to promulgate appropriate rules and regulations for the administration and enforcement of the provisions of this Act.

Sec. 12. In any reduction in personnel in any civilian service of any Federal agency, competing employees shall be released in accordance with Civil Service Commission regulations which shall give due effect to tenure of employment, military preference, length of service, and efficiency ratings: *Provided,* That the length of time spent in active service in the armed forces of the United States of each such employee shall be credited in computing length of total service: *Provided further,* That preference employees whose efficiency ratings are "good" or better shall be retained in preference to all other competing employees and that preference employees whose efficiency ratings are below "good" shall be retained in preference to competing nonpreference employees who have equal or lower efficiency ratings: *And provided further,* That when any or all of the functions of any agency are transferred to, or when any agency is replaced by, some other agency, or agencies, all preference employees in the function or functions transferred or in the agency which is replaced by some other agency shall first be transferred to the replacing agency, or agencies, for employment in positions for which they are qualified, before such agency, or agencies, shall appoint additional employees from any other source for such positions.

Sec. 13. Any preference eligible who has resigned or who has been dismissed or furloughed may, at the request of any appointing officer, be certified for, and appointed to, any position for which he may be eligible in the civil service, Federal, or District of Columbia, or in any establishment, agency, bureau, administration, project, or department, temporary or permanent.

Sec. 14. No permanent or indefinite preference eligible, who has completed a probationary or trial period employed in the civil service, or in any establishment, agency, bureau, administration, project, or department, hereinbefore referred to shall be discharged, suspended for more than thirty days, furloughed without pay, reduced in rank or compensation, or debarred for future appointment except for such cause as will promote the efficiency of the service and for reasons given in writing, and the person whose discharge, suspension for more than thirty days, furlough without pay, or reduction in rank or compensation is sought shall have at least thirty days' advance written notice (except where there is reasonable cause to believe the employee to be guilty of a crime for which a sentence of imprisonment can be imposed), stating any and all reasons, specifically and in detail, for any such proposed action; such preference eligible shall be allowed a reasonable time for answering the same personally and in writing, and for furnishing affidavits in support of such answer, and shall have the right to appeal to the Civil Service Commission from an adverse decision of the administrative officer so acting, such appeal to be made in writing within a reasonable length of time after the date of receipt of notice of such adverse decision: *Provided,* That such preference eligible shall have the right to make a personal appearance, or an appearance through a designated representative, in accordance with such reasonable rules and regulations as may be issued by the Civil Service Commission; after investigation and consideration of the evidence submitted, the Civil Service Commission shall submit its findings and recommendations to the proper administrative officer and shall send copies of same to the appellant or to his designated representative: *Provided further,* That the Civil Service Commission may declare any such preference eligible who may have been dismissed or furloughed without pay to be eligible for the provisions of section 15 hereof.

Sec. 15. Any preference eligible, who has been furloughed, or separated without delinquency or misconduct, upon request, shall have his name placed on all appropriate civil-service registers and/or on all employment lists, for every position for which his qualifications have been established, as maintained by the Civil Service Commission, or as shall be maintained by any agency or project of the Federal Government, or of the District of Columbia, in the order as provided in section 7 hereof, and shall then be eligible for recertification and reappointment in the order and according to the procedure as provided for in sections 7 and 8 hereof.

No appointment shall be made from an examination register of eligibles, except of ten-point preference eligibles, when there are three or more names of preference eligibles on any appropriate reemployment list for the position to be filled.

Sec. 16. Any preference eligible who has resigned shall, upon request to the Civil Service Commission, have his name again placed on all proper civil-service registers for which he may have been qualified, in the order as provided for in section 7 hereof, and shall then be eligible for recertification and reappointment in the order, and according to the procedure, as provided for in sections 7 and 8 hereof.

Sec. 17. The term "Civil Service Commission" or "Commission" as used in this Act shall mean the present United States Civil Service Commission or any body or person who may by law succeed to its powers and duties, or any of them, or which or who may be designated by law to perform any specific duty and possess any specific power concerning matters covered by this Act.

Sec. 18. All Acts and parts of Acts inconsistent with the provisions hereof are hereby modified to conform herewith, and this Act shall not be construed to take away from any preference eligible any rights heretofore granted to, or possessed by, him under any existing law, Executive order, civil-service rule or regulation, of any department of the Government or officer thereof.

Sec. 19. It shall be the authority and duty of the Civil Service Commission in all cases under the classified civil service to make and enforce appropriate rules and regulations to carry into full effect the provisions, intent, and purpose of this Act and such Executive orders as may be issued pursuant thereto and in furtherance thereof.

Sec. 20. Nothing contained in this Act is intended to apply to any position in or under the legislative or judicial branch of the Government or to any position or appointment which by the Congress is required to be confirmed by, or made with, the advice and consent of the United States Senate: *Provided, however,* That the provisions of this Act shall apply to appointments under Public Law Numbered 720, Seventy-fifth Congress, third session, approved June 25, 1938.

Sec. 21. If any part of this Act shall be found to be unconstitutional, the rest of it shall be considered as in full force and effect.

Approved June 27, 1944.

2. Government Corporation Control Act (1945)*

Be it enacted by the Senate and House of Representatives of the United States of America in Congress assembled, That this Act may be cited as the "Government Corporation Control Act."

Declaration of Policy

Sec. 2. It is hereby declared to be the policy of the Congress to bring Government corporations and their transactions and operations under annual scrutiny by the Congress and provide current financial control thereof.

Title I—Wholly Owned Government Corporations

Sec. 101. As used in this Act the term "wholly owned Government corporation" means the Commodity Credit Corporation; Federal Intermediate Credit Banks; Production Credit Corporations; Regional Agricultural Credit Corporations; Farmers Home Corporation; Federal Crop Insurance Corporation; Federal Farm Mortgage Corporation; Federal Surplus Commodities Corporation; Reconstruction Finance Corporation; Defense Plant Corporation; Defense Supplies Corporation; Metals Reserve Company; Rubber Reserve Company; War Damage Corporation; Federal National Mortgage Association; the RFC Mortgage Company; Disaster Loan Corporation; Inland Waterways Corporation; Warrior River Terminal Company; The Virgin Islands Company; Federal Prison Industries, Incorporated; United States Spruce Production Corporation; Institute of Inter-American Affairs; Institute of Inter-American Transportation; Inter-American Educational Foundation, Incorporated; Inter-American Navigation Corporation; Prencinradio, Incorporated; Cargoes, Incorporated; Export-Import Bank of Washington; Petroleum Reserves Corporation; Rubber Development Corporation; U.S. Commercial Company; Smaller War Plants Corporation; Federal Public Housing Authority (or United States Housing Authority) and including public housing projects financed from appropriated funds and operations thereof; Defense Homes Corporation; Federal Savings and Loan Insurance Corporation; Home Owners' Loan

* 59 Stat. 557 (1945). Title III, "General Provisions," which contains detailed provisions on deposits, auditing, etc., is not included herein.

Corporation; United States Housing Corporation; Panama Railroad Company; Tennessee Valley Authority; and Tennessee Valley Associated Cooperatives, Incorporated.

Sec. 102. Each wholly owned Government corporation shall cause to be prepared annually a budget program, which shall be submitted to the President through the Bureau of the Budget on or before September 15 of each year. The Bureau of the Budget, under such rules and regulations as the President may establish, is authorized and directed to prescribe the form and content of, and the manner in which such budget program shall be prepared and presented. The budget program shall be a business-type budget, or plan of operations, with due allowance given to the need for flexibility, including provision for emergencies and contingencies, in order that the corporation may properly carry out its activities as authorized by law. The budget program shall contain estimates of the financial condition and operations of the corporation for the current and ensuing fiscal years and the actual condition and results of operation for the last completed fiscal year. Such budget program shall include a statement of financial condition, a statement of income and expense, an analysis of surplus or deficit, a statement of sources and application of funds, and such other supplementary statements and information as are necessary or desirable to make known the financial condition and operations of the corporation. Such statements shall include estimates of operations by major types of activities, together with estimates of administrative expenses, estimates of borrowings, and estimates of the amount of Government capital funds which shall be returned to the Treasury during the fiscal year or the appropriations required to provide for the restoration of capital impairments.

Sec. 103. The budget programs of the corporations as modified, amended, or revised by the President shall be transmitted to the Congress as a part of the annual Budget required by the Budget and Accounting Act, 1921. Amendments to the annual budget programs may be submitted from time to time.

Budget programs shall be submitted for all wholly owned Government corporations covering operations for the fiscal year commencing July 1, 1946, and each fiscal year thereafter.

Sec. 104. The budget programs transmitted by the President to the Congress shall be considered and, if necessary, legislation shall be enacted making available such funds or other financial resources as the Congress may determine. The provisions of this section shall not be construed as preventing wholly owned Government corporations from carrying out and financing their activities as authorized by existing law, nor shall any provisions of this section be construed as affecting in any way the provisions of section 26 of the Tennessee Valley Authority Act, as amended. The provisions of this section shall not be construed as affecting the existing authority of any wholly owned Government corporation to make contracts or other commitments without reference to fiscal-year limitations.

Sec. 105. The financial transactions of wholly owned Government corporations shall be audited by the General Accounting Office in accordance with the principles and procedures applicable to commercial corporate transactions and under such rules and regulations as may be prescribed by the Comptroller General of the United States: *Provided,* That such rules and regulations may provide for the retention at the offices of such corporations, in whole or in part, of any accounts of accountable officers, covering corporate financial transactions, which are required by existing law to be settled and adjusted in the General Accounting Office, and for the settlement and adjustment of such accounts in whole or in part upon the basis of examinations in the course of the audit herein provided, but nothing in this proviso shall be construed as affecting the powers reserved to the Tennessee Valley Authority in the Act of November 21, 1941 (55 Stat. 775). The audit shall be conducted at the place or places where the accounts of the respective corporations are normally kept. The representatives of the General Accounting Office shall have access to all books, accounts, financial records, reports, files, and all other papers, things, or property belonging to or in use by the respective corporations and necessary to facilitate the audit, and they shall be afforded full facilities for verifying transactions with the balances or securities held by depositaries, fiscal agents, and custodians. The audit shall begin with the first fiscal year commencing after the enactment of this Act.

Sec. 106. A report of each such audit for each fiscal year ending on June 30 shall be made by the Comptroller General to the Congress not later than January 15 following the close of the fiscal year for which such audit is made. The report shall set forth the scope of the audit and shall include a statement (showing intercorporate relations) of assets and liabilities, capital and surplus or deficit; a statement of surplus or deficit analysis; a statement of income and expense; a statement of sources and application of funds; and such comments and information as may be deemed necessary to keep Congress informed of the operations and financial condition of the several corporations, together with such recommendations with respect thereto as the Comptroller General may deem advisable, including a report of any impairment of capital noted in the audit and recommendations for the return of such Government capital or the payment of such dividends as, in his judgment, should be accomplished. The report shall also show specifically any program, expenditure, or other financial transaction or undertaking observed in the course of the audit, which, in the opinion of the Comptroller General, has been carried on or made without authority of law. A copy of each report shall be furnished to the President, to the Secretary of the Treasury, and to the corporation concerned at the time submitted to the Congress.

Sec. 107. Whenever it is deemed by the Director of the Bureau of the Budget, with the approval of the President, to be practicable and in the public interest that any wholly owned Government corporation be treated with respect to its appropriations, expenditures, receipts, accounting, and other fiscal matters as if it were a Government agency other than a corporation, the Director shall include in connection with the budget program of such corporation in the Budget a recommendation to that effect. If the Congress approves such recommendation in connection with the budget program for any fiscal year, such corporation, with respect to subsequent fiscal years, shall be regarded as an establishment other than a corporation for the purposes of the Budget and Accounting Act, 1921, and other provisions of law relating to appropriations, expenditures, receipts, accounts, and other fiscal matters, and shall not be subject to the provisions of this Act other than this section. The corporate entity shall not be affected by this section.

Title II—Mixed-Ownership Government Corporations

Sec. 201. As used in this Act the term "mixed-ownership Government corporations" means (1) the Central Bank for Cooperatives and the Regional Banks for Cooperatives, (2) Federal Land Banks, (3) Federal Home Loan Banks, and (4) Federal Deposit Insurance Corporation.

Sec. 202. The financial transactions of mixed-ownership Government corporations for any period during which Government capital has been invested therein shall be audited by the General Accounting Office in accordance with the principles and procedures applicable to commercial corporate transactions and under such rules and regulations as may be prescribed by the Comptroller General of the United States. The audit shall be conducted at the place or places where the accounts of the respective corporations are normally kept. The representatives of the General Accounting Office shall have access to all books, accounts, financial records, reports, files, and all other papers, things, or property belonging to or in use by the respective corporations and necessary to facilitate the audit, and they shall be afforded full facilities for verifying transactions with the balances or securities held by depositaries, fiscal agents, and custodians. The audit shall begin with the first fiscal year commencing after the enactment of this Act.

Sec. 203. A report of each such audit for each fiscal year ending on June 30 shall be made by the Comptroller General to the Congress not later than January 15, following the close of the fiscal year for which such audit is made. The report shall set forth the scope of the audit and shall include a statement (showing intercorporate relations) of assets and liabilities, capital and surplus or deficit; a statement of surplus or deficit analysis; a statement of income and expense; a statement of sources and application of funds; and such comments and information as may be deemed necessary to keep Congress informed of the operations and financial condition of, and the use of Government capital by, each such corporation, together with such recommendations with respect thereto as the Comptroller General may deem advisable, including a report of any impairment of capital or lack of sufficient capital noted in the audit and recommendations for the return of such Government capital or the payment of such dividends as, in his judgment, should be accomplished. The report shall also show specifically any program, expenditure, or other financial transaction or undertaking observed in the course of the audit, which, in the opinion of the Comptroller General, has been carried on or made without authority of law. A copy of each report shall be furnished to the President, to the Secretary of the Treasury, and to the corporation concerned at the time submitted to the Congress.

Sec. 204. The President shall include in the annual Budget any recommendations he may wish to make as to the return of Government capital to the Treasury by any mixed-ownership corporation.

3. Employment Act of 1946*

Section 1. This Act may be cited as the "Employment Act of 1946."

Declaration of Policy

Sec. 2. The Congress hereby declares that it is the continuing policy and responsibility of the Federal Government to use all practicable means consistent with its needs and obligations and other essential considerations of national policy, with the assistance and cooperation of industry, agriculture, labor, and State and local governments, to coordinate and utilize all its plans, functions, and resources for the purpose of creating and maintaining, in a manner calculated to foster and promote free competitive enterprise and the general welfare, conditions under which there will be afforded useful employment opportunities, including self-employment, for those able, willing, and seeking to work, and to promote maximum employment, production, and purchasing power.

Sec. 3. (a) The President shall transmit to the Congress within sixty days after the beginning of each regular session (commencing with the year 1947) an economic report (hereinafter called the "Economic Report") setting forth (1) the levels of employment, production, and purchasing power obtaining in the United States and such levels needed to carry out the policy declared in section 2; (2) current and foreseeable trends in the levels of employment, production, and purchasing power; (3) a review of the economic program of the Federal Government and a review of economic conditions affecting employment in the United States or any considerable portion thereof during the preceding year and of their effect upon employment, production, and purchasing power; and (4) a program for carrying out the policy declared in section 2, together with such recommendations for legislation as he may deem necessary or desirable.

(b) The President may transmit from time to time to the Congress reports supplementary to the Economic Report, each of which shall include such supplementary or revised recommendations as he may deem necessary or desirable to achieve the policy declared in section 2.

(c) The Economic Report, and all supplementary reports transmitted under subsection (b), shall, when transmitted to Congress, be referred to the joint committee created by section 5.

* 60 Stat. 33 (1946).

Council of Economic Advisers to the President

Sec. 4. (a) There is hereby created in the Executive Office of the President a Council of Economic Advisers (hereinafter called the "Council"). The Council shall be composed of three members who shall be appointed by the President, and by and with the advice and consent of the Senate, and each of whom shall be a person who, as a result of his training, experience, and attainments, is exceptionally qualified to analyze and interpret economic developments, to appraise programs and activities of the Government in the light of the policy declared in section 2, and to formulate and recommend national economic policy to promote employment, production, and purchasing power under free competitive enterprise. Each member of the Council shall receive compensation at the rate of $15,000 per annum. The President shall designate one of the members of the Council as chairman and one as vice chairman, who shall act as chairman in the absence of the chairman.

(b) The Council is authorized to employ, and fix the compensation of, such specialists and other experts as may be necessary for the carrying out of its functions under this Act, without regard to the civil-service laws and the Classification Act of 1923, as amended, and is authorized, subject to the civil-service laws, to employ such other officers and employees as may be necessary for carrying out its functions under this Act, and fix their compensation in accordance with the Classification Act of 1923, as amended.

(c) It shall be the duty and function of the Council—

(1) to assist and advise the President in the preparation of the Economic Report;

(2) to gather timely and authoritative information concerning economic developments and economic trends, both current and prospective, to analyze and interpret such information in the light of the policy declared in section 2 for the purpose of determining whether such developments and trends are interfering, or are likely to interfere, with the achievement of such policy, and to compile and submit to the President studies relating to such developments and trends;

(3) to appraise the various programs and activities of the Federal Government in the light of the policy declared in section 2 for the purpose of determining the extent to which such programs and activities are contributing, and the extent to which they are not contributing, to the achievement of such policy, and to make recommendations to the President with respect thereto;

(4) to develop and recommend to the President national economic policies to foster and promote free competitive enterprise, to avoid economic fluctuations or to diminish the effects thereof, and to maintain employment, production, and purchasing power;

(5) to make and furnish such studies, reports thereon, and recommendations with respect to matters of Federal economic policy and legislation as the President may request.

(d) The Council shall make an annual report to the President in December of each year.

(e) In exercising its powers, functions and duties under this Act—

(1) the Council may constitute such advisory committees and may consult with such representatives of industry, agriculture, labor, consumers, State and local governments, and other groups, as it deems advisable;

(2) the Council shall, to the fullest extent possible, utilize the services, facilities, and information (including statistical information) of other Government agencies as well as of private research agencies, in order that duplication of effort and expense may be avoided.

(f) To enable the Council to exercise its powers, functions, and duties under this Act, there are authorized to be appropriated (except for the salaries of the members and the salaries of officers and employees of the Council) such sums as may be necessary. For the salaries of the members and the salaries of officers and employees of the Council, there is authorized to be appropriated not exceeding $345,000 in the aggregate for each fiscal year.

Joint Committee on the Economic Report

Sec. 5. (a) There is hereby established a Joint Committee on the Economic Report, to be composed of seven Members of the Senate, to be appointed by the President of the Senate, and seven Members of the House of Representatives, to be appointed by the Speaker of the House of Representatives. The party representation on the joint committee shall as nearly as may be feasible reflect the relative membership of the majority and minority parties in the Senate and House of Representatives.

(b) It shall be the function of the joint committee—

(1) to make a continuing study of matters relating to the Economic Report;

(2) to study means of coordinating programs in order to further the policy of this Act; and

(3) as a guide to the several committees of the Congress dealing with legislation relating to the Economic Report, not later than May 1 of each year (beginning with the year 1947) to file a report with the Senate and House of Representatives containing its findings and recommendations with respect to each of the main recommendations made by the President in the Economic Report, and from time to time to make such other reports and recommendations to the Senate and House of Representatives as it deems advisable.

(c) Vacancies in the membership of the joint committee shall not affect the power of the remaining members to execute the functions of the joint committee, and shall be filled in the same manner as in the case of the original selection. The joint committee shall select a chairman and a vice chairman from among its members.

(d) The joint committee, or any duly authorized subcommittee thereof, is authorized to hold such hearings as it deems advisable, and, within the limitations of its appropriations, the joint committee is empowered to appoint and fix the compensation of such experts, consultants, technicians, and clerical and stenographic assistants, to procure such printing and binding, and to make such expenditures, as it deems necessary and advisable. The cost of stenographic services to report hearings of the joint committee, or any subcommittee thereof, shall not exceed 25 cents per hundred words. The joint committee is authorized to utilize the services, information, and facilities of the departments and establishments of the Government, and also of private research agencies.

(e) There is hereby authorized to be appropriated for each fiscal year, the sum of $50,000, or so much thereof as may be necessary, to carry out the provisions of this section, to be disbursed by the Secretary of the Senate on vouchers signed by the chairman or vice chairman.

4. Administrative Procedure Act (1946)*

Section 1. This Act may be cited as the "Administrative Procedure Act."

Definitions

Sec. 2. As used in this Act—

(a) *Agency.*—"Agency" means each authority (whether or not within or subject to review by another agency) of the Government of the United States other than Congress, the courts, or the governments of the possessions, Territories, or the District of Columbia. Nothing in this Act shall be construed to repeal delegations of authority as provided by law. Except as to the requirements of section 3, there shall be excluded from the operation of this Act (1) agencies composed of representatives of the parties or of representatives of organizations of the parties to the disputes determined by them, (2) courts martial and military commissions, (3) military or naval authority exercised in the field in time of war or in occupied territory, or (4) functions which by law expire on the termination of present hostilities, within any fixed period thereafter, or before July 1, 1947, and the functions conferred by the following statutes: Selective Training and Service Act of 1940; Contract Settlement Act of 1944; Surplus Property Act of 1944.

(b) *Person and Party.*—"Person" includes individuals, partnerships, corporations, associations, or public or private organizations of any character other than agencies. "Party" includes any person or agency named or admitted as a party, or properly seeking and entitled as of right to be admitted as a party, in any agency proceeding; but nothing herein shall be construed to prevent an agency from admitting any person or agency as a party for limited purposes.

(c) *Rule and Rule Making.*—"Rule" means the whole or any part of any agency statement of general or particular applicability and future effect designed to implement, interpret, or prescribe law or policy or to describe the organization, procedure, or practice requirements of any agency and includes the approval or prescription for the future of rates, wages, corporate or financial structures or reorganizations thereof, prices, facilities, appliances, services or allowances therefor or of valuations, costs, or accounting, or practices bearing upon any of the foregoing. "Rule making" means agency process for the formulation, amendment, or repeal of a rule.

---

* 60 Stat. 324 (1946).

(d) *Order and Adjudication.*—"Order" means the whole or any part of the final disposition (whether affirmative, negative, injunctive, or declaratory in form) of any agency in any matter other than rule making but including licensing. "Adjudication" means agency process for the formulation of an order.

(e) *License and Licensing.*—"License" includes the whole or part of any agency permit, certificate, approval, registration, charter, membership, statutory exemption, or other form of permission. "Licensing" includes agency process respecting the grant, renewal, denial, revocation, suspension, annulment, withdrawal, limitation amendment, modification, or conditioning of a license.

(f) *Sanction and Relief.*—"Sanction" includes the whole or part of any agency (1) prohibition, requirement, limitation, or other condition affecting the freedom of any person; (2) withholding of relief; (3) imposition of any form of penalty or fine; (4) destruction, taking, seizure, or withholding of property; (5) assessment of damages, reimbursement, restitution, compensation, costs, charges or fees; (6) requirement, revocation, or suspension of a license; or (7) taking of other compulsory or restrictive action. "Relief" includes the whole or part of any agency (1) grant of money, assistance, license, authority, exemption, exception, privilege, or remedy; (2) recognition of any claim, right, immunity, privilege, exemption, or exception; or (3) taking of any other action upon the application or petition of, and beneficial to, any person.

(g) *Agency Proceeding and Action.*—"Agency proceeding" means any agency process as defined in subsections (c), (d), and (e) of this section. "Agency action" includes the whole or part of every agency rule, order, license, sanction, relief, or the equivalent or denial thereof, or failure to act.

Public Information

Sec. 3. Except to the extent that there is involved (1) any function of the United States requiring secrecy in the public interest or (2) any matter relating solely to the internal management of an agency—

(a) *Rules.*—Every agency shall separately state and currently publish in the Federal Register (1) descriptions of its central and field organization including delegations by the agency of final authority and the established places at which, and methods whereby, the public may secure information or make submittals or requests; (2) statements of the general course and method by which its functions are channeled and determined, including the nature and requirements of all formal or informal procedures available as well as forms and instructions as to the scope and contents of all papers, reports, or examinations; and (3) substantive rules adopted as authorized by law and statements of general policy or interpretations formulated and adopted by the agency for the guidance of the public, but not rules addressed to and served upon named persons in accordance with law. No person shall in any manner be required to resort to organization or procedure not so published.

(b) *Opinions and Orders.*—Every agency shall publish or, in accordance with published rule, make available to public inspection all final opinions or orders in the adjudication of cases (except those required for good cause to be held confidential and not cited as precedents) and all rules.

(c) *Public Records.*—Save as otherwise required by statute, matters of official record shall in accordance with published rule be made available to persons properly and directly concerned except information held confidential for good cause found.

Rule Making

Sec. 4. Except to the extent that there is involved (1) any military, naval, or foreign affairs function of the United States or (2) any matter relating to agency management or personnel or to public property, loans, grants, benefits, or contracts—

(a) *Notice.*—General notice of proposed rule making shall be published in the Federal Register (unless all persons subject thereto are named and either personally served or otherwise have actual notice thereof in accordance with law) and shall include (1) a statement of the time, place, and nature of public rule making proceedings; (2) reference to the authority under which the rule is proposed; and (3) either the terms or substance of the proposed rule or a description of the subjects and issues involved. Except where notice or hearing is required by statute, this subsection shall not apply to interpretative rules, general statements of policy, rules of agency organization, procedure, or practice, or in any situation in which the agency for good cause finds (and incorporates the finding and a brief statement of the reasons therefor in the rules issued) that notice and public procedure thereon are impracticable, unnecessary, or contrary to the public interest.

(b) *Procedures.*—After notice required by this section, the agency shall afford interested persons an opportunity to participate in the rule making through submission of written data, views, or arguments with or without opportunity to present the same orally in any manner; and, after consideration of all relevant matter presented, the agency shall incorporate in any rules adopted a concise general statement of their basis and purpose. Where rules are required by statute to be made on the record after opportunity for an agency hearing, the requirements of sections 7 and 8 shall apply in place of the provisions of this subsection.

(c) *Effective Dates.*—The required publication or service of any substantive rule (other than one granting or recognizing exemption or relieving restriction or interpretative rules and statements of policy) shall be made not less than thirty days prior to the effective date thereof except as otherwise provided by the agency upon good cause found and published with the rule.

(d) *Petitions.*—Every agency shall accord any interested person the right to petition for the issuance, amendment, or repeal of a rule.

Adjudication

Sec. 5. In every case of adjudication required by statute to be determined on the record after opportunity for an agency hearing, except to the extent that there is involved (1) any matter subject to a subsequent trial of the law and the facts de novo in any court; (2) the selection or tenure of an officer or employee of the United States other than examiners appointed pursuant to section 11; (3) proceedings in which decisions rest solely on inspections, tests, or elections; (4) the conduct of military, naval, or foreign affairs functions; (5) cases in which an agency is acting as an agent for a court; and (6) the certification of employee representatives—

(a) *Notice.*—Persons entitled to notice of an agency hearing shall be timely informed of (1) the time, place and nature thereof; (2) the legal authority and jurisdiction under which the hearing is to be held; and (3) the matters of fact and law asserted. In instances in which private persons are the moving parties, other parties to the proceeding shall give prompt notice of issues controverted in fact or law; and in other instances agencies may by rule require responsive pleading. In fixing the times and places for hearings, due regard shall be had for the convenience and necessity of the parties or their representatives.

(b) *Procedure.*—The agency shall afford all interested parties opportunity for (1) the submission and consideration of facts, arguments, offers of settlement, or proposals of adjustment where time, the nature of the proceeding, and the public interest permit, and (2) to the extent that the parties are unable so to determine any controversy by consent, hearing, and decision upon notice and in conformity with sections 7 and 8.

(c) *Separation of Functions.*—The same officers who preside at the reception of evidence pursuant to section 7 shall make the recommended decision or initial decision required by section 8 except where such officers become unavailable to the agency. Save to the extent required for the disposition of ex parte matters as authorized by law, no such officer shall consult any person or party on any fact in issue unless upon notice and opportunity for all parties to participate; nor shall such officer be responsible to or subject to the supervision or direction of any officer, employee, or agent engaged in the performance of investigative or prosecuting functions for any agency. No officer, employee, or agent engaged in the performance of investigative or prosecuting functions for any agency in any case shall, in that or a factually related case, participate or advise in the decision, recommended decision, or agency review pursuant to section 8 except as witness or counsel in public proceedings. This subsection shall not apply in determining applications for initial licenses or to proceedings involving the validity or application of rates, facilities, or practices of public utilities or carriers; nor shall it be applicable in any manner to the agency or any member or members of the body comprising the agency.

(d) *Declaratory Orders.*—The agency is authorized in its sound discretion, with like effect as in the case of other orders, to issue a declaratory order to terminate a controversy or remove uncertainty.

Ancillary Matters

Sec. 6. Except as otherwise provided in this Act—

(a) *Appearance.*—Any person compelled to appear in person before any agency or representative thereof shall be accorded the right to be accompanied, represented, and advised by counsel or, if permitted by the agency, by other qualified representative. Every party shall be accorded the right to appear in person or by or with counsel or other duly qualified representative in any agency proceeding. So far as the orderly conduct of public business permits, any interested person may appear before any agency or its responsible officers or employees for the presentation, adjustment, or determination of any issue, request, or controversy in any proceeding (interlocutory, summary, or otherwise) or in connection with any agency function. Every agency shall proceed with reasonable dispatch to conclude any matter presented to it except that due regard shall be had for the convenience and necessity of the parties or their representatives. Nothing herein shall be construed either to grant or to deny to any person who is not a lawyer the right to appear for or represent others before any agency or in any agency proceeding.

(b) *Investigations.*—No process, requirement of a report, inspection, or other investigative act or demand shall be issued, made, or enforced in any manner or for any purpose except as authorized by law. Every person compelled to submit data or evidence shall be entitled to retain or, on payment of lawfully prescribed costs, procure a copy or transcript thereof, except that in a nonpublic investigatory proceeding the witness may for good cause be limited to inspection of the official transcript of his testimony.

(c) *Subpenas.*—Agency subpenas authorized by law shall be issued to any party upon request and, as may be required by rules of procedure, upon a statement or showing of general relevance and reasonable scope of the evidence sought. Upon contest the court shall sustain any such subpena or similar process or demand to the extent that it is found to be in accordance with law and, in any proceeding for enforcement, shall issue an order requiring the appearance of the witness or the production of the evidence or data within a reasonable time under penalty of punishment for contempt in case of contumacious failure to comply.

(d) *Denials.*—Prompt notice shall be given of the denial in whole or in part of any written application, petition, or other request of any interested person made in connection with any agency proceeding. Except in affirming a prior denial or where the denial is self-explanatory, such notice shall be accompanied by a simple statement of procedural or other grounds.

Hearings

Sec. 7. In hearings which section 4 or 5 requires to be conducted pursuant to this section—

(a) *Presiding Officers.*—There shall preside at the taking of evidence (1) the agency, (2) one or more members of the body which comprises the agency, or (3) one or more examiners appointed as provided in this Act; but nothing in this Act shall be deemed to supersede the conduct of specified classes of proceedings in whole or part by or before boards or other officers specially provided for by or designated pursuant to statute. The functions of all presiding officers and of officers participating in decisions in conformity with section 8 shall be conducted in an impartial manner. Any such officer may at any time withdraw if he deems himself disqualified; and upon the filing in good faith of a timely and sufficient affidavit of personal bias or disqualification of any such officer, the agency shall determine the matter as a part of the record and decision in the case.

(b) *Hearing Powers.*—Officers presiding at hearings shall have authority, subject to the published rules of the agency and within its powers, to (1) administer oaths and affirmations, (2) issue subpenas authorized by law, (3) rule upon offers of proof and receive relevant evidence, (4) take or cause depositions to be taken whenever the ends of justice would be served thereby, (5) regulate the course of the hearing, (6) hold conferences for the settlement or simplification of the issues by consent of the parties, (7) dispose of procedural requests or similar matters, (8) make decisions or recommend decisions in conformity with section 8, and (9) take any other action authorized by agency rule consistent with this Act.

(c) *Evidence.*—Except as statutes otherwise provide, the proponent of a rule or order shall have the burden of proof. Any oral or documentary evidence may be received, but every agency shall as a matter of policy provide for the exclusion of irrelevant, immaterial, or unduly repetitious evidence and no sanction shall be imposed or rule or order be issued except upon consideration of the whole record or such portions thereof as may be cited by any party and as supported by and in accordance with the reliable, probative, and substantial evidence. Every party shall have the right to present his case or defense by oral or documentary evidence, to submit rebuttal evidence, and to conduct such cross-examination as may be required for a full and true disclosure of the facts. In rule making or determining claims for money or benefits or applications for initial licenses, any agency may, where the interest of any party will not be prejudiced thereby, adopt procedures for the submission of all or part of the evidence in written form.

(d) *Record.*—The transcript of testimony and exhibits, together with all papers and requests filed in the proceeding, shall constitute the exclusive record for decision in accordance with section 8 and, upon payment of lawfully prescribed costs, shall be made available to the parties. Where any agency decision rests on official notice of a material fact not appearing in the evidence in the record, any party shall on timely request be afforded an opportunity to show the contrary.

Decisions

Sec. 8. In cases in which a hearing is required to be conducted in conformity with section 7—

(a) *Action by Subordinates.*—In cases in which the agency has not presided at the reception of the evidence, the officer who presided (or, in cases not subject to subsection (c) of section 5, any other officer or officers qualified to preside at hearings pursuant to section 7) shall initially decide the case or the agency shall require (in specific cases or by general rule) the entire record to be certified to it for initial decision. Whenever such officers make the initial decision and in the absence of either an appeal to the agency or review upon motion of the agency within time provided by rule, such decision shall without further proceedings then become the decision of the agency. On appeal from or review of the initial decisions of such officers the agency shall, except as it may limit the issues upon notice or by rule, have all the powers which it would have in making the initial decision. Whenever the agency makes the initial decision without having presided at the reception of the evidence, such officers shall first recommend a decision, except that in rule making or determining applications for initial licenses (1) in lieu thereof the agency may issue a tentative decision or any of its responsible officers may recommend a decision or (2) any such procedure may be omitted in any case in which the agency finds upon the record that due and timely execution of its functions imperatively and unavoidably so requires.

(b) *Submittals and Decisions.*—Prior to each recommended, initial, or tentative decision, or decision upon agency review of the decision of subordinate officers, the parties shall be afforded a reasonable opportunity to submit for the consideration of the officers participating in such decisions (1) proposed findings and conclusions, or (2) exceptions to the decisions or recommended decisions of subordinate officers or to tentative agency decisions, and (3) supporting reasons for such exceptions or proposed findings or conclusions. The record shall show the ruling upon each such finding, conclusion, or exception presented. All decisions (including initial, recommended, or tentative decisions) shall become a part of the record and include a statement of (1) findings and conclusions, as well as the reasons or basis therefor, upon all the material issues of fact, law, or discretion presented on the record; and (2) the appropriate rule, order, sanction, relief, or denial thereof.

Sanctions and Powers

Sec. 9. In the exercise of any power or authority—

(a) *In General.*—No sanction shall be imposed or substantive rule or order be issued except within jurisdiction delegated to the agency and as authorized by law.

(b) *Licenses.*—In any case in which application is made for a license required by law the agency, with due regard to the rights or privileges of all the interested parties or adversely affected persons and with reasonable dispatch, shall set and complete any proceedings required to be conducted pursuant to sections 7 and 8 of this Act or other proceedings required by law and shall make its decision. Except in cases of willfulness or those in which public health, interest, or safety requires otherwise, no withdrawal, suspension, revocation, or annulment of any license shall be lawful unless, prior to the institution of agency proceedings therefor, facts or conduct which may warrant such action shall have been called to the attention of the licensee by the agency in writing and the licensee shall have been accorded opportunity to demonstrate or achieve compliance with all lawful requirements. In any case in which the licensee has, in accordance with agency rules, made timely and sufficient application for a renewal or a new license, no license with reference to any activity of a continuing nature shall expire until such application shall have been finally determined by the agency.

Judicial Review

Sec. 10. Except so far as (1) statutes preclude judicial review or (2) agency action is by law committed to agency discretion—

(a) *Right of Review.*—Any person suffering legal wrong because of any agency action, or adversely affected or aggrieved by such action within the meaning of any relevant statute, shall be entitled to judicial review thereof.

(b) *Form and Venue of Action.*—The form of proceeding for judicial review shall be any special statutory review proceeding relevant to the subject matter in any court specified by statute or, in the absence or inadequacy thereof, any applicable form of legal action (including actions for declaratory judgments or writs of prohibitory or mandatory injunction or habeas corpus) in any court of competent jurisdiction. Agency action shall be subject to judicial review in civil or criminal proceedings for judicial enforcement except to the extent that prior, adequate, and exclusive opportunity for such review is provided by law.

(c) *Reviewable Acts.*—Every agency action made reviewable by statute and every final agency action for which there is no other adequate remedy in any court shall be subject to judicial review. Any preliminary, procedural, or intermediate agency action or ruling not directly reviewable shall be subject to review upon the review of the final agency action. Except as otherwise expressly, required by statute, agency action otherwise final shall be final for the purposes of this subsection whether or not there has been presented or determined any application for a declaratory order, for any form of reconsideration, or (unless the agency otherwise requires by rule and provides that the action meanwhile shall be inoperative) for an appeal to superior agency authority.

(d) *Interim Relief.*—Pending judicial review any agency is authorized, where it finds that justice so requires, to postpone the effective date of any action taken by it. Upon such conditions as may be required and to the extent necessary to prevent irreparable injury, every reviewing court (including every court to which a case may be taken on appeal from or upon application for certiorari or other writ to a reviewing court) is authorized to issue all necessary and appropriate process to postpone the effective date of any agency action or to preserve status or rights pending conclusion of the review proceedings.

(e) *Scope of Review.*—So far as necessary to decision and where presented the reviewing court shall decide all relevant questions of law, interpret constitutional and statutory provisions, and determine the meaning or applicability of the terms of any agency action. It shall (A) compel agency action unlawfully withheld or unreasonably delayed; and (B) hold unlawful and set aside agency action, findings, and conclusions found to be (1) arbitrary, capricious, an abuse of discretion, or otherwise not in accordance with law; (2) contrary to constitutional right, power, privilege, or immunity; (3) in excess of statutory jurisdiction, authority, or limitations, or short of statutory right; (4) without observance of procedure required by law; (5) unsupported by substantial evidence in any case subject to the requirements of sections 7 and 8 or otherwise reviewed on the record of an agency hearing provided by statute; or (6) unwarranted by the facts to the extent that the facts are subject to trial de novo by the reviewing court. In making the foregoing determinations the court shall review the whole record or such portions thereof as may be cited by any party, and due account shall be taken of the rule of prejudicial error.

Examiners

Sec. 11. Subject to the civil-service and other laws to the extent not inconsistent with this Act, there shall be appointed by and for each agency as many qualified and competent examiners as may be necessary for proceedings pursuant to sections 7 and 8, who shall be assigned to cases in rotation so far as practicable and shall perform no duties inconsistent with their duties and responsibilities as examiners. Examiners shall be removable by the agency in which they are employed only for good cause established and determined by the Civil Service Commission (hereinafter called the Commission) after opportunity for hearing and upon the record thereof. Examiners shall receive compensation prescribed by the Commission independently of agency recommendations or ratings and in accordance with the Classification Act of 1923, as amended, except that the provisions of paragraphs (2) and (3) of subsection (b) of section 7 of said Act, as amended, and the provisions of section 9 of said Act, as amended, shall not be applicable. Agencies occasionally or temporarily insufficiently staffed may utilize examiners selected by the Commission from and with the consent of other agencies. For the purposes of this section, the Commission is authorized to make investigations, require reports by agencies, issue reports, including an annual report to the Congress, promulgate rules, appoint such advisory committees as may be deemed necessary, recommend legislation, subpena witnesses or records, and pay witness fees as established for the United States courts.

Construction and Effect

Sec. 12. Nothing in this Act shall be held to diminish the constitutional rights of any person or to limit or repeal additional requirements imposed by statute or otherwise recognized by law. Except as otherwise required by law, all requirements or privileges relating to evidence or procedure shall apply equally to agencies and persons. If any provision of this Act or the application thereof is held invalid, the remainder of this Act or other applications of such provision shall not be affected. Every agency is granted all authority necessary to comply with the requirements of this Act through the issuance of rules or otherwise. No subsequent legislation shall be held to supersede or modify the provisions of this Act except to the extent that such legislation shall do so expressly. This Act shall take effect three months after its approval except that sections 7 and 8 shall take effect six months after such approval, and no procedural requirement shall be mandatory as to any agency proceeding initiated prior to the effective date of such requirement.

5. Organization for National Security (1947 and 1949)*

The National Security Act of 1947 and the National Security Act Amendments of 1949

Declaration of Policy

"Sec. 2. In enacting this legislation, it is the intent of Congress to provide a comprehensive program for the future security of the United States; to provide for the establishment of integrated policies and procedures for the departments, agencies, and functions of the Government relating to the national security; to provide three military departments, separately administered, for the operation and administration of the Army, the Navy (including naval aviation and the United States Marine Corps), and the Air Force, with their assigned combat and service components; to provide for their authoritative coordination and unified direction under civilian control of the Secretary of Defense but not to merge them; to provide for the effective strategic direction of the armed forces and for their operation under unified control and for their integration into an efficient team of land, naval, and air forces but not to establish a single Chief of Staff over the armed forces nor an armed forces general staff (but this is not to be interpreted as applying to the Joint Chiefs of Staff or Joint Staff)."

Title I—Coordination for National Security

National Security Council

Sec. 101. (a) There is hereby established a council to be known as the National Security Council (hereinafter in this section referred to as the "Council").

The President of the United States shall preside over meetings of the Council: *Provided,* That in his absence he may designate a member of the Council to preside in his place.

---

* 61 Stat. 343 (1947) and 63 Stat. 412 (1949). The language herein is taken from the 1947 Act, as amended in 1949. Substitutions and additions from 1949 are indicated by quotation marks. Much of the detailed language is omitted, including: section 103, National Security Resources Board; sections 203 and 204, concerning personnel authorities; sections 208-210, containing certain detailed provisions about the Air Force and the Armed Forces Policy Council; section 213, Munitions Board; section 214, Research and Development Board; the entirety of Title III—Miscellaneous; and sections 405-411, which provide for working capital funds, management funds, and certain accounting provisions.

The function of the Council shall be to advise the President with respect to the integration of domestic, foreign, and military policies relating to the national security so as to enable the military services and the other departments and agencies of the Government to cooperate more effectively in matters involving the national security.

"The Council shall be composed of—

(1) the President;

(2) the Vice President;

(3) the Secretary of State;

(4) the Secretary of Defense;

(5) the Chairman of the National Security Resources Board; and

(6) the Secretaries and Under Secretaries of other executive departments and of the military departments, the Chairman of the Munitions Board, and the Chairman of the Research and Development Board, when appointed by the President by and with the advice and consent of the Senate, to serve at his pleasure."

(b) In addition to performing such other functions as the President may direct, for the purpose of more effectively coordinating the policies and functions of the departments and agencies of the Government relating to the national security, it shall, subject to the direction of the President, be the duty of the Council—

(1) to assess and appraise the objectives, commitments, and risks of the United States in relation to our actual and potential military power, in the interest of national security, for the purpose of making recommendations to the President in connection therewith; and

(2) to consider policies on matters of common interest to the departments and agencies of the Government concerned with the national security, and to make recommendations to the President in connection therewith.

(c) The Council shall have a staff to be headed by a civilian executive secretary who shall be appointed by the President, and who shall receive compensation at the rate of $10,000 a year. The executive secretary, subject to the direction of the Council, is hereby authorized, subject to the civil-service laws and the Classification Act of 1923, as amended, to appoint and fix the compensation of such personnel as may be necessary to perform such duties as may be prescribed by the Council in connection with the performance of its function.

(d) The Council shall, from time to time, make such recommendations, and such other reports to the President as it deems appropriate or as the President may require.

Central Intelligence Agency

Sec. 102. (a) There is hereby established under the National Security Council a Central Intelligence Agency with a Director of Central Intelligence, who shall be the head thereof. The Director shall be appointed by the President, by and with the advice and consent of the Senate, from among the commissioned officers of the armed services or from among individuals in civilian life. The Director shall receive compensation at the rate of $14,000 a year.

(b)

(1) If a commissioned officer of the armed services is appointed as Director then—

(A) in the performance of his duties as Director, he shall be subject to no supervision, control, restriction, or prohibition (military or otherwise) other than would be operative with respect to him if he were a civilian in no way connected with the Department of the Army, the Department of the Navy, the Department of the Air Force, or the armed services or any component thereof; and

(B) he shall not possess or exercise any supervision, control, powers, or functions (other than such as he possesses, or is authorized or directed to exercise, as director) with respect to the armed services or any component thereof, the Department of the Army, the Department of the Navy, or the Department of the Air Force, or any branch, bureau, unit or division thereof, or with respect to any of the personnel (military or civilian) of any of the foregoing.

(2) Except as provided in paragraph (1), the appointment to the office of Director of a commissioned officer of the armed services, and his acceptance of and service in such office, shall in no way affect any status, office, rank, or grade he may occupy or hold in the armed services, or any emolument, perquisite, right, privilege, or benefit incident to or arising out of any such status, office, rank, or grade. Any such commissioned officer shall, while serving in the office of Director, receive the military pay and allowances (active or retired, as the case may be) payable to a commissioned officer of his grade and length of service and shall be paid, from any funds avail-

able to defray the expenses of the Agency, annual compensation at a rate equal to the amount by which $14,000 exceeds the amount of his annual military pay and allowances.

(c) Notwithstanding the provisions of section 6 of the Act of August 24, 1912 (37 Stat. 555), or the provisions of any other law, the Director of Central Intelligence may, in his discretion, terminate the employment of any officer or employee of the Agency whenever he shall deem such termination necessary or advisable in the interests of the United States, but such termination shall not affect the right of such officer or employee to seek or accept employment in any other department or agency of the Government if declared eligible for such employment by the United States Civil Service Commission.

(d) For the purpose of coordinating the intelligence activities of the several Government departments and agencies in the interest of national security, it shall be the duty of the Agency, under the direction of the National Security Council—

(1) to advise the National Security Council in matters concerning such intelligence activities of the Government departments and agencies as relate to national security;

(2) to make recommendations to the National Security Council for the coordination of such intelligence activities of the departments and agencies of the Government as relate to the national security;

(3) to correlate and evaluate intelligence relating to the national security, and provide for the appropriate dissemination of such intelligence within the Government using where appropriate existing agencies and facilities: *Provided,* That the Agency shall have no police, subpoena, law-enforcement powers, or internal-security functions: *Provided further,* That the departments and other agencies of the Government shall continue to collect, evaluate, correlate, and disseminate departmental intelligence: *And provided further,* That the Director of Central Intelligence shall be responsible for protecting intelligence sources and methods from unauthorized disclosure;

(4) to perform, for the benefit of the existing intelligence agencies, such additional services of common concern as the National Security Council determines can be more efficiently accomplished centrally;

(5) to perform such other functions and duties related to intelligence affecting the national security as the National Security Council may from time to time direct.

(e) To the extent recommended by the National Security Council and approved by the President, such intelligence of the departments and agencies of the Government, except as hereinafter provided, relating to the national security shall be open to the inspection of the Director of Central Intelligence, and such intelligence as relates to the national security and is possessed by such departments and other agencies of the government, except as hereinafter provided, shall be made available to the Director of Central Intelligence for correlation, evaluation, and dissemination: *Provided, however,* That upon the written request of the Director of Central Intelligence, the Director of the Federal Bureau of Investigation shall make available to the Director of Central Intelligence such information for correlation, evaluation, and dissemination as may be essential to the national security.

(f) Effective when the Director first appointed under subsection (a) has taken office—

(1) the National Intelligence Authority (11 Fed. Reg. 1337, 1339, February 5, 1946) shall cease to exist; and

(2) the personnel, property, and records of the Central Intelligence Group are transferred to the Central Intelligence Agency, and such Group shall cease to exist. Any unexpended balances of appropriations, allocations, or other funds available or authorized to be made available for such Group shall be available and shall be authorized to be made available in like manner for expenditure by the Agency.

"Title II—The Department of Defense

"Sec. 201. (a) There is hereby established, as an Executive Department of the Government, the Department of Defense, and the Secretary of Defense shall be the head thereof.

"(b) There shall be within the Department of Defense (1) the Department of the Army, the Department of the Navy, and the Department of the Air Force, and each such department shall on and after the date of enactment of the National Security Act Amendments of 1949 be military departments in lieu of their prior status as Executive Departments, and (2) all other agencies created under title II of this Act."

The Secretary of Defense

"Sec. 202. (a) There shall be a Secretary of Defense, who shall be appointed from civilian life by the President, by and with the advice and consent of the Senate: *Provided,* That a person who has within ten years been on active duty as a commissioned officer in a Regular component of the armed services shall not be eligible for appointment as Secretary of Defense.

"(b) The Secretary of Defense shall be the principal assistant to the President in all matters relating to the Department of Defense. Under the direction of the President, and subject to the provisions of this Act, he shall have direction, authority, and control over the Department of Defense.

"(c)

"(1) Notwithstanding any other provision of this Act, the combatant functions assigned to the military services by sections 205 (e), 206 (b), 206 (c), and 208 (f) hereof shall not be transferred, reassigned, abolished, or consolidated.

"(2) Military personnel shall not be so detailed or assigned as to impair such combatant functions.

"(3) The Secretary of Defense shall not direct the use and expenditure of funds of the Department of Defense in such manner as to effect the results prohibited by paragraphs (1) and (2) of this subsection.

"(4) The Departments of the Army, Navy, and Air Force shall be separately administered by their respective Secretaries under the direction, authority, and control of the Secretary of Defense.

"(5) Subject to the provisions of paragraph (1) of this subsection no function which has been or is hereafter authorized by law to be performed by the Department of Defense shall be substantially transferred, reassigned, abolished or consolidated until after a report in regard to all pertinent details shall have been made by the Secretary of Defense to the Committees on Armed Services of the Congress.

"(6) No provision of this Act shall be so construed as to prevent a Secretary of a military department or a member of the Joint Chiefs of Staff from presenting to the Congress, on his own initiative, after first so informing the Secretary of Defense, any recommendation relating to the Department of Defense that he may deem proper.

"(d) The Secretary of Defense shall not less often than semi-annually submit written reports to the President and the Congress covering expenditures, work and accomplishments of the Department of Defense, accompanied by (1) such recommendations as he shall deem appropriate, (2) separate reports from the military departments covering their expenditures, work and accomplishments, and (3) itemized statements showing the savings of public funds and the eliminations of unnecessary duplications and overlappings that have been accomplished pursuant to the provisions of this Act.

"(e) The Secretary of Defense shall cause a seal of office to be made for the Department of Defense, of such design as the President shall approve, and judicial notice shall be taken thereof.

"(f) The Secretary of Defense may, without being relieved of his responsibility therefor, and unless prohibited by some specific provision of this Act or other specific provision of law, perform any function vested in him through or with the aid of such officials or organizational entities of the Department of Defense as he may designate."

Department of the Army

Sec. 205. (a) The Department of War shall hereafter be designated the Department of the Army, and the title of the Secretary of War shall be changed to Secretary of the Army. Changes shall be made in the titles of other officers and activities of the Department of the Army as the Secretary of the Army may determine.

(b) All laws, orders, regulations, and other actions relating to the Department of War or to any officer or activity whose title is changed under this section shall, insofar as they are not inconsistent with the provisions of this Act, be deemed to relate to the Department of the Army within the Department of Defense or to such officer or activity designated by his or its new title.

(c) The term "Department of the Army" as used in this Act shall be construed to mean the Department of the Army at the seat of government and all field headquarters, forces, reserve components, installations, activities, and functions under the control or supervision of the Department of the Army.

(d) The Secretary of the Army shall cause a seal of office to be made for the Department of the Army, of such design as the President may approve, and judicial notice shall be taken thereof.

(e) In general the United States Army, within the Department of the Army, shall include land combat and service forces and such aviation and water transport as may be organic therein. It shall be organized, trained, and equipped primarily for prompt and sustained combat incident to operations on land. It shall be responsible for the preparation of land forces necessary for the effective prosecution of war except as otherwise assigned and, in accordance with integrated joint mobilization plans, for the expansion of peacetime components of the Army to meet the needs of war.

Department of the Navy

Sec. 206. (a) The term "Department of the Navy" as used in this Act shall be construed to mean the Department of the Navy at the seat of government; the headquarters, United States Marine Corps; the entire operating forces of the United States Navy, including naval aviation, and of the United States Marine Corps, including the reserve components of such forces; all field activities, headquarters, forces, bases, installations, activities, and functions under the control or supervision of the Department of the Navy; and the United States Coast Guard when operating as a part of the Navy pursuant to law.

(b) In general the United States Navy, within the Department of the Navy, shall include naval combat and service forces and such aviation as may be organic therein. It shall be organized, trained, and equipped primarily for prompt and sustained combat incident to operations at sea. It shall be responsible for the preparation of naval forces necessary for the effective prosecution of war except as otherwise assigned, and, in accordance with integrated joint mobilization plans, for the expansion of the peacetime components of the Navy to meet the needs of war.

All naval aviation shall be integrated with the naval service as part thereof within the Department of the Navy. Naval aviation shall consist of combat and service and training forces, and shall include land-based naval aviation, air transport essential for naval operation, all air weapons and air techniques involved in the operations and activities of the United States Navy, and the entire remainder of the aeronautical organization of the United States Navy, together with the personnel necessary therefor.

The Navy shall be generally responsible for naval reconnaissance, antisubmarine warfare, and protection of shipping.

The Navy shall develop aircraft, weapons, tactics, technique, organization and equipment of naval combat and service elements; matters of joint concern as to these functions shall be coordinated between the Army, the Air Force, and the Navy.

(c) The United States Marine Corps, within the Department of the Navy, shall include land combat and service forces and such aviation as may be organic therein. The Marine Corps shall be organized, trained, and equipped to provide fleet marine forces of combined arms, together with supporting air components, for service with the fleet in the seizure or defense of advanced naval bases and for the conduct of such land operations as may be essential to the prosecution of a naval campaign. It shall be the duty of the Marine Corps to develop, in coordination with the Army and the Air Force, those phases of amphibious operations which pertain to the tactics, technique, and equipment employed by landing forces. In addition, the Marine Corps shall provide detachments and organizations for service on armed vessels of the Navy, shall provide security detachments for the protection of naval property at naval stations and bases, and shall perform such other duties as the President may direct: *Provided,* That such additional duties shall not detract from or interfere with the operations for which the Marine Corps is primarily organized. The Marine Corps shall be responsible, in accordance with integrated joint mobilization plans, for the expansion of peacetime components of the Marine Corps to meet the needs of war.

Department of the Air Force

Sec. 207. (a) Within the Department of Defense there is hereby established an executive department to be known as the Department of the Air Force, and a Secretary of the Air Force, who shall be the head thereof. The Secretary of the Air Force shall be appointed from civilian life by the President, by and with the advice and consent of the Senate.

(b) [Repealed]

(c) The term "Department of the Air Force" as used in this Act shall be construed to mean the Department of the Air Force at the seat of government and all field headquarters, forces, reserve components, installations, activities, and functions under the control or supervision of the Department of the Air Force.

(d) There shall be in the Department of the Air Force an Under Secretary of the Air Force and two Assistant Secretaries of the Air Force, who shall be appointed from civilian life by the President by and with the advice and consent of the Senate.

(e) The several officers of the Department of the Air Force shall perform such functions as the Secretary of the Air Force may prescribe.

(f) So much of the functions of the Secretary of the Army and of the Department of the Army, including those of any officer of such Department, as are assigned to or under the control of the Commanding General, Army Air Forces, or as are deemed by the Secretary of Defense to be necessary or desirable for the operations of the Department of the Air Force or the United States Air Force, shall be transferred to and vested in the Secretary of the Air Force and the Department of the Air Force: *Provided,* That the National Guard Bureau shall, in addition to the functions and duties performed by it for the Department of the Army, be charged with similar functions and duties for the Department of the Air Force, and shall be the channel of communication between the Department of the Air Force and the several States on all matters pertaining to the Air National Guard: *And provided further,* That, in order to permit an orderly transfer, the Secretary of Defense may, during the transfer period hereinafter prescribed, direct that the Department of the Army shall continue for appropriate periods to exercise any of such functions, insofar as they relate to the Department of the Air Force, or the United States Air Force or their property and personnel. Such of the property, personnel, and records of the Department of the Army used in the exercise of functions transferred under this subsection as the Secretary of Defense shall determine shall be transferred or assigned to the Department of the Air Force.

(g) The Secretary of the Air Force shall cause a seal of office to be made for the Department of the Air Force, of such device as the President shall approve, and judicial notice shall be taken thereof.

Joint Chiefs of Staff

"Sec. 211. (a) There is hereby established within the Department of Defense the Joint Chiefs of Staff, which shall consist of the Chairman, who shall be the presiding officer thereof but who shall have no vote; the Chief of Staff, United States Army; the Chief of Naval Operations; and the Chief of Staff, United States Air Force. The Joint Chiefs of Staff shall be the principal military advisers to the President, the National Security Council, and the Secretary of Defense.

"(b) Subject to the authority and direction of the President and the Secretary of Defense, the Joint Chiefs of Staff shall perform the following duties, in addition to such other duties as the President or the Secretary of Defense may direct:

"(1) preparation of strategic plans and provision for the strategic direction of the military forces;

"(2) preparation of joint logistic plans and assignment to the military services of logistic responsibilities in accordance with such plans;

"(3) establishment of unified commands in strategic areas;

"(4) review of major material and personnel requirements of the military forces in accordance with strategic and logistic plans;

"(5) formulation of policies for joint training of the military forces;

"(6) formulation of policies for coordinating the military education of members of the military forces; and

"(7) providing the United States representation on the Military Staff Committee of the United Nations in accordance with the provisions of the Charter of the United Nations.

"(c) The Chairman of the Joint Chiefs of Staff (hereinafter referred to as the 'Chairman') shall be appointed by the President, by and with the advice and consent of the Senate, from among the Regular officers of the armed services to serve at the pleasure of the President for a term of two years and shall be eligible for one reappointment, by and with the advice and consent of the Senate, except in time of war hereafter declared by the Congress when there shall be no limitation on the number of such reappointments. The Chairman shall receive the basic pay and basic and personal money allowances prescribed by law for the Chief of Staff, United States Army, and such special pays and hazardous duty pays to which he may be entitled under other provisions of law.

"(d) The Chairman, if in the grade of general, shall be additional to the number of officers in the grade of general provided in the third proviso of section 504 (b) of the Officer Personnel Act of 1947 (Public Law 381, Eightieth Congress) or, if in the rank of admiral, shall be additional to the number of officers having the rank of admiral provided in section 413 (a) of such Act. While holding such office he shall take precedence over all other officers of the armed services: *Provided,* That the Chairman shall not exercise military command over the Joint Chiefs of Staff or over any of the military services.

"(e) In addition to participating as a member of the Joint Chiefs of Staff in the performance of the duties assigned in subsection (b) of this section, the Chairman shall, subject to the authority and direction of the President and the Secretary of Defense, perform the following duties:

"(1) serve as the presiding officer of the Joint Chiefs of Staff;

"(2) provide agenda for meetings of the Joint Chiefs of Staff and assist the Joint Chiefs of Staff to prosecute their business as promptly as practicable; and

"(3) inform the Secretary of Defense and, when appropriate as determined by the President or the Secretary of Defense, the President, of those issues upon which agreement among the Joint Chiefs of Staff has not been reached."

"Joint Staff

"Sec. 212. There shall be, under the Joint Chiefs of Staff, a Joint Staff to consist of not to exceed two hundred and ten officers and to be composed of approximately equal numbers of officers appointed by the Joint Chiefs of Staff from each of the three armed services. The Joint Staff, operating under a Director thereof appointed by the Joint Chiefs of Staff, shall perform such duties as may be directed by the Joint Chiefs of Staff. The Director shall be an officer junior in grade to all members of the Joint Chiefs of Staff."

"Title IV—Promotion of Economy and Efficiency Through
Establishment of Uniform Budgetary and Fiscal Procedures and
Organizations

"Comptroller of Department of Defense

"Sec. 401.(a) There is hereby established in the Department of Defense
the Comptroller of the Department of Defense, who shall be one of the
Assistant Secretaries of Defense.

"(b) The Comptroller shall advise and assist the Secretary of Defense in
performing such budgetary and fiscal functions as may be required to
carry out the powers conferred upon the Secretary of Defense by this Act,
including but not limited to those specified in this subsection. Subject to
the authority, direction, and control of the Secretary of Defense, the
Comptroller shall—

"(1) supervise and direct the preparation of the budget estimates of the Department of Defense; and

"(2) establish, and supervise the execution of—
"(A) principles, policies, and procedures to be followed in connection with organizational and administrative matters relating to—
"(i) the preparation and execution of the
budgets,
"(ii) fiscal, cost, operating, and capital property accounting,
"(iii) progress and statistical reporting,
"(iv) internal audit, and
"(B) policies and procedures relating to the expenditure and collection of funds administered by the Department of Defense; and

"(3) establish uniform terminologies, classifications, and procedures in all such matters."

*"Military Department Budget and Fiscal Organization—
Departmental Comptrollers*

"Sec. 402. (a) The Secretary of each military department, subject to the
authority, direction, and control of the Secretary of Defense, shall cause
budgeting, accounting, progress and statistical reporting, internal audit
and administrative organization structure and managerial procedures
relating thereto in the department of which he is the head to be organized
and conducted in a manner consistent with the operation of the Office of
the Comptroller of the Department of Defense.

"(b) There is hereby established in each of the three military departments a Comptroller of the Army, a Comptroller of the Navy, or a Comptroller of the Air Force, as appropriate in the department concerned. There shall, in each military department, also be a Deputy Comptroller. Subject to the authority of the respective departmental Secretaries, the comptrollers of the military departments shall be responsible for all budgeting, accounting, progress and statistical reporting, and internal audit in their respective departments and for the administrative organization structure and managerial procedures relating thereto. The Secretaries of the military departments may in their discretion appoint either civilian or military personnel as comptrollers of the military departments. Departmental comptrollers shall be under the direction and supervision of, and directly responsible to, either the Secretary, the Under Secretary, or an Assistant Secretary of the respective military departments: *Provided,* That nothing herein shall preclude the comptroller from having concurrent responsibility to a Chief of Staff or a Chief of Naval Operations, a Vice Chief of Staff or a Vice Chief of Naval Operations, or a Deputy Chief of Staff or a Deputy Chief of Naval Operations, if the Secretary of the military department concerned should so prescribe. Where the departmental comptroller is not a civilian, the Secretary of the department concerned shall appoint a civilian as Deputy Comptroller."

"Performance Budget

"Sec. 403. (a) The budget estimates of the Department of Defense shall be prepared, presented, and justified, where practicable, and authorized programs shall be administered, in such form and manner as the Secretary of Defense, subject to the authority and direction of the President, may determine, so as to account for, and report, the cost of performance of readily identifiable functional programs and activities, with segregation of operating and capital programs. So far as practicable, the budget estimates and authorized programs of the military departments shall be set forth in readily comparable form and shall follow a uniform pattern.

"(b) In order to expedite the conversion from present budget and accounting methods to the cost-of-performance method prescribed in this title, the Secretary of each military department, with the approval of the President and the Secretary of Defense, is authorized and directed, until the end of the second year following the date of enactment of this Act, to make such transfers and adjustments within the military department of which he is the head between appropriations available for obligation by such department in such manner as he deems necessary to cause the obligation and administration of funds and the reports of expenditures to reflect the cost of performance of such programs and activities.

Reports of transfers and adjustments made pursuant to the authority of this subsection shall be made currently by the Secretary of Defense to the President and the Congress."

"Obligation of Appropriations

"Sec. 404. In order to prevent overdrafts and deficiencies in any fiscal year for which appropriations are made, on and after the beginning of the next fiscal year following the date of enactment of this Act appropriations made to the Department of Defense or to the military departments, and reimbursements thereto, shall be available for obligation and expenditure only after the Secretary of Defense shall approve scheduled rates of obligation, or modifications thereof: *Provided,* That nothing in this section shall affect the right of the Department of Defense to incur such deficiencies as may be now or hereafter authorized by law to be incurred."

---

6. Concluding Report of the Commission on Organization of the Executive Branch of the Government
First Hoover Commission (1949)*

Executive Authority and Accountability

It was a frequent finding of our various task forces that the President and his department heads do not have authority commensurate with the responsibility they must assume. In many instances authority is either lacking or is so diffused that it is almost impossible to hold anyone completely accountable for a particular program or operation. This ten-

* The Commission on Organization of the Executive Branch of the Government, *Concluding Report* (Washington, D.C.: Government Printing Office, 1949), pp. 5-33, and 37-44. Excluded herein are: the introduction, the sections dealing with red tape, areas requiring further study, and the danger of piecemeal attack, some of the illustrative material, and all charts and diagrams.

dency is dangerous and can, if extended far enough, lead to irresponsible government.

At the present time the President lacks authority to organize the agencies of the executive branch for the most effective discharge of his executive duties. While powers to reorganize have been granted to Presidents in the past, they have been intermittent and subject to many limitations and exclusions, thus seriously diminishing their effectiveness.

Likewise, the recent tendency to create by statute interdepartmental committees with specific duties and memberships has limited the President's authority to choose his advisors. Examples of such agencies are the National Security Council and the National Security Resources Board.

Similarly, statutory powers have often been granted directly to subordinate officers in such a way as to deny authority in certain areas to the President or to a department head. A case in point is the statutory authority of the Army Corps of Engineers to prepare river development plans—authority completely outside of the control of either the Secretary of the Army or the President.

In the critical area of national security, the Secretary of Defense has only a coordinating relation to the Army, Navy, and Air Force. He cannot hire and fire subordinates except on his immediate staff. Almost all appointive power not in the President's hands is vested in the subordinate service secretaries. The Defense Secretary has inadequate powers over the budget and expenditures and he possesses no authority to reorganize the Military Establishment, whose machinery is rigidly prescribed by statute.

Furthermore, where executive duties are assigned to the independent regulatory commissions the President's authority is also weakened. An example of this is the power of the Maritime Commission to operate and charter ships without regard to the views of the President.

Similarly, in the field of administrative management services, executive authority and discretion have been so weakened by rigid and detailed statutes and regulations that the effectiveness of these services has been impaired.

Likewise, requirements affecting recruitment, selection, pay increases, and dismissal of employees, intended to insure fairness and merit in personnel administration, have actually become so detailed and precise as to deprive department heads and their supervisors of important management prerogatives necessary to perform an effective and efficient job.

In another area—fiscal management—no one in the executive branch has authority to set up a central accounting system. Such an instrument is absolutely essential to management and fiscal control. The influence of the Comptroller General—an agent of the Congress—in the determination of executive expenditures also seriously impairs the authority and discretion of the President and his department heads.

Still another basic weakness is to be found in the outmoded appropriation system which concentrates on detailed listings of positions and materials rather than on well-defined functional programs. This prevents the wisest expenditure of public monies; and often diffuses the spending power among so many organization units that it becomes impossible to hold any one person or unit accountable for accomplishing program objectives.

Finally, the enormous amount of detailed substantive legislation is still another feature of present practices which is not conducive to the most effective administration of the public business. There are, for example, 199 statutes affecting personnel management alone in the Department of Agriculture. Disposition of surplus property is governed by over 369 separate laws. The Bureau of Indian Affairs is required to administer over 5,000 statutes and 370 treaties; and the laws which govern the operations of the Reclamation Bureau run to no less than 803 pages.

It is not any one of these factors alone but, like the Lilliputian threads that bound Gulliver, it is the total complex of these restrictions—lack of organization authority; grants of independent executive powers to subordinate officials; restrictive controls over personnel; divided controls over accounting and preaudit of expenditures; diffusion of the spending power of appropriations; overly detailed legislation—that weakens the powers of management in the executive branch and makes it difficult if not impossible to fix responsibility.

Solution The solution to this problem will require some fundamental and far-reaching changes in present legislative and administrative practices. The Commission's recommendations to the Congress are covered in detail in a number of its previous reports and need not be repeated at length here. However, the reforms required must provide that sufficient authority be delegated to the President and to his department heads to permit them to carry out responsibilities that have been assigned to them by the Constitution and the Congress.

The President should be granted continuing authority to submit reorganization plans covering all agencies of the executive branch, without exception; such plans to be presented to Congress, and to become effective unless disapproved within 60 days by concurrent resolution of both houses. This authority is necessary if the machinery of government is to be made adaptable to the ever changing requirements of administration and if efficiency is to become a continuing rather than a sporadic concern of the Federal Government.

The department heads must be free, with presidential approval, to reorganize their departments in the ways that, in their judgment, best suit the requirements of efficiency and economy. This means that the internal organization structure of executive agencies should not be prescribed by legislation.

The related practice of determining the precise functions and membership of coordinating and advisory bodies by statute should be discontinued in favor of more general enabling legislation which would provide a flexible framework within which the President can act.

Detailed legislation, including rigid itemized appropriation language which unnecessarily limits executive discretion and initiative, should also be avoided.

In the further interest of responsible management, independent grants of executive authority not subject to the control of the Chief Executive should not be made to department heads and subordinate officials.

The purely executive functions of quasi-legislative and quasi-judicial agencies, too, should be brought within the regular executive departments, thus placing these responsibilities within the ambit of executive control.

Likewise, departmental authority over personnel management must be strengthened by permitting those charged with management responsibilities to exercise more discretion in such phases of personnel administration as recruiting, selection, promotions, pay administration, and dismissals.

Finally, the President must have more authority to determine the kind of fiscal reporting he needs to obtain reliable information and to maintain sound fiscal controls.

These changes are the first steps necessary to achieve not only increased efficiency and economy in the Government, but also a greater measure of accountability of the executive branch to Congress.

Sharpening the Tools of Management

Beyond the need for greater executive authority and discretion, the President and top officials in the executive branch require more adequate tools in the areas of fiscal management, personnel, supply, and housekeeping services, if the public business is to be conducted efficiently and economically.

Fiscal

In the first of these areas—fiscal management—there are glaring weaknesses to be found in the budget process, in accounting controls, and in the appropriation structure.

The budget process is weakest at the departmental level where it should be strongest. The budget document itself, because of its size and complexity and its concentration on services and materials to be bought rather than programs to be undertaken, is a relatively ineffective tool of management. Perhaps the underlying reason for this is the outmoded appropriation structure, which is exceedingly complex, overly detailed in certain areas and much too broad in others, and is based upon the requirements of organizational units rather than work programs.

The apportionment system is ineffective in controlling overspending. Insufficient attention is given to the revenue side of the budget; and constant difficulty of interpretation is caused by the intermingling of current operating expenditures and capital outlays, and, in certain instances, by failure to disclose subsidies.

There is no formal accounting plan for the Government as a whole. As a consequence there is no place where the complete financial picture of our Government can be seen. Complete and current financial information cannot be obtained since Federal accounting is a mixture of the cash basis of accounting and the accrual basis; and it does not include supply accounting.

Responsibility for fiscal accounts—those relating to revenues, custody of funds, disbursements, public debt, and the currency—rests with the Treasury. Yet the Comptroller General, an agent of Congress, prescribes the form and procedure for administrative appropriation and fund accounting in the executive branch.

As a result we have not had, to this day, a system of accounting that shows the Government's true revenues and expenses for any year, that provides for property or cost accounting, or for a positive control of assets, liabilities, and appropriations.

Solution In our report on budgeting and accounting we propose far-reaching changes in these areas. In order to produce a budget plan which will be a more understandable and useful instrument, both to the President and to Congress, we recommend that the budget document be completely recast along the lines of work programs and functions. Such a document, which we designate as a "performance budget," would analyze the work of Government departments and agencies according to their major functions, activities, or projects. It would thus concentrate attention on the work to be done or service to be rendered rather than on things to be acquired such as personal services, contractual services, supplies, materials, and equipment. A performance budget, moreover, would facilitate congressional and executive control by clearly showing the scope and magnitude of each Federal activity. It could also show the relationships between the volume of work to be done and the cost of the work, a measurement which cannot be made under the present system.

However, in order to obtain the full benefit of the performance budget, the appropriation structure would have to be simplified and adjusted to mesh with the budget plan.

The initial stages of budget preparation at the operational level also need to be strengthened. This will both insure better planning and relieve the Office of the Budget of the burden of detailed revisions at that level.

To further assist the President in tightening controls over spending, an Office of the Accountant General should be established under the Secretary of the Treasury with authority to prescribe general accounting methods and to enforce accounting procedures in the executive branch. These methods and procedures should be subject to the approval of the Comptroller General within the powers presently conferred upon him by the Congress.

The Accountant General should have the responsibility, on a report basis, of combining agency accounts into summary accounts of the Government and of producing complete financial reports for the information of the President, the Congress, and the public. The accounts should be kept on an accrual basis and should cover all revenues, receipts, funds, appropriations, expenditures, supplies, properties, and securities of the Federal Government.

When this new system is installed, it will make possible the development of an apportionment system that can provide what is now seriously lacking—proper executive control over the spending of appropriations.

Finally, the Commission recommends that the General Accounting Office's costly practice of minutely examining millions of expenditure vouchers be discontinued so far as possible and be replaced by spot-sampling audits at the various Government agencies. In addition to reducing costs without impairing control, it would free the legislature's auditor for more comprehensive and effective post-auditing duties.

These changes in budgeting, accounting, and auditing methods must be made if sound practices in fiscal management and clearer fiscal accountability of the executive branch to the Congress are to be assured.

Personnel

Probably no problem in the management of the Government is more important than that of obtaining and retaining a capable and conscientious body of public servants. Unfortunately, personnel practices in the Federal Government give little room for optimism that these needs are being met.

The Civil Service Commission has not been organized to develop as a really effective staff arm of the President. Planning and administration of the personnel program have not kept pace with the tremendous expansion of employment in the Government.

The centralization of personnel transactions in the Civil Service Commission and in the departmental personnel offices has resulted in unjustifiable delays in handling personnel problems.

Recruitment machinery has been slow, impersonal, and cumbersome. Many personnel procedures are unnecessarily complicated; and the rigidity of certain of them does not permit the necessary latitude of judgment and discretion that operating officials need to do the most effective management job.

Insufficient attention has been given to such positive aspects of sound personnel management as developing better supervisor-employee relations, training, promotion, and incentives for superior performance. In short, the system is not constituted so as to attract and retain sufficient qualified people for the Government's tasks.

These criticisms should not be construed, however, as a reflection on the vast majority of our Federal employees, who are conscientious, hardworking, and devoted, but rather upon a system which has not fully kept pace with the needs of the Federal Government.

Solution In our report on personnel management we make several recommendations to improve the quality of personnel administration in the Government. We recommend that the personnel system be decentralized so that the operating agencies of the Government will perform the day-to-day tasks of recruitment, selection, position classification, and other aspects of personnel management, under standards to be approved and enforced by the Civil Service Commission.

This will free the Commission from the details of centralized control of personnel operations and transactions, and permit its chairman to concentrate on planning and personnel standards, and on assisting the President and his department heads in developing sound and active personnel management programs.

The chairman of the Civil Service Commission not only should serve as the President's principal staff advisor on civil service problems, but also should direct the Commission's operations.

On the agency level the personnel function should be represented in top management. The departments themselves, in recruiting employees, should use more active and attractive methods; and apply selection methods which will both give their supervisors wider latitude of judgment and insure that appointments are being made on a merit, and not on a political, basis.

To improve employee performance, line supervisors should play a greater role in the selection, advancement, and removal of employees.

Forms and procedures in personnel processes should be simplified. Increased emphasis should be given to such matters as employee participation in management problems, in-service training, promotions, and the human relations aspect of management.

Salaries, pitifully low in the higher levels . . . must be substantially increased to attract and retain employees with first-rate abilities. This need was emphasized again and again by almost all of our task forces: by our task forces on personnel, on supply, on medical services, on budgeting and accounting, by our management engineering consultants, and by many other experts working in the various fields of our work.

Finally, all positions in the service with the exception of top level policy jobs should be filled by merit system methods.

All these improvements are necessary if we are to achieve a higher degree of competency, efficiency, and accountability in the Federal service.

General Services

In several of the chief housekeeping services of the Government—supply, records management, and building maintenance—there are shocking instances of wasteful practices and poor business management.

Supply

In the field of supply our task force reported that no large private corporation could long survive if it practiced the waste and extravagance in supply operations which is condoned in the Federal Government.

There is no adequate central organization to coordinate Government purchasing. Purchasing operations are unplanned and have degenerated largely into the routine practice of soliciting bids and awarding contracts to the lowest bidder. Purchasing officers, moreover, lack information and funds necessary to schedule purchases so as to take maximum advantage of favorable market conditions. They have failed to develop cost records and other management tools essential to performing an effective job of purchasing.

There are too many storage warehouses, many improperly located and carrying duplicating inventories. Because most agencies lack stock-control systems which indicate agency needs, and because of the general practice of investing appropriation balances at the end of the fiscal year in supplies, practically all agencies have excessive stocks on hand.

The attention of most traffic personnel is directed to auditing transportation bills. Very few employees are engaged in activities concerned with improving traffic management and reducing costs.

There is considerable evidence that many commodities requiring specifications do not have them; and many existing specifications are out of date. Standards are generally described in terms of physical characteristics or composition of product rather than in terms of performance required.

There is no uniformity in the quality of inspection or standard practice as to what types of commodities should be inspected. The Federal Government has no uniform system of cataloging which permits identification or classification of materials used by Federal agencies. There have been as many as 17 unrelated systems of property identification in use at one time. Some agencies maintain no property controls whatever; and numerous others have not inventoried their property in years. This situation has resulted in the piling up of costly duplicating inventories throughout the Government and waste of the taxpayers' money.

Solution   Putting the Government supply operations on a businesslike basis can result in enormous savings. The Government is now spending more than $6 billion a year for material, supplies, and equipment. While no one knows exactly what the Government owns, total military and civilian warehouse inventories have been estimated at $27 billion.

In order to place the supply operation on an efficient basis a number of things must be done.

First, the jungle of unduly restrictive statutes, conflicting decisions, and regulations must be swept away and supplanted by a code which will establish basic principles for an effective supply system.

A central supply agency should be created within an Office of General Services to develop, on behalf of the President, policies and regulations designed to assist the civilian operating departments in establishing efficient supply practices—practices which would give proper attention to all phases of supply such as specifications, purchasing, traffic management, inspection, property identification, storage and issue, and property utilization. The agency would also serve as the central purchasing and storage center for common use items.

Records and Building Management

The problem of records management likewise provides fertile ground for substantial economies. Government records have accumulated at a tremendous rate during the past 20 years. They now occupy about 18 million square feet of space, equivalent to 6 buildings each the size of the Pentagon. At least 50 percent of these records are not currently used, yet many are housed in expensive office space and equipment.

Building management practices, also, are loose. No one knows exactly what property the Government owns and leases; and policies and practices on leasing and other aspects of property management differ widely.

Solution Here again we need an Office of General Services attached to
the Executive Office. Through a Bureau of Records Management, it
would supervise the destruction of useless records, and should transfer
records not required for current operation to strategically located record
centers throughout the country where they could be stored at a fraction of
present costs. This organization should also assist the departments in
developing more efficient and economical records management practices.

Similar economies can be obtained in the operation and maintenance of
public buildings. Authority now vested in the Public Buildings Administration should be expanded and assigned to an Office of General Services
which, in addition to regular duties of operation and maintenance, would
prepare and issue standards of efficiency in building management,
supervise space allotments, prepare standard leases and deeds, and maintain a record of buildings leased and owned by the Government.

The strengthening of each of these tools of management—fiscal, personnel, general services—now woefully inadequate, is essential for improved operation of the executive branch.

The Wastes of Overlapping and Duplication

There is probably no place in the Government where waste is more
conspicuous than in the overlapping services of the Government. Many of
these duplicating and competing services have stubbornly survived
through repeated exposures and attempts at reorganization. Our reports
and those of the task forces give numerous examples of overlapping and
duplication throughout the Government. Here, for the purpose of high-
lighting the problem and pointing the way toward its solution, we shall
briefly cite only three. [The three, dealing with water resource development, land and forestry management, and hospital construction are omitted herein.]

Solution In several of our reports we recommend putting an end to
such wasteful competition by consolidating these overlapping services.
We also propose bringing the major construction activities together in one
agency.

In addition to this, a Board of Impartial Review of all major public
works is required in the President's Office to insure that projects planned
are feasible, are supported by adequate basic data, are not in conflict with
other works projects, and are being completed with utmost efficiency.

Moreover, to avoid other overlapping and duplication, as for example
in the field of statistics, we recommend that the President's authority and
staff of the Office of the Budget be strengthened. Likewise, to coordinate

the various scientific research programs we recommend the creation of a National Science Foundation.

Finally, in order to provide the President with the necessary information and control of all executive programs we recommend that a position of Staff Secretary be created to keep him informed on current programs. The President will thus be able to achieve better coordination of executive activities.

These basic changes in organization supplemented by additional coordinating and planning devices are vital to the elimination and prevention of tremendous wastes in money and manpower in the Government.

Decentralization Under Centralized Control

As a general rule, economy can be achieved in administration by centralizing services common to all agencies. There is a limit, however, in the size and complexity of Government beyond which it is no longer feasible to furnish services centrally without creating serious bottlenecks, delays, and confusion. As a result, the services become more costly and less efficient than if performed by the agencies themselves.

This point has long been reached in the operations of the Federal Government. It is no longer conceivable that personnel transactions for 2 million employees could be processed centrally, or that 3 million purchase orders for $6 billion worth of goods could be handled on a central basis. Yet in the fields of personnel, budgeting, and supply our task forces have found overcentralized operations which are resulting in inefficient and expensive management.

Our task forces also found many instances where headquarters officials in Washington still cling to the power to make decisions even in matters of minor importance. This, too, has resulted in interminable delays in getting things done, has stultified initiative in the field services, and has resulted in decisions being made which have not taken due account of variations in local conditions.

Solution   While a considerable amount of decentralization has already taken place, the necessity for further decentralization of operations under proper central controls is badly needed and has been a recurring theme in our various reports.

In our report on personnel management we recommend that recruitment, selection, and other processes of personnel administration be decentralized to the agencies under standards to be approved and enforced by the Civil Service Commission. Within the agencies themselves we recommend that a similar decentralization of personnel management be made to their field units and operating supervisors.

In our report on budgeting and accounting we recommend that the bulk of the work in the preparation of budget estimates be performed in the operating departments; that accounting reports be kept by the operating departments under a central accounting system.

With the exception of common-use items, we have recommended purchasing by departments under uniform standards prescribed by a central supply agency.

In substantive matters, too, we have recommended that a greater measure of authority be delegated to the field services of the operating departments. This will require that the headquarters agencies concentrate their attention more and more on developing policies which are unmistakably clear. They must also give more attention to establishing standards of performance and to improving their systems of reporting and inspection to insure that policies are carried out.

Reorganization by Major Purpose

Improvements in such areas as authority, management tools, coordination, planning, procedures, and decentralization are not sufficient in themselves to bring about the maximum degree of efficiency in the operations of the Government. The organization structure of the executive branch must also undergo radical revision. Similarly, the departments and agencies themselves must be reorganized.

There are at present too many separate agencies to permit adequate attention and direction from the President. Many closely related functions also are so scattered that in certain fields such as labor, transportation, or medical services no one is charged with considering the problem as a whole.

Furthermore, many agencies contain functions which are totally unrelated to each other, if not inconsistent; creating a lack of central purpose and greatly increasing the problems of internal coordination.

Several areas of conflict, duplication and overlapping, at least partially due to faulty organization, have been cited.

In our previous reports we have made numerous recommendations designed to improve the organization structure of the executive branch, as well as the internal structure of the various departments and agencies. . . . Our studies have shown conclusively that the areas presenting the greatest problems of duplication and coordination are those in which services of a similar nature are located in different agencies in the executive branch. This dispersion of related functions has led to interagency rivalries and conflicts which have been extremely wasteful and costly.

Solution   In recommending reorganization changes it has been our constant objective to achieve the greatest possible degree of unity in the departmental structure. We have been mindful, too, of the excessive burden on the President of having so many agencies report to him. In our first report we recommended, as a desirable goal, the reduction of the total number of agencies reporting to the President to about one-third of their present number. While it has not been entirely possible to reach this objective, we have, nevertheless, made recommendations which will reduce the total number of agencies so reporting, to what, in our judgment, is the smallest number feasible if a maximum unity of purpose in each department is also to be achieved.

To strengthen the organization of the principal central staff services we have recommended a consolidation of the functions of supply, records management, and buildings management in an Office of General Services.

To restore the Treasury Department to its historic role in fiscal matters and to remove from it operations which are unrelated to its major purpose, we have recommended that the Bureau of Narcotics, the Coast Guard, and the Bureau of Federal Supply be transferred to other departments and that the Treasury become the focal point for the proposed central accounting system.

To integrate the scattered transportation functions of the executive branch, we have recommended combining within a single transportation service in the Department of Commerce such related functions as those of the Maritime Commission relating to the construction, operation, charter and sale of ships, the Coast Guard, the National Advisory Committee for Aeronautics, the Public Roads Administration, the Office of Defense Transportation, and certain transportation safety functions of the Civil Aeronautics Board and Interstate Commerce Commission.

To remove the major areas of overlapping and duplication, we have recommended that the functions of flood control and river and harbor improvement work of the Army Corps of Engineers be consolidated with the Reclamation Service within the Department of the Interior. Similarly, we have recommended that the Bureau of Land Management in Interior be consolidated with the Forest Service in Agriculture.

Finally, in the field of labor we have recommended that several important labor and manpower functions such as the Bureau of Employment Security, Bureau of Employees Compensation, and Selective Service System be transferred to the Department of Labor.

These are typical examples of reorganization proposals that we have made to achieve greater over-all efficiency and improved coordination in the executive branch by grouping services and activities according to major purpose.

Contents by Topic

Budget and Finance

Note: Reference to parts and sections are entered for the convenience of the reader for documents which relate to a range of topics, only sections of which are applicable to the specific subject matter that is segregated in this topical table of contents. When parts or sections are not specified, the meaning is: that most or all of the document is relevant to the topic; or that it is difficult or impossible to segregate and identify sections of the document according to topics; or that the document itself is too short to make identification useful.

Departments, Agencies, and Offices

General Government Organization and Reorganization

Goals and Principles

Local Government

National Defense

Personnel and Civil Service

Presidency

Protection of Citizens' Rights